Appalachian Odyssey

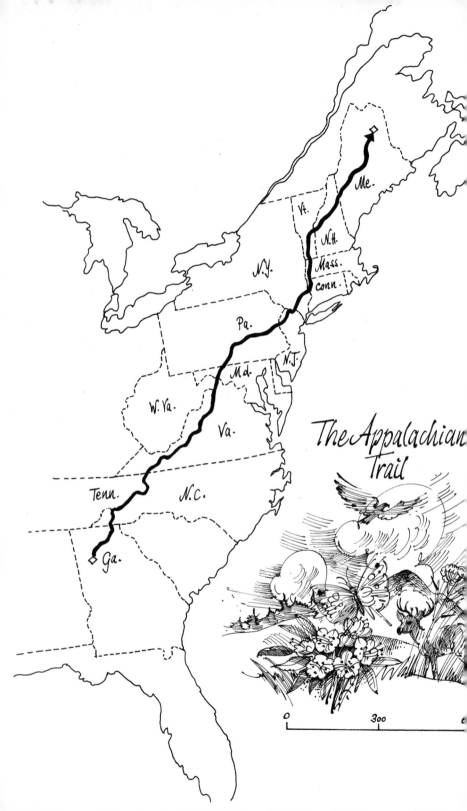

The Appalachian Trail

Appalachian Odyssey

Walking the Trail from

Georgia to Maine

By STEVE SHERMAN and
JULIA OLDER

With a Foreword by Edward Abbey

The Stephen Greene Press

BRATTLEBORO • VERMONT

The authors are grateful to the editor of the *Hollow Spring Review of Poetry*, in which the poem, "Appalachian Root Woman," on page 69, first appeared.

Text copyright © 1977 by Steve Sherman and Julia Older

Foreword copyright © 1977 by Edward Abbey

This book has been produced in the United States of America.

It is designed by R. L. Dothard Associates and published by The Stephen Greene Press, Brattleboro, Vermont 05301

LIBRARY OF CONGRESS CATALOGING IN PUBLICATION DATA
Sherman, Steve, 1938–
    Appalachian odyssey.

    Bibliography: p.
    Includes index.
    1. Appalachian Trail.   2. Appalachian Mountains—Description and travel.
3. Sherman, Steve, 1938–   4. Backpacking—Appalachian Mountains.
I. Older, Julia, 1941–   joint author.
II. Title.
GV199.42.A68S53   917.4   76-50269
ISBN 0-8289-0294-1
ISBN 0-8289-0295-X pbk.
    77 78 79 80 81 9 8 7 6 5 4 3 2 1

Contents

Dedicated to our
German pot handle, French sleeping bags,
English water jug, Swedish stove,
Japanese whistles, Swiss Army knife,
California packs, Wisconsin boots,
Colorado tent, and Mom and Dad

For special help we thank Kay and Scott Taylor of Peterborough, New Hampshire; Robert Ray of the First National Bank of Peterborough; Claudia Spohnholz of the MacDowell Colony, New Hampshire; and Judy and Arthur Ginsburg of Silver Spring, Maryland.

The Appalachian Trail, and Beyond

A FOREWORD

Appalachia. Appalachia . . . Good God I lived there, in the northern fringe, on a little sub-marginal farm in western Pennsylvania, for the first eighteen years of my life.

Eighteen years. Good God. Finally rescued by Hitler and the war (*The* war), the draft, the United States Army, God bless them all. Otherwise, who knows, I might still be there driving a coal truck for the strippers, or teaching English to sullen delinquents with TV-shriveled minds in some grimy small-town high school, or even—God, the soul curls to think of it—traipsing the Appalachian Trail from end to end, for *fun*! for *recreation*! for *re*-creation!

Well, so I escaped. But my brother Howard, he's still living back there, making a living, driving coal trucks, building gasification plants (he's a high steel man), raising three wild kids. But he has guts, unlike me. And my mother, and old man, they're still there, surviving in their little house by the side of the road where the forty-ton supertrucks thunder past every thirty minutes, shaking the foundations. The farm was sold, years ago, and the old house burned down, and the wild blackberry are taking over the fields that the strip-miners didn't get to first, and over that whole remembered country-side of childhood now hangs the awful shroud of industry. On a clear day you can see for maybe two miles. Powerlines draped from hill to hill. Constant traffic on the dense network of highways that look, on a map, like the red breakdown of varicose veins. Trailerhouse slums and "mobile-home" ghettos spreading across the slopes of abandoned farms. Most working people in America can no longer afford to live in true houses, no longer have enough free time to build a real home for themselves.

But in the burgeoning towns and cities the skyscraper banks rise up, tombs of tinted glass and frosty steel, towering above the surrounding tracts of fiberboard and plywood, aluminum and formica, where the serfs live. Death to the land. Death to all the old American dreams. How absolutely prescient was Oliver Goldsmith when he wrote, two centuries ago, of a similar malaise falling on England:

> *Ill fares the land, to hastening ills a prey,*
> *Where wealth accumulates, and men decay.*

No need to go on with this dirge. Harry Caudill has said it all, much better, in *Night Comes to the Cumberlands* and in his recent book, *The Watches of the Night*.

Thus our native Appalachia. In large part a commercial, industrial, profiteering wasteland, America's first great National Sacrifice Area. (There will be others.) But the wonder of it all is that some of the original beauty of the land yet remains. The flame azalea still blooms in the Big Smokies, and the blue phlox, the Mayapple, the mandrake, the rhododendron, the toadshade, the trillium, the showy orchis, the hobblebush, the dogwood, the wild chokecherry. In our Appalachian autumn a multitude of ancient hardwoods burst out in seventeen different shades of red, gold, rust, the hues of October in infinite number. From Georgia up to Maine, the rush of spring-green, the exultance of ten thousand different species of flowers, and then in the fall the movement of color in reverse, from north to south. Lonesome farmhouses still hiding back on red-dog roads, down in hardscrabble hollows, up near the summits of cloud-shaded hills. Coon dogs baying at the smoky moon. The winding streams, the covered bridges, the deep woods where the deer still flourish—now more than ever!—and the black bear still raid the hogpen, the chickencoop, the backpacker's portable kitchen.

The backpacker? Who else? For through the middle of this capitalist squalor and naturalist splendor runs the Appalachian Trail, a ridiculous footpath 2,000 miles long running the length of the Appalachian Mountains, up and down a thousand peaks, in and out of a thousand valleys, across a thousand meadows, through a thousand forest glades. Myself, I've walked only a few short stretches of it in Great Smokies National Park. But like almost everyone who's heard of it, or come across it, the idea—the *ideal!*—of some year actually getting into harness and walking the entire Trail has always haunted the back of my mind. It's one of those outdoor dream-adventures we all dream and very few have the nerve to realize. Like traversing the Grand Canyon from end to end; like hitchhiking through the Sahara and into the Congo past the Mountains of the Moon down the planet's awesome curve to the Kalihari Desert and the Cape of Good Hope; like skiing down Fujiyama; like personally inspecting each and every active volcano on the face of the earth.

Many talk, many write. Some do. Steve Sherman and Julia Older are two who've done it. This is their book about the walk and it's a good book. In it you'll find everything you ever wanted to know about hiking the Great Hike. Everything and then some—none of the misery has been left out, none of the tedium, none of the chiggers, snakes, mosquitoes, or odd-ball fellow hikers, and none of the glory, exaltation and satisfaction either. They say they'll do it again sometime and I, for one, believe them. (You may not.)

Appalachia is in trouble, but that's not news, the whole country's in trouble, under assault by the insatiable demands of an insane expanding economy and what the journalist Tom Wolfe (of New York; no kin to the real Thomas Wolfe, the writer) calls a "happiness explosion." Fueled more by Valium, alcohol and the St. Vitus Dance than by happy people, this explosion is real all the same, and its destructive disruption of the North American continent condemns our children and our grandchildren to a form of poverty heretofore unknown in human history: confinement for life to a wonderful department store set in the midst of a steaming junkyard three thousand miles wide. They will not love us for it.

But wait a minute! One thin ray of hope shines through the smog and uproar. One thin bright ray: it is the conscience of the American people beginning to stir at last, beginning finally to question and sometimes even resist the Master Plan of industry and technocracy. From the consciousness of loss and danger rises the glow of a national earth-use morality. We call it environmentalism; the conservationist cause; the light of sanity and moderation. Julia Older and Steve Sherman speak for that cause, not with a sermon, as I do here, but with the implicit meaning of their experience. In this *Appalachian Odyssey* they have voted with their feet. All over America a million others are doing the same. Some day soon these votes must count—and be counted.

EDWARD ABBEY

Home, Pennsylvania

Preface

Most couples start out with a mortgage on a new house or maybe a brand-new bouncing six-pounder to add to the general census. It didn't work out that way for us. Our sweet nothings were transformed overnight into wild romantic chatter about lightweight sleeping bags, lightweight foods, and lightweight lives. "Why don't we hike the whole Appalachian Trail?" "Why not?"

We met over a novel and a collection of poetry we were working on at the MacDowell Colony, a writer's and artist's retreat in the backwoods of Peterborough, New Hampshire. One of us had arrived from São Paulo, Brazil, a concrete Bird of Paradise with more than six million inhabitants, a congested, burgeoning, poverty-stricken, pollution-mindless international cog in the grinding gears of industry and progress. The other had flown in from Fairbanks, Alaska, where oil greed has turned old-timers and outsiders alike into money-mad maniacs of the dollar bill.

In transit from these outposts, we had both stopped awhile in New York and Boston to renew our kinship with hardcore urban life. Fortunately, two Americans of foresight, Marian MacDowell and Benton MacKaye, saved us from more seamy examples of civilized terrorism. Mrs. MacDowell, wife of the American composer Edward MacDowell, had established the Colony, quiet, secluded, wooded, and lofty. The Colony and nearby snow-capped Mt. Monadnock, as pristine as when Thoreau climbed it, joined to focus our dream. We wanted to get away from it all, to go back to the roots of our origin, to hike Benton MacKaye's Appalachian Trail.

Now usually men propose a primrose path. Steve proposed walking a 2,000-mile footpath from Georgia to Maine through the wilderness of the Appalachians, the longest continuously marked trail in the world. Julia accepted. Besides, we wouldn't have to pay rent.

Steve, having bicycled across the continent and written about his experiences, knew that for ideas to pass from true confessions to true stories, commitment is merely the beginning. So with the Boy Scout–Girl Scout motto burned into our hearts, we prepared to "Be Prepared."

First on our list was to read every book and pamphlet on the Appalachian Trail. Benton MacKaye, a visionary, first conceived of a continuous trail as the backbone of a natural primitive environment. The article in which he expounded his idea in 1921 sparked interest among existing northeast hiking and outdoor clubs. The following year the first section of the Trail was opened and marked in the Palisades Interstate Park, New York. The Trail, originally estimated at 1,200 miles, was completed in 1937. Major growth of urban areas near the Trail has since caused it to be re-routed through more scenic and isolated regions, resulting in an additional 800 miles.

Today, hikers may follow diamond-shaped galvanized metal markers ⩜ as well as painted white trail blazes from Springer Mountain, Georgia, all the way to Mt. Katahdin, Maine. Along the summits and down the valleys, a chain of more than 230 lean-tos provide hikers with shelter from the elements. A 35-mile stretch of exposed mountaintops in the Presidentials of the White Mountain Range, however, forces hikers to lodge in Appalachian Mountain Club huts.

In 1968, the Appalachian Trail was designated a National Scenic Trail by Act of Congress. Through the National Trails System Act, the Appalachian Trail comes under the jurisdiction of the Secretary of the Interior, with the United States Forest Service assuming responsibility for those parts of the Trail that pass over Forest Service land. Individual hiking clubs continue to maintain sections of the Trail within their states.

These clubs join with their organization and representation to form the Appalachian Trail Conference, which meets every other year. Club members, public officials, life members, and individual members meet to discuss Trail-related problems with the Board of Managers, composed of Conference officers and three persons each from the six districts into which the Trail is divided.

These districts are: 1. Southern District (Georgia and North Carolina in the Great Smoky Mountains); 2. Unaka District (North Carolina from Big Pigeon River, Tennessee and Southern Virginia); 3. Maryland and Virginia District (Northern Virginia, West Virginia, and Maryland); 4. Pennsylvania District (all sections of Pennsylvania); 5. New York and New Jersey District (all sections of these states); 6. New England District (all sections of Connecticut, Massachusetts, Vermont, New Hampshire and Maine).

We were to walk through fourteen states. We had three months till countdown in mid-April, when the mountain crests would be warm enough to receive us. Three months to foot our bill, to tone our flabby muscles, to get rid of our sedentary writers' cramps.

One author we read told us he lost twenty pounds hiking the Trail in the first two weeks. We started swallowing cookies by the cookie sheetful, eating spaghetti by the pasta pound, drinking milk by the carton gallon, all to stave off visions of blowing from the mountains like dandelion fluff. For training we climbed ice-encrusted Mt. Monadnock when no other fool ventured out of house to turn over the motor of his car. The day we shelled out $100 for lug sole hiking boots was the first big economic point of no return. We looked each other straight in the eye and clomped out the door for our daily five-mile forced march. Those three months of preparation were a time of wonder and doubt.

Why were we hiking the Appalachian Trail? Because we wanted to touch the land directly, to re-confirm our trust in the slow but unconquerable ascendancy of nature over man, to test, to accomplish, to learn. Were the rumors right that most of the waters of our country were contaminated? Was there no place to hear the living rhythms of the woods? And what about America the Beautiful—another jaded catchphrase to divert the truth that our cities were ugly?

Benton MacKaye wrote, "The old pioneer opened through a forest a path for the spread of civilization. His work was nobly done and life of the town and city is in consequence well upon the map throughout our country. Now comes the great task of holding this life in check—for it is just as bad to have too much urbanization as too little. America needs her forests and her wild spaces quite as much as her cities and her settled places."

Three months is not a long time to sprout an idea such as ours and cook it in your wok. We were fortunate, however. We may not have been altogether footloose in our four-pound clod-hopping boots, but we were fancy free and, above all, optimistic that what we would discover between the blisters and blizzards would be worth 4½ months of our lives, worth spending our wad. We had gone the nine-to-five route like everyone else, but we had each reached the same conclusion individually: Time is only of consequence when you are pursuing your own disciplines and beliefs.

We walked from south to north, the idea being to follow spring as it blossomed northward, and to miss the blackfly season at the beginning of summer in Maine. The latter reason was the better one. Hikers we met venturing from north to south looked as if they had stumbled from a science fiction scenario. As for our revery of spring, we were not prepared for the wintry landscape and the snow flurries that awaited us on April 11 in the South. Our super-light, ultra-modern sleeping bags worked mostly on theory, one miscalculation that we would correct next trip.

At times we remembered Benton MacKaye's warning about too much urbanization. Interstate highways loomed too close to the Trail in the middle states. At times the body was more willing than the spirit to trudge ahead.

Despite our bellyaching about the Stekoahs in North Carolina and the rock flats of Pennsylvania, the crowds in the White Mountains and the zealous backpack haters, were the trials of our Odyssey worth it? Did we return home believers in America the Beautiful and Americans the Beautiful People?

Perhaps not believers as much as fighters. What good we saw we wanted to save with the same ornery determination as a wiry Georgia mountain woman we met who took her shotgun to some strangers at her mailbox. "I love these mountains," she said, "and nobody's going to ruin them if I can help it." We wanted to preserve the silence and peace of Georgia, the majestic flora and fauna of the Smokies, from encroachments by greed and poor taste. We learned that the biggest fight is against the slick offenders who bribe and cajole, hoodwinkers such as logging companies that present a public image of environmental concern when in fact too many of them are raping our land and polluting our rivers. The Androscoggin River in Maine and New Hampshire is Exhibit A.

We gnashed our teeth at recreation managers and their law enforcement procedures that have evolved from a need to protect the interests of the majority, the weekend candy-wrapper droppers. The minority backpacker in turn receives short shrift. In some instances, we were too surprised by this discrimination to call into question why state and national forests, parks and trails, were set apart in the first place. Certainly, Benton MacKaye was not talking about ski trails, snowmobile runs, and enforced overnight paid lodging when he proposed the Appalachian Trail six decades ago.

Still, in contrast to the man who chased us off his lawn in Bethel, Maine, or the hutboy who ordered us onto a tent platform in the White Mountains, people like Walter and Emily Cherry were always smiling and ready to offer us a cup of soup or chauffeur us from town back to the Trail. The din of our doubts and perturbances was always superseded by the hush of the woods, the taste of cold sweet spring water bubbling from the base of a cool dark rock, the tangential flight of a sparrow hawk following us over the mountain crests.

We held tight to sights of running deer and free-wheeling birds, of good, friendly back-country folk, and a thousand peaks and valleys. When the rain crashed against our tent and lightning zapped the living daylights out of us, we sensed that not far away a wood thrush shared our misery and would rejoice with high sweet trills when the storm subsided. Even some golden anniversaries don't hinge on such shared adversity and joy.

S.S.
J.O.

Hancock, New Hampshire

Georgia

78 MILES

On Springer Mountain in northern Georgia we signed the register, a rusty metal pulpit with a stubby pencil and scraps of notebook paper. Our signatures joined the scribbles of other conquerors: "Going all the way"; "End to End!"; "Georgia to Maine on the AT."

Then, hoping to give back to the Appalachian Trail some

of the new life that we expected to gain by hiking it, we gouged holes in the still-hard dirt and sowed the earth with zinnia seeds. A packet of marigold seeds we kept to plant on Mt. Katahdin, the Trail's northern terminus in Baxter State Park, Maine, fourteen states and two thousand miles away.

Exuberant, we followed the two-by-six-inch white paint stripes interspersed on tree trunks along the Trail. Our first day showed us what we could expect in Georgia. Persephone and Spring had not yet risen from the underworld. With icy invitation, the wind gusted through the barren maples and oaks. Dead vines were rolled like barbed wire at the foot of skeletal trees. The scant signs of color in the wintry landscape were rhododendron leaves winnowing through the sunlight and a few chestnut-sided warblers, brave vanguard of that cold April 11, 1973.

Before long we felt like this worn landscape. Our calves were throbbing, our feet sore, our backs aching. Two hours later we arrived at Big Stamp Gap and the lean-to, a bare, three-sided enclosure with an earth-gravel floor. We could not imagine anyone wanting to sleep on the slanting ground under this rudimentary roof with the wind blowing down the valley into the open side.

Altogether, more than 230 shelters provided refuge for hikers along the entire Trail. If the shelters were all like this one, to us the better choice seemed obvious—a flat spot of Mother Earth. In minutes our man-and-woman tent provided a waterproof, windproof home behind a giant fallen oak to protect us from the cold blasts.

We followed a blue-blaze trail to fetch fresh water flowing from a slab-rock crevice on a hillside about 150 yards from camp. Then, with windbreaker hoods drawn tight around our faces, and wearing scarecrow brown gardening gloves, we gathered pieces of dry wood, built a fire, and prepared a hot chicken-and-rice dinner. Soon the Chicken Supreme, with a packet of sherry, no less, bubbled in the cooking pot. A standing rib roast and a bottle of Chateau Lafite back home in Hancock, New Hampshire, would not have tasted better.

That night, according to our pocket thermometer, the temperature dropped to eighteen degrees. We were as vulnerable as cacti in the arctic. Exhausted from the climb and the constant effort to keep warm, we got ready for bed. Most people get undressed for bed, but not us. We donned longjohns and thermal long-sleeve shirts. Over that we put on our summer sweat shirts, and over them sweaters and jeans. We put on two pairs of socks and cotton gloves. Then we crawled into our zip-together, newest-thing-on-the-market sleeping bags, and tied down the tent flap.

Whoever wrote "I've Got My Love to Keep Me Warm" never slept on the Appalachian Trail in Georgia in early spring. We trembled with the cold, squirmed and shivered, quaked and shuddered. We curled into each other, hugged each other, tossed and turned. We spent half the night playing single sack, double sack, sack in sack, all the while taking long swigs of Southern Comfort we brought to warm our blood.

We were discovering our first major mistake—the purchase of two French sleeping bags designed on the body-heat reflection principle. The bags weighed scarcely more than 1½ pounds each, a bonanza find in our pursuit of the lightest packs possible. They were specified to provide comfort in weather down to thirty-six degrees.

Through this long, freezing, first night on the Trail we wondered why indeed we had started from the south instead of the north. Yet from research and personal experience, we did know that April was far too cold to hike comfortably from Maine. Besides, we wanted to follow the unfolding fan of spring, hoping that the blackfly season of the north would be over by the time we reached Maine.

Part of our research back home had been to find exactly

where Springer Mountain, Georgia, was located. Every atlas in the library ignored this first mountain peak of our adventure. Even on the day we boarded the Southern Railroad in Washington, D.C., for Gainesville, Georgia, we still didn't know exactly where Springer Mountain was. Willie, the train porter, added to our insecurity. "No, sir. That's a long way. Makes me tired just thinking about it. I don't even like riding that long way in a car. Now you watch out for snakes, hear? May is matin' season, you know. Two thousand miles. You ain't going to make it."

At the Greyhound bus station in Gainesville, we learned that no public transportation to Amicalola Falls and Springer Mountain was available. We hired a taxi, and an hour later watched the driver pocket two ten-dollar traveler's checks when he left us at the entrance to the ranger station of the Chattahoochee National Forest.

As we headed toward the ranger's cabin, snow swirled over the valley of bare trees. This was Georgia, the Deep South? Our decision to postpone the first climb until the snow let up was only one of many such decisions about the elements that we had to make along the Trail. We were not procrastinating, but we did not want to submit our bodies to the possibility of frostbite. Later, we heard stories of an older newspaperman who set out from Georgia in early March and suffered so badly from frostbitten fingers that he had to be treated by a doctor.

Biding our time, we rented a cozy cabin with plenty of hot water and a fully-equipped kitchen at Amicalola Falls. The National Forest maintains several of these cabins for tourists and hunters. All night the wind raged and rattled the glass. When we awoke it was cold but clear. We could get under way at last.

Up the steep, seven-mile approach trail we climbed to Springer Mountain (3,782 feet), the southern terminus of the Appalachian Trail, grandfather of all hiking trails in the

United States, the longest continuously marked trail in the world. With the first five days of food in our packs, we signed the Trail register.

That had been the day before. Now, in our freezing camp at Big Stamp Gap, we awoke shivering. Fortunately, the wind had died down. Forgetting our exalted purpose, like zombies we stared at geysers bubbling up from our breakfast grits. Then the smell of sizzling bacon alerted our senses. Sunlight fell on our camp. An azure butterfly, like a flying violet, led us to the Trail. It was going to be all right.

We struggled up and down mountainsides these early days of the hike, stopping frequently to rest, catch our breath, and look at the tips of the great Blue Ridge Mountains corrugating the land as far as the eye could see.

This sub-range of the Chattahoochee Mountains was not an easy one for the novice hiker. Springer Mountain already proved that. Every two hours we stopped by a stream to wipe our faces with cool water. What a novelty not to have to turn a faucet. Water was everywhere, miniature waterfalls over rocks, thin rivulets meandering toward the valleys, hidden springs gushing as if from nowhere to form small clear pools in the moss-covered culverts. Our toes unsocked and cooling in one of those streams, we sat side by side eating raisins and Cracker Jacks, vying for the prize of a shiny bauble ring that Julia wore in her boot strap a few hundred miles. The raisins, we found, lasted longer in our stomachs: Every raisin a calorie, every calorie a step.

Our bodies stiffened early in the hiking day. Often, only the words in the guidebook kept us going, urging us on to the next shelter where spring water, firewood, and a flat tent site—we hoped—awaited us for a comfortable night's sleep. A sleepless night was as bad as no water, two sleepless nights, disaster.

A quiet desperation set inside our psyches during these

beginning days. We had not yet toned our hiking muscles or truly learned our pace and walking rhythms. We didn't know what we could do, and so the rush to move forward filled our heads with a drive to reach water before night. The thought of trapping ourselves somewhere in the unmanageable dark haunted us. Our backlog of experience was too scant to abandon ourselves to patterns not yet fully ingrained.

One day we kept seeing the distinct footprints of Vibram lug soles. We feared that the next shelter would be taken, not that we wanted the shelter, but already we had become accustomed to the silence of an unpeopled world. Fatigued, we climbed Hawk Mountain. Spurred on by yellow violets growing mysteriously every twenty feet, we reached the top and shaded our eyes from the brilliant sun, low in the afternoon sky. A hawk swooped around the summit and glided overhead, neck craned, wings splayed, to eye the intruders.

We were right. When we reached Gooch Gap shelter, smoke lazed up through the treetops. Our shoulders slumped when we saw the lean-to already inhabited. The ground around the shelter heaved and swelled, rough sailing for a tent. Since the taciturn couple didn't appreciate us any more than we did them ("Well, have they gone yet?" the man whispered to the woman) we found a site farther on in a cozy grove of white pines that whistled in the wind.

While one of us got water at a nearby spring, the other built a fire, soon to be standard procedure. Whenever apart, we kept in touch by blowing dime-store whistles. One whistle meant: *Where are you?* Two: *Come here.* Three: *Help!*

After a dinner of chipped beef and instant potatoes, we secured all the food in big plastic bags and pulleyed them into a tree, making sure no food was in or near the tent for marauding bear and raccoon.

Then with flute in hand Julia went off to serenade the full

moon's rising and all the unseen creatures that skirred through the night.

> *The moon spills down the narrows*
> *of trunks and spreads in golden rivulets*
> *over last year's leaves,*
> *while this year's, papery and new,*
> *shimmer like displaced water*
> *shot off the mainstream.*
> *How can we sleep when these light rivers*
> *run under our tent and glimmer*
> *through our closed eyes?*

At dawn a phoebe came by the tent singing her friendly two-note name. The brisk morning called for something special. We sat in front of the fire warming our fingers, stirring our hash browns, and deciding what to get in Suches, the first grocery-town since the start of our hike four days ago. We walked 2¼ miles off the Trail on a gravel road that rolled through small country farms.

This one-telephone-booth town was the first stop for most long-distance Trail hikers. Like a crescent, Suches lined the banks of a lake surrounded with rounded hills and lush green meadows and pastures. The sky that day was as clear as the spring water we were drinking from the Appalachians.

The original general store was equipped with everything from shovels to soda pop. An iron pot-bellied stove squatted opposite the front door. The wooden floor creaked underfoot. Cooking pots and garden hoes hung on nails high on the walls. We bought what we could get from our list, the priority being moleskin bandages for blisters. We had to settle for hamburger buns in place of French bread, and macaroni and cheese instead of Quiche Lorraine.

"We get a lot of hikers round this time," the tall slim man in coveralls said from the cashier's counter. "Where you-uns from?"

"New Hampshire."

"Hiking the Trail, huh?"

"Yep."

"Well, anything you need, you just ask for it."

When we asked for hooch, he was startled. "Why, this a dry county." So we asked for pocket-size notebooks. He rummaged around and came up with just what we wanted —notepads advertising Bull of the Woods Chewing Tobacco and Dental Sweet Snuff. We bought a half-dozen fresh eggs, a pound of Cheddar cheese, two spoons (our experimental plastic ones broke), and four Eskimo Pies to eat on the spot.

The man couldn't find any flannel sleeping bag linings, so his wife telephoned the new general store across the lake. "You two go over yonder," she said, "and they'll fix you up with something."

We bought four yards of flannel material to make a floral mummy liner. Two local elderly women at the counter saw the material and, like blood grandmothers, unfolded the yardage and said, "Why isn't this perfect material. You could make a lovely dress with this, my dear. Is that what you're going to do?"

"Not really. It's cold at night and all we've got are summer sleeping bags. We're going to make inner linings to help keep us warm."

"A good idea. Really, it is," one grandmother said excitedly to the other. "She could sew it like this, and then tack this together here, and then make it so it's all open here at the top. It'd be perfect, wouldn't it?" Everyone agreed.

We ate lunch by the side of the lake. Julia played her flute, which she backpacked in a crush-proof box made of cardboard and cloth. The Bach sonata beckoned three waterthrush warblers chirping and fluttering beside the rapids where we sat.

Warmed, full, and feeling befriended by Suches, we hiked on and arrived at Winfield Scott State Park later in the afternoon. The park was closed. It was still winter in Georgia, and nobody with any interest in outdoor comfort vacationed in early April. The park was so placid and restrained that it alarmed us on sight, a reaction totally unexpected. The dark lake was dotted white with unmoving ducks and geese. Not a breath stirred; not a branch moved, nor a bird's wing, nor a squirrel. The stone picnicking shelters stood in muted sullenness as if the myriad voices of last summer were straining for emancipation. What lurked in the silence we didn't know, but we both—separately, then together—felt the tension mount.

The caretaker met us at the entrance. "Park's closed for restoration," the man said. "One of the cabins burned down and we have to replace it, but help yourself to the wood. Here, do you want some water?"

He was balding and paunchy. His belt was strapped below his hanging belly. He examined us a second too long, and once too many times, for us to be at ease. Nonetheless, we did need water. We filled our water jug, an ingenious spigot roll-up plastic container made in England. We thanked the caretaker and walked toward the building he indicated as a possible overnight camp.

Not a soul was in sight, and we continued to feel uneasy, though we could not place the cause. We checked out a roof shelter with fireplace, cement floor, and tables, but decided on our old stand-by, the soft ground. We separated to gather kindling. What was it about this place? We were used to the no-people scene—in fact we luxuriated in solitude. The caretaker's truck was parked on the other side of the lake. If the park was closed, what was he doing?

Suddenly, at the edge of the lake, in a clump of head-high pine trees about twenty feet in front of us, we saw a dead deer, shot recently, its body angled in a grotesque death, legs contorted into an ugly tangle, eyes staring nowhere.

"What do we do?"

"I don't know, but I don't like this place. It gives me the creeps. Creepy Lake."

"Let's go."

We grabbed the water jug and rushed into the woods. At first we were lost, but we soon found the trail connecting to the main AT. We hiked as if being followed. For two miles we virtually ran over the mountain ridges until the approaching night caught us. We didn't know where we were or what we ran from. All we knew was that once again we were surrounded by our friends, the living deer and the sounds of a trickling freshet.

After several forays into the trees, we found a spot in a depression to block the wind and quickly set up camp in the dark and cold. The trees creaked in the wind and enveloped us with their large bony black trunks and leafless limbs, making jumping shadows in the night, keeping us alert. We re-named this site the Witchy Woods Camp. Since our Primus camp stove wouldn't ignite, we cooked macaroni and cheese over a fire in a circle of rocks. The light from the fire flickered our silhouettes as high as the oaks that encircled us. We were alone and nervously keen to the slightest sound beyond the comforting range of firelight.

Again we slept little that night, and cursed ourselves for not bringing down sleeping bags. Without fail, the cold nights and hot days forced a rhythm into our appreciation of the backwoods.

Because it was the weekend, we met twenty-one people on Blood Mountain (4,458 feet), re-named Mt. Blood, Sweat, and Tears after the climb. At the top we stuck our heads into the windowless four-walled shelter. Three hikers were rolling up their sleeping bags on the dirt floor. The remains of a fire smoldered in the central stone fireplace.

"Have a good sleep?" we asked.

"Man, last night there were rats running around here as big as cats."

Tinfoil envelopes and tins from freeze-dried dinners were scattered in a pile near the dry kindling. This Skid Row on a mountaintop made us hurry back into the light and fresh air.

By noon of this, our fifth day on the Trail we were sweating in our summer shirts. The warmth was welcome, for it was resurrecting the earth. The spotted yellow trout lilies floated among the dark green galax leaves that covered the forest floor. May apple leaves unwhorled, fiddleheads uncurled. Congregations of bluets stared up bright-eyed as we passed.

The Neels Gap forest ranger, short, heavy-bellied, and loquacious, greeted us as we entered his way station. "You're numbers 63 and 64 this year," he told us after we signed the register. "That's how many Trail hikers are heading for Maine this year so far. You two look like you're carrying the lightest packs. No, I take that back. One hiker came in here with hardly anything. He said he wasn't carrying nothing except a five-pound bag of mixed nuts. Another girl and her dog came in. She was walkin' barefoot. Her blisters were so big she couldn't put on her boots. You know what? Only about five of those passing through here will make it to Katahdin."

We performed our ablutions in the lodge lavatories and washed our dirty socks and bodies with hot water. For lunch we lopped off slices of a one-pound salami and added them to cheese sandwiches on cocktail rye. Lunches were that simple. We sampled an assortment of candy bars from the vending machine, and set off to the woods again, our socks bobbing dry on our packs.

At an outcrop of granite and grass high on an unnamed rise, we rested and lolled in the sun to enjoy the expanse of Blue Ridge Mountains that gullied the earth below us. A black vulture eased his way on a thermal updraft toward us on a swoop of inspection. Perhaps our bright red nylon packs caught his eye. Perhaps he saw our Snickers candy bars. More than likely he was asserting his presence as the keeper of this dominion. He eased lower so that we could see the light patches on the underside of each spread wing. For a time we studied each other at eye level, a special treat that no downtown skyscraper affords. This bird, with its five-foot wingspread, was both command and beauty, a scouting warrior of the sky, a passing tribute to the wilds of the high mountains.

By the end of the first full week we were doing nine to ten miles per day instead of seven. We were learning that it paid to select a campsite early. One night we picked a moss-covered ledge, and, to insure double comfort, we pushed dry leaves under our poncho ground covering. The ponchos, we discovered, were far from waterproof in a heavy rain, but served well as ground covers, makeshift entrance roofs, pack covers, bathrobes in laudromats, pack padding when the portable pot handle stuck us in the back, windbreaks in high altitudes, rainwater collectors.

We were learning much about nature as well. The warblers, quick and small, defied identification, yet we spotted chestnut-sided and black and white warblers. In our plastic zip-lock offices, we carried paperback bird, flower, and tree books (minus the covers and several pages, which we thought added unnecessary weight). Dogwood was blossoming, not just white but yellow and pink. White bloodroot and scarlet wake-robins, bright harbingers of spring, advertised themselves against the drab forest floor. Still, the trees on the ridges refused to green.

Again we needed provisions. The sorghum syrup we poured from a plastic baby bottle onto our grits was nearly gone. Also, the ground Brazilian coffee we boiled camp style proved too much trouble. We were out of chipped beef and instant potatoes. The hickory-smoked ham bought in Suches disappeared in a day. Our appetites were growing as fast as the mountain dandelions. Each night we were famished, each morning we were famished.

On the way to Helen a turkey hunter gave us a lift to town. It had just started to rain. A mile later we passed another hunter hunkering down by a compact fire over which he was frying country ham and eggs in a black iron skillet. Rain drops dripping from his gray hat sizzled in the grease.

"See any turkey?" our driver asked.

"Not a one. Ol' Jack Anderson saw four."

"Did he fire any?"

"Nope. Said he counted seven deer this mornin'. That's the way it is. In turkey season you see deer. In deer season you see turkey."

We drove through the drizzle to a camp where other hunters congregated. It was the first day of the season. We hadn't flushed any wild turkey, but we heard many gobbling sounds in the night.

At our next site the rain continued without letup, and the drive to break camp and head out onto the Trail diminished to zero. We decided to remain in camp the entire day to rest and recuperate. We hadn't realized how exhausted we were.

That night, while we were fetching water at the spring, our flashlights discovered a brilliant orange newt. The spring rains brought out the snails, salamanders, and other semi-aquatic creatures and plant life. One day, while heating vegetable soup on a soggy log, we happened on a jellyfish-like blob among the fiddleheads. Often while climbing the slick sides of mountains, we came across what by all appearances seemed the land version of a starfish (later classified as a star puff-ball). Also, we began sharing the Trail with scores of centipedes, and told them outright,

Centipedes, even with one hundred legs
you aren't going as far as we are.

At lunch Steve, nicknamed Dr. Namrehs, popped blisters on his heel, toes, and soles. Dr. Redlo assisted with sterilizing flames for the needle. After inserting the needle, we drained the blisters, applied antiseptic ointment, and covered them with moleskin pads.

Both of us suffered from sore left feet. We had to relieve the pressure on blisters by removing one of two socks from the left foot, though we kept both socks on the right foot. It didn't make sense, unless perhaps the left foot of most people is larger than the right, and shoe manufacturers do not allow for this discrepancy. In any case, we shared a sore left foot syndrome.

Dr. Redlo, her feet toughened from walking in sandals the previous year, suffered other physical discomfiture. Outside of Deep Gap (they were all deep) while scaling a 4,420-foot nameless peak, a tight knot formed at the back of her left leg. Fortunately, our medicine kit contained Ben-Gay, which was applied immediately, freely, and effectively.

Shortly afterward, two young hikers came through the gap, stopped, and talked. One had hiked many parts of the Appalachian Trail in the South and spoke with aplomb. He restrained his wonder at meeting people who were actually hiking the entire Trail in one season. "Well, if you make it through Stekoah to the Smokies in a couple of weeks," he said, the frown of authority creasing his forehead, "if you make it that far, then you'll make it the whole way."

We had heard about the twenty-five-mile Stekoah section in North Carolina. Along with Mahoosuc Notch in Maine, it was considered one of the most challenging parts of the Trail.

The rains came again, this time spraying us under power of a mountain-high wind. We hiked up from Tray Mountain Gap and into a storm cloud thick with driving rain that struck us horizontally in the face. Visibility shrank to thirty feet. We reached the summit of the mountain and, according to the Trail guidebook, were to be rewarded with one of the most sweeping panoramas in that section of the country. Instead, we walked eye level with a cold April tempest. The rain soaked our jeans and shirts; the snaps from our ponchos had yanked loose. The only comfort about our ponchos was their color—bright yellow and orange. With the hoods up, we resembled a joyous holy order. Our brown cotton garden gloves turned into sponges, our socks blotters, our jeans candlewicks.

The sky was unkind to us that day. The Trail was, too, for it turned to mud and slick logs and rocks as dangerous as wet marble steps. We plodded on, if only to hike down from the driving rain and torment to relief in the shallow gulches where the woods, barren as they were, at least offered some protection.

We hoped for a motel and hot shower, but the next town turned out to be Browning's Gas Station. The store shelves were sparsely stocked with grits, antique corn flakes, pig hocks, and candy bars. The nearest head of lettuce was six miles away. Two tourist cabins out back were closed, but Mr. Browning offered us an old school bus converted to living quarters. Would we take that?

Browning owned the store, but Geneva, a small wiry old mountain woman who wore white cotton string in her hair and tattered tennis shoes, ran it. Browning offered us a lift into Hiawassee to pick up some fresh produce while he bought a tank of butane gas for the stove in the bus. Our quarters were somewhat less than we expected, but they were a piece of paradise out of the downpour.

At Geneva's invitation, we tromped mud all through her house to use her bath facilities. The next morning we chatted with this feisty Georgian. "I love these mountains," she said, "and nobody's going to ruin them if I can help it. Nobody can take 'em away. We're mountain folk and you got to protect the ground you stand on. Most of you-uns are real nice, but one mornin' I was lookin' out the window and saw two girls stealin' postage from my mailbox. Well, I took my shotgun to 'em and they shore did clear out. Don't you blame me?"

The rain continued. We waited for a break in the clouds, which came about ten o'clock. When we were three hundred yards beyond the store, Mr. Browning chugged up in his pickup and gave us a ride to the Trail, some parts of which he had walked himself. One time, he was chasing his hogs that had taken off into the woods with wild boar.

"When I found one of my hogs, I tied a bell to its neck," he said. "Whole lot of mine come in and we sugar cured every one of them."

At Plumorchard Gap we descended to a crosstrail with a large garbage heap and eight hikers lolling against their packs. Overpopulation gave us claustrophobia. We filled our water bag and walked farther up the Trail to privacy. The intermittent sun called for celebration. A dinner of fried country-smoked ham smothered in bread dressing with chives, garlic, sausage, and dry mustard, along with mashed potatoes garnished with knife-slivers of Cheddar cheese, came out of our packs. Magic. We topped it all with a tisane of freshly-picked wintergreen leaves and eased into sleep, dreaming of North Carolina.

Virginia · Tennessee
Johnson City
Great Smoky Mountains
Nat'l Park
Mt. Guyot
Clingman's Dome · Mt. Leconte
ngWater
helter
Fontana Lake
Cheoah
Bald
Sweetwater Gap
Stekoah Gap
Wesser
Rocky Bald
Black
Bald
Sassafras Gap
Tellico Bald
ahala State
Park
Wayah
Bald
Loafer's Glory
North Carolina
Georgia · South Carolina

Hot Springs
Rocky Bluff Campground
Little Pigeon River
Asheville
1" = 28 Miles
North
Carolina

North Carolina

229 MILES

In North Carolina the Trail bordered the Tennessee state line. Often the hiker crossed over, unaware of having passed into the adjacent state. This tended to become confusing and embarrassing, especially if you told someone how much you liked North Carolina and he calmly informed you that you were in Tennessee.

17

We entered North Carolina on April 20. Soon, we noticed a pronounced economic difference between North Carolina and Georgia. In the towns on the Trail, such as Wesser and Hot Springs, the mountain people were better off. No doubt tourism contributed to this affluence. More than seven million people passed through the Great Smoky Mountains National Park each year. Also, a big land boom was on, and retired people were buying property near the many rivers and lakes.

One road contractor we spoke with claimed that North Carolina had 73,000 miles of roads, more than any other state. However, 60,000 miles were unpaved. Hunters enjoyed this back-country access, and large resorts on the scale of Nantahala and Fontana Dam were tucked away in the lush woodlands of North Carolina's valleys.

Loafer's Glory wasn't a resort. It was a general store on the way to Wayah Bald, and a shining example of the old-time drugstore, hardware store, and grocery store rolled into one. We filled every item on our list except Ben-Gay, left behind at Browning's bus in Georgia.

"Here," the storekeeper said, handing us a brown medicine bottle. "This is jes' what you-uns need. I guarantee it'll cure y'all."

We unscrewed the lid. One whiff was enough to cure the devil. Brown's Liniment. Contents: Pine tar (turpentine), and alcohol. The directions bragged, "Use freely on sore area. Good for man and beast." We took it.

Outside in the sun we loafed and ate spoonfuls of Neapolitan ice cream, the "large economy size," a half gallon. Then we got to work, removing cardboard from cereal boxes, taking nuts out of cans, pouring instant soups and sauces from tinfoil packets. The first time we eliminated all the cardboard, paper and tinfoil from our food supply, we weighed it just for fun—nearly three pounds of Madison Avenue packaging!

That night we camped in the Nantahala State Park, one of

the many efficiently managed, clean parks along the Trail. After freely applying Brown's Liniment "for man and beast," we decided it would serve better as starter fuel. At sunset, with the eastern full moon rising like a pumpkin out of season, we ate a dinner of chipped beef and gravy over instant potatoes and skillet biscuits that rose fluffy and triumphant. Beef was salted and preserved by the early American settlers. Today salted chipped beef was still a versatile meat that traveled well. We always soaked the beef shreds to tone down the salt before creaming them with flour and instant milk or packaged gravy. For dessert we stewed prunes, and the next day regretted it.

Despite having to run off into the bushes once too often, we managed to hike the 3.7 miles up 5,336-foot Wayah Bald in one hour and thirty-five minutes, a 2.4-mile-per-hour pace that astounded us when we calculated it at the summit. We had been on the Trail for two weeks and, although we wanted to think that our Southern grits and sorghum syrup were the telling factors in this burst of energy, our bodies and spirits were growing stronger. The Trail was ours. This was not a weekend excursion into the trees. This was a commitment to walking together in back-country North America. Already we were nurturing a friendship with the woods. What awaited, we hoped, was a mature intimacy with the wilderness.

At the Wayah Bald lookout tower, which resembled a medieval turret, we shaded our eyes from the midmorning sun and pirouetted slowly for a complete 360 degrees. The sweeping circle of horizon rolled from our station as if the land were a pond rippling endlessly outward. We enjoyed our first unobstructed view of the Nantahala Mountain Range. To the north the rugged peaks of Stekoah looked like fabric cut out with pinking shears. The mountaintops faded into a steel-gray haze, erasing the distance. These mountains were old and tolerant, most of them formed prior to Paleozoic times in the Precambrian period, when only the most primitive aquatic plants existed. What we were looking at was "Old Appalachia," and from our vantage point we pivoted toward the new.

A brown thrasher sat in a budding silverbell tree singing his repertoire, aria after aria, his tail vibrating and flapping on the more grandiose trills.

The microscopic and the macroscopic surrounded us. All we had to do was look. The more we looked the more we saw. It was all there and alive. On the way down from Wayah Bald we sat on a log to rest and have a snack of almonds and mincemeat. British soldiers, a lichen, marched the grooved bark of the log, a kind of toothpick army dressed in red. Two deer browsing along a stream leapt from us when a twig snapped. They crashed through the dry branches and disappeared up a hillside, their white-tailed rumps as slick as their strides.

The Trail offered a pleasant path high along the sides of Tellico, Black, and Rocky Balds before a steep 1,400-yard grade to the Wesser Bald firetower. At a junction in the gap a truck pulled up on the gravel fire road and a young boy and older man jumped out. "You see a boy come by here? We was supposed to meet him at three o'clock."

"Where'd he start?" we asked.

"Can't rightly say. Think it was Wesser. Yeah, that's where. You seen 'im?"

This man and boy were just two of several people we had met looking for hikers on the Trail. This always amazed us, because unless you were a hiker yourself and knew the terrain, it was impossible to designate the exact minute you would be somewhere.

At Amicalola Falls, Georgia, the ranger told us about two small boys, without food or water, who were dropped off by careless parents. Then they drove on to wait for the boys at the falls. What they hadn't counted on was that the hike by Trail took at least two days. People on wheels have a difficult time judging distances.

Now this grandfather and his grandson stood before us flabbergasted as we told them that if the boy had started in Wesser at noon the day before, they'd probably have to wait until nightfall to pick him up.

A few minutes later a battered green pickup truck full of family and friends bounded past us down the road. We waved to the half dozen boys and girls in the back load bed. "Happy Easter!" the woman in the passenger seat called as the truck clanked by. We sat down on a nearby stump and reflected. This was our thirteenth hiking day, of that we were sure, but Easter?

The days of festivity, the national holidays, the news of Washington had disappeared into the shade of another world. Our concentration was focused on staying alive—food, shelter, water, sleep, protection from the unknown, planning for the immediate future, maintaining supplies, restoring our tired bodies, re-creating our sagging spirits, moving on, moving on. How could this two thousand-year-old celebration elude us? Easter momentarily brought us back to the other world, like an aroma akin to an old family recipe nobody makes anymore. Now our exhaustion took precedence as we climbed upward toward the firetower, pushing over the other side before nightfall.

We found that this growing sense of belonging to the woods held fast from one campsite to another. Each day brought us a new site to pitch our tent, set up our kitchen, roll out our bedroom, stake out our bathroom, select our storage room. We were finding that each new house turned into "home" in about half an hour. We continually marveled that a strange campsite could become so intimate, cozy and personally ours.

One morning we awoke just outside of Wesser, North

Carolina, a railway stop on an obsolete track. And it was spring. Trillium and yellow fritillaria bowed their heads as we passed. Fiddlehead ferns tuned to the sun's rising baton. We shouted deafening eulogies to the dogwood, spring beauties, flowering almond. The honeysuckle accosted our lungs, and old apple trees pumped out their clouds of heavy blossoms. The butterflies' Rorschach wings skimmed the shale above the river.

"What is this place?"

"Wesser Creek Canyon."

"It can't be that. Let's re-name it. How about Gorgeous Gorge?"

The smaller streams meshed into one another until finally all of them united in Wesser Creek, a boulder-filled river rushing headlong down the mountainside. We followed the river as it moved closer to the bottom of the canyon and a dirt road with the first house with plowed fields, and finally a row of houses on the brown dusty road that eventually turned to asphalt. We followed the white blazes on fence posts and telephone poles through this country settlement. Across the fields where the dark green spruces lined the forest edges like a stage backdrop, dogwood blossoms hung loose and free in mid-sky. The delicate spots of white floated idly past the heavy oaks, pines, and firs.

The small town of Wesser was the starting point of the notorious rugged twenty-five-mile section of the Trail that led toward Stekoah Gap. We stood at the center of town, a filling station–store, and wondered where we would go for a much-needed rest. The motel was closed. A gargantuan flatbed truck pulled up. "Where you headed?"

We mouthed the standard response, which never evoked the same reaction. "We're walking the Appalachian Trail from Georgia to Maine, two thousand miles."

"Well, now, that calls for a celebration. Too bad we're going the other way or we'd give you a lift. George, give them folk somethin' to eat."

A thick, hairy arm reached out the window. "Here. Mrs. Carter baked this special for us. Don't taste whole wheat bread like this no more."

George broke off a hunk of cheese and handed it down with the bread. "How long you-uns reckon it'll take?"

"Five months."

"Wow, that's a long time." The driver leaned over. "I'd do it myself but I'm a married man. Got kids to feed. Take it you ain't got no kids."

We were doing something he might have done earlier in his life if a Depression and World War hadn't lurked in the wings. Our spirits uplifted by these strangers' interest and kindness, we walked uphill three miles toward a resort called Nantahala Village. We stopped at Charlie's Drive-in for lunch. The owner, waitress, and cook placed two king-size cheeseburgers in front of us. "Why, ain't I seen you on the Appalachian Trail?" she asked. She was the one who had yelled Happy Easter a couple of days before.

It was a pleasant feeling to meet someone we knew. Usually on the Trail people passed each other—the extent of their friendship. "You know," she chatted, "I'm from Tennessee and we're just home folk. In the Wesser firetower we met some boys from Chicago. Well, I had some Easter eggs with me and I wanted to give 'em some. You know what they did? Just laughed. I was just tryin' to be good, like I am to everybody. You know, I'd never go north for love nor money. I love these Smokies too much." We set off carrying a Coke, compliments of the house.

Nantahala Village was an all-inclusive resort providing a relaxed atmosphere on two hundred acres overlooking Fontana Lake and the Great Smokies. We were given a small rustic cabin, which to us was the Ritz. Hot water, clean sheets, dogwood bobbing in the breeze outside the window, and a plump wood thrush with a black speckled belly officiating on a nearby branch.

That night we dressed up (i.e. combed our hair and put

on a clean sweat shirt and thirty-year-old Navy sweater), to eat in the dining room. After finishing off cold cucumber soup, roast beef, mountain rainbow trout, string beans, hush puppies, candied yams, sauerkraut, a chef's salad, blueberry muffins, biscuits, and hot tea, we ordered a rhubarb tart and lemon meringue pie à la mode. The waitress, who had been frantically running back and forth to the kitchen ever since we sat down, tried to keep her cool. Rhubarb tart à la mode, yes. But lemon meringue pie à la mode?

Our two days of rest were dry. Naturally, after we were back on the Trail an hour it began to drizzle. Well, we would up Stekoah, rain and all. Fortitude, perseverance, doggedness, grit, and all those charming qualities, wear down when climbing a mountain so steep your heels won't flatten against the ground. We clocked our progress at a mile an hour.

At Jump-up, a rocky edge so precipitous it demanded a special title, we began to feel like woodpeckers climbing a tree trunk. Occasionally, logs were laid across the Trail to help the hiker reach the next level a foot-and-a-half away. No tree-holds were available for balance, let alone to pull ourselves upward. Pebbles slid from underfoot. We toppled back and forth under the precarious weight of our packs, slipped, sweated, and cursed. We struggled up three or four steps at a time.

"Who routed this stupid Trail?"

"They're nuts. Crazy, damn fools. What do they think we are? Giraffes?"

At the top we stored the impression of deep V valleys left by this upheaval of rock edges. The Jump-up formed the brim of a spinach-green drop down the mountainside, a dizzy spill as forbidding from the top as from the bottom. We scanned the terrain we had covered. In the faint distance we saw the minute matchstick outline of the firetower on Wesser Bald. We had climbed up and down those ridge lines that stretched behind us. Amazed by this discovery we asked ourselves if we were actually capable of such a feat? What else were we capable of?

Next morning, once more in the rain, we approached Sassafras Gap from a sixty-five-degree descent on a muddy, rocky, chute of peril. Our boots gouged foot-long slip marks in the mud. Our hands, only slightly protected by the seventy-nine-cent gardening gloves, slipped down the slick limbs and shoots we grabbed to steady our falls.

At the bottom we met two boys wearing green plastic garbage bags over their packs. They watched as we skidded down, hanging onto trees and do-si-do–ing around brush and slippery logs. "Hey, you guys must be wearing good boots. You're the first ones we've seen headed down the gap that haven't fallen." We vouched for our Chippewas.

Many hiking books had strongly emphasized the importance of good boots. We selected these particular boots because they were light enough to provide flexibility, yet strong enough to give support. The cushion ankle tops, back, and "Kush-n-Kollar" gave us added comfort. After Stekoah, many thru-hikers were already sending away for a second pair of boots. Our quarter-inch lug soles were still as good as new.

After eulogizing our boots, we remarked that the two hikers looked like figures out of a carnival with their rain suits and garbage bags. "Walking this Trail in the rain *is* a carnival," they answered.

Stekoah taught us a lot about hiking on wet mountains. Often our pack shoulder straps would loosen with continued stress, and then on descents the pack weight shifted from side to side. This was extremely dangerous, and we made a habit of checking our straps and weight balance before heading down.

Also, we discovered that the Trail was most dangerous where it was worn. So we aimed for the borders of mulch and pebbles, avoiding flat, slippery stones and branches. We reminded ourselves with a checklist:

	VERY SLIPPERY	SLIPPERY	SAFER
Wet stone	X		
Wet leaves			X
Wet pine needles		X	
Mud	X		
Mulch			X
Sand			X

Through a gauzy storm cloud that soaked us to the skin, we climbed Cheoah Bald (5,036 feet). Except for a colossal surge of unbridled optimism, we would have remained in our sleeping bags to wait out the rain. At the top of Cheoah, where visibility shrank to a thirty-foot maximum, all we saw were each other's glum faces. It was too wet to stop, too wet to remove our dripping ponchos and water-heavy packs, even too wet to heed the calls of nature. The elements were indifferent. We passed the wooden marker at the summit with barely a glance and proceeded down the steep far side of the mountain.

In the persistent rain and cold, we were becoming experts of body circulation. In the morning, no matter how chilly it was at breakfast, after a few hundred feet of hiking, a long-sleeved shirt and nylon windbreaker provided adequate—and often too much—warmth. As soon as we stopped for snacks, we would keep a sweater handy to slip on against sudden chill. In Georgia and North Carolina quite often we wore gloves. Our pack straps cut off circulation to the hands, and a great deal of time we suffered from cold fingers.

Just after we got the tent up at Sweetwater Gap, more rain fell. It rained all night and, although our tent was waterproof, the downpour, the bolts of lightning, the booms of thunder, rocked our brains too much to sleep. We lay in our isolated campsite listening to the thunder like some mighty stamp hammer of the sky trying to flatten the mountaintops. The explosions of lightning shot through the tent with the intensity of searchlights in a desperate World War. When the mighty thunder vibrated among the canyons below, and even shook the little sag we were camped in, we definitely knew we were under attack. Our only hope was that the enemy lightning would never discover us in our tiny clump of trees. If it did, we prayed that we wouldn't be fried to death between the aluminum layers of our reflector sleeping bags.

When the morning sun burned off enough clouds to make a show, we broke camp. The rufous-sided towhees cavorted and tried to cheer us up as they followed along the Trail singing their monotonous greetings.

Yes, if you made it through the Stekoahs to the Smokies alive, you stood a good chance to make it to Maine.

As we walked, we saw several sleepy communities tucked neatly in place at the bottom of long green valleys. We had an advantage over the people living in them; we could see the next settlement over the mountains. Then again, they could see our viewpoint peak, and several others denied from where we stood.

The Trail edged one of the crests that could have been any old part of the planet, were we humans not possessed with naming everything. At times we ourselves wanted to be nameless, too, so we could become even closer to these mountains which the maps called the Great Smokies.

We marveled at the gigantic culverts of earth filled with crawling mist. On one side was a vast boil of steam, on the other, an empty cauldron of durable rock, a vat of mountainside waiting for the next helping of cloud and fog. The valleys took their turns. This misty, magical region changed face sometimes in a matter of minutes. Knobs of mountaintops, surrounded at their bases by the smoke of this eerie world, floated like islands. Head clouds led the solid banks, dutiful platoons, well-disciplined and correct. They wisped ahead of the pack, testing the lay of the land, poking gingerly ahead, scouting what valleys could be occupied with ease.

We stopped and, like children, made pictures from the drifting scenes. Witches' heads. Eagle wings. Monster noses. Granny fingers. Clipper ships. Dragon jaws. Many of these images had come from T. H. White's *Sword in the Stone*, which we were reading each night by the campfire. Enchanted, we listened as Merlin the wizard changed Wart, the young King Arthur, into a kestrel and took him to the falconry to learn how to be a hawk. Wart's transformations into, first, a fish, then a bird, and finally a snake, became our own transformations on the Trail, made walking more imaginative, and gave us added insight when we did spot a sparrow hawk or a black snake.

On April 27 we came down once more into the valley, this time at Fontana Dam Village. The delicate mitrewort and wild iris grew taller with each raindrop as we grew damper, grumpier, and impatient for a shower of a different temperature.

> *I'm walkin' the Appalachian Trail.*
> *My feet are in blisters*
> *and my body's sore as hell.*
> *For six straight days*
> *I seen nothin' but rain.*
> *To walk the Trail*
> *from Georgia to Maine, Lord,*
> *you got to be insane, Lord,*
> *you got to be insane.*

We hiked the last six miles to Fontana Dam Village in rain, fog, and mist on a steep, slippery, muddy trail that at times doubled as an aqueduct. We had perspired over precipitous cliffs, through pernicious precipitation, and if we made light of it, this was the only way to relieve the tension of quivering knees, sore spines, and blistered feet. Dr. Redlo now joined Dr. Namrehs at his blister-popping sessions, shouting "Hallelujah!" and praying for salvation and calluses.

I'm walkin' the Appalachian Trail,
and I haven't gotten far,
but I sure could use another candy bar.
My pack is creakin' like a lonesome friend.
Sure do wonder when this Trail will end, Lord,
sure do wonder if this Trail will end.

Fontana Village had that look of an army installation, complete with PX and shooting range. We rented a small cottage in the subdivision of three hundred tourist accommodations, and made for the cafeteria filled with conventioning artisans from the Appalachians. Both of us were interested in crafts, but the meeting was not open to outsiders, especially outdoor outsiders.

In the warmth of our cabin, we read three bags full of mail that had waited for us at the post office. Then we strung out our wet tent and newly-washed clothes across the living room. The place looked like wash day in the Italian quarter of New York City.

By chance, we ran into another thru-hiker who informed us that we would be unable to hike the seventy-one miles of the Trail through the Great Smoky Mountains National Park without a fire permit. Subsequently, we telephoned the Park ranger who met us to issue the permit and also schedule nightly stopovers at the Trail shelters. Because of problems with bear, tenting in the Smokies was permitted only at official campgrounds.

Rested and refreshed, we crossed the bridge-walk over 480-foot Fontana Dam, one of the five original Tennessee Valley Authority reservoir projects of 1933. Slowly, we ascended to the ridge line. One by one, the wild geraniums and velvet lady slippers, the rue anemones and lilies of the valley disappeared. Once more we walked a barren crest as yet untouched by spring. The southern tulip and buckeye trees remained dormant. A few hardy chartreuse sassafras mittens shot through the layer of dead leaves.

We arrived at the Spring Water Shelter in midafternoon. Our permit indicated that we had to stay here on April 29. The shelter was a three-sided stone enclosure with a link fence to keep the bear out. Or was it to keep us in? Going for water wasn't a problem, since a muddy rivulet ran right past the door. We joined six other hikers in the dark cavern and took turns, two by two, huddling around a small fireplace stuck as an afterthought in the corner. We took off our packs and selected two of the twelve chicken wire double-decker bunks. The shelter pretended to sleep twelve, but three of the bunks were torn and sagging. Other hikers ambled in, rubbed their frosty fingers, and sidled toward the fireplace. The warmth was make-believe.

We started our Primus in the hope of warming our stomachs and bodies. A backpacking German shepherd ambled over and nosed our pots. He looked as miserable and hungry as the rest of us. We cooked spaghetti with dehydrated tomato sauce, adding slivers of garlic, dehydrated onions, and plenty of oregano, the secret to Italian cookery. In two minutes the spaghetti was gone, and we were scraping freshly pulled sassafras roots for tea. Root beer aroma filled the air. Sassafras was a discovery that took us scores of wrong identifications and two states to find.

Everyone hit the sack early. A freezing wind funneled down the ravine and into a crack between the stone wall and tin roof. A latecomer clanged the gate and fumbled around in the dark, opening and shutting plastic bags. We huddled in our summer bags; the flannel jersey inserts from Suches, Georgia, were slight help. We wore every stitch of clothing, but froze anyway. Our teeth chattered. Restlessly, we turned on the creaky wire bunks. We had planned to make our nightly trips together, so in case Smoky the Bear came by to say hello we would have help. Our metabolism accelerated because of the cold, and both of us got up, trying to aim our flashlights beyond the downy warm bodies of the other sleepers. The bare branches caught the stars and wore them like Christmas lights. It was a breathtaking spectacle. It was a cold spectacle. We returned to the frosty touch of nylon and shivered until dawn. Everyone woke up. We didn't have to.

We started a fire from the coals in the fireplace. The only other wide-awake hiker wore the number 26 on his shirt and stirred raisins into his oatmeal while scrutinizing a list, every once in a while muttering, "Twenty miles. No, let's see, twenty-two. If I do twenty-two . . ."

Just as we were leaving, he approached us. "Hey, I'm Jersey. Are you going into town? I sure could use a sweat shirt. Could you just drop this post card in the mailbox for me?"

We agreed that if we decided to leave the ridge, we'd drop off the card. For half an hour we sat on a log and mulled over the situation. We were ill-equipped for cold nights, and would never reach Maine if sleepless nights continued.

The Great Smoky Mountains National Park provides many alternatives to campers and hikers, developed and primitive campsites in the valleys, as well as shelters on the Appalachian Trail. We decided to head for the warmth of the lowland and a telephone to call for a down bag.

The Park showed off a variety of scapes we would not have seen had we stuck to the ridge line. We passed from stands of Virginia pine and balsam fir into meadows of greening raspberry and blueberry shrubs. Aware that this was bear country, we whistled the theme song from the "Bridge on the River Kwai" and other zesty favorites, repeating our repertoire ad nauseam. This vocal concert was enough to scare any living creature within hearing.

The foliage became thicker and greener as we descended.

Giant mountain hemlocks and red pines towered over the Trail. Rivers gurgled over mammoth boulders. We crossed one churning white water creek after another as if they, too, were flowering like the trillium and spring beauties. The light spiraled down through the tangled growth. Was this the Congo or the Smokies? Some of the trees grew 100 to 150 feet high, with girths as large as California redwoods.

At the Park headquarters we arranged to have a down bag mailed to us at Hot Springs, about a week's hike up the Trail. We bought new tree and wildflower books, since our old ones were dogeared. We had already spotted and identified most of their entries. The ranger gave us Campsite 22, a special out-of-the-way primitive spot for backpackers.

Certain that we had taken a wrong turn on the way to the site, we stopped at the edge of what looked like a gravel pit. Then we came to a small faded signpost: *Campsite 22*. It pointed down a flooded road, decidedly not a promising route. After a quarter-mile, however, we came to the rapids of the West Prong of Little Pigeon River. The site was idyllic. Nobody else was there. It was perched high above the deafening river on a flat embankment covered with Virginia pines. Its added feature was warmth, for pines, we noticed, seemed to trap the sun's heat under the bowers of needles.

The next morning after a snug, welcome sleep, and a breakfast of granola and coffee, we intended to hike the highest mountain on the Appalachian Trail, 6,642-foot Clingman's Dome. But when a scarlet tanager landed on a nearby hawthorn bush we asked ourselves why we shouldn't stay, fish, read, flute, and relax. Clingman's Dome had been there a few millenniums. It could wait another day.

Campsite 22 became the prototype of what a park or forest can offer the tenter. We spent the day taking time to wonder at the life force surrounding us—from a bully-loud river to towering tulip trees and the red ants that rushed along mounds of brown pine needles. We sniffed lilies of the valley like addicts. The flaming azaleas warmed us with their soda fountain colors. We walked past the mountain laurel that earlier had been dormant and now looked as if it had been decorated with sugar rosettes from a cake decorator.

Although we wanted to stay at Campsite 22 longer, our goal prodded us on. We did not look forward to hiking back to the frigid mountain saddlebacks. As we suspected, the closer we came to the summit of Clingman's Dome, the colder the air. By the time we reached the forests of balsam and Frazier fir, scattered patches of snow had turned into uniform blankets.

The summit observation tower took a prize in architecture second only to the Guggenheim Museum in New York City, and very much in the chambered nautilus style. With apprehension we looked ahead at the snow and snow clouds over Mounts Guyot and Le Conte.

Tourists dressed for summer skidded in patent leather Easter shoes down the path. Some threw snowballs. Others photographed this phenomenon more to be expected in the skiing country of the West—sun and snow together. The snow might have been a novelty to vacationers, but to us it was a disappointment. We would be unable to continue along the crest in snowy weather with flimsy summer sleeping bags.

Once more we walked off the heights, and headed for Cosby Cove Campground. Later, we were picked up by a vacationing couple from Michigan on their way to Florida. The husband hardly said a word. The wife said they had seen no wildlife in the Park and were extremely disappointed. We presumed they meant bear and deer. No, they had seen nothing, she insisted.

"Have you taken any of the trails?" we asked incredulously, thinking of the wildflowers so abundant that we had once gone only one mile in two hours because we could not pass them up. Forest carpets of wild geranium and marshmallow, vervain, groundsel, Solomon's seal, jack-in-the-pulpit, not to mention the trees—American basswood with their huge heart leaves, the delicate compound hickory frond, the distinct fan-shaped blackjack oak leaf and the star leaf of the liquidambar were everywhere. Weren't these wildlife?

"No, we haven't been on the trails," the wife admitted. "I don't like to get out of the car because of snakes. I'm deathly afraid of them."

In vain, we tried to convince them there was nothing to be afraid of if they were sensible. They seemed afraid of everything: rattlesnakes, bear, skunks, burning out their brakes in the mountains. We wondered from which wellspring came the courage to pick us up.

The next day we hiked 16½ miles, and camped in the only available clearing near our planned water source, a site we called Poison Ivy Alley. Awhile back, we had met another thru-hiking couple, Jerry and Alice. Alice told us when she was young she and her girl friend were to give a piano recital. The day before the performance they put their heads together to figure a way out of the ordeal. They went into the backwoods and vigorously rubbed their arms and hands with poison ivy. "My girl friend went to bed. She had to be shot with cortisone. Her eyes were swollen shut," Alice lamented. "But I didn't get one blister and had to play the recital anyway."

We laughed at Alice's story. However, as a precaution we carried a plastic bottle of Caladril. Also, we wiped off our jeans with our all-purpose sponge.

That night two barred owls, commonly known as eight-hooters, hooted at us from their hidden perches. Later, a whip-poor-will (or perhaps chuck-will's-widow), whistled ceaselessly into the night until we turned the harping into hypnotism and fell asleep.

The next day—May 4—we walked seventeen miles, past cascades falling down mossy-black gneiss tiers much like Japanese terrace gardens. Through this exquisite terrain we often found ourselves talking to the flowers, trees, birds, and salamanders. The birds were first to respond, but we kept trying with the others.

We often saw things on the Trail not wholly animal, vegetable, or mineral. These included small coins, discarded and moldy sweat shirts, freeze-dried foods, boots, blankets, and so on. At Poison Ivy Alley we met three hikers who picked up a packet of freeze-dried strawberries and a pair of brand-new Indian moccasins. Unfortunately, none of us wore size ten. We all agreed that this shedding of earthly belongings might lighten packs but was an eyesore and a discredit to the hikers doing it.

We walked through grazing land and rolling hills as surrealistic and cryptic as the lone muscular oaks standing watch through the haze. The valleys and weathered farm buildings stood guard against outsiders like us.

Fog settled over the Trail. Occasionally, the fog lifted to disclose a cheerful purple finch or a pair of goldfinches (always two), bobbing up and down like yoyos along Max Patch Road. A towhee followed us in the weeds along the barbed wire fence. Ravens lifted their large sleek wings and propelled themselves toward the hilltop in the glimmering sunlight. Patches of more fog lifted, and hillside meadows, green, tree-full, and luxurious, appeared above a kidney-shaped pond, no doubt full of hungry trout.

We passed a forsaken farmhouse. A wet Coke bottle sat on a table next to the porch swing dripping rain. An abandoned Buick that was gutted and left to rot in the stubby field suddenly appeared through the fog. Maybe its creaking hood listing in the wind signaled secrets in the mist ahead. Four sodden dogs growled and snarled from behind the old carcass. A white furry bitch befriended us, the others hung back, teeth bared, hackles up. Their masters were nowhere near the tired clapboard house with its tilting porch roof, or the sagging barn with the rusty plow idle by the side door.

All at once the wind shifted and again we coasted into oblivion. Our feet were soaked, hands freezing, and, alas, our snacks had dwindled to a rationing low, an undeniable energy crisis. Through experience we found that shivering steals too much energy, and if your teeth chatter you might as well sit down to eat until they stop.

This was the night of the great invention—a hot water canteen. The initial heat relaxed us enough to get to sleep before the early morning chill set in.

In Hot Springs our first stop was at the post office to see if our down sleeping bag had arrived. It hadn't. Disappointed, we headed for Henderson's Cafe, where all Appalachian Trail hikers congregated. We ambled into the hiker's cheapie motel to take a look. Mr. Henderson greeted us. "Here's the key. Look it over yourself."

"There's hot water, isn't there?" we asked.

"Oh, no, you'll have to go down to the river to fetch the water." He smiled.

When we saw the room we didn't smile. It smelled of disinfectant, and if there was hot water it was only because the pipes were in the sun. We never could figure out why hikers chose the most uncomfortable, dingy rooming houses and motels. At most, they were usually only a dollar cheaper. We walked down Main Street, a strange mixture of the old and the new. Several store fronts were empty. A competing motel turned out to be an oasis with an airy comfortable room, a large bath, a stock of the latest magazines, a television, and gratis postcards and envelopes.

The next morning we headed straight for the post office. Still no bag. The postmaster suggested we come back the next day, Sunday. He was one of many postmasters who went out of their way to help us and other hikers.

One day in a motel was a luxury we could afford. Two days were not. We headed out of town to Rocky Bluff Campground. Though the grounds were ten years old they retained their originality and did for campgrounds what Frank Lloyd Wright did for houses. Each site was completely tucked away from the road. Most were terraced, with a level sand tentsite and a separate cooking picnic area with a stone fireplace. Water pumps were located close to all sites. Wood was provided in abundance at no charge. The lavatory facilities were built with skylights and were well ventilated and clean.

At sunrise the next morning we walked the three miles into Hot Springs. The postmaster was there but not our bag. Another long-distance call assured us it would be waiting in Erwin, Tennessee. We had become accustomed to self-sufficiency on the Trail and didn't like to impose on friends a thousand miles away. We were wasting time arranging and worrying about the down sleeping bag. Day by day summer was approaching, and we had that bungling feeling that when we finally did get the bag it would be three pounds of dead weight.

On Monday morning as we hiked down Main Street (for the third and, we hoped, the last time), we wondered if every Appalachian Trail hiker arrived in Hot Springs at once. Bushy-faced hikers leaned against the post office and read their mail. A girl in a dirty T-shirt and pigtails asked where the laundromat was. Other hikers accosted the general store and sat on the steps in the sun eating ice cream and Hostess Twinkies. One hiker stood outside the phone booth cursing because he lost a dime. Packs lined Henderson's Cafe, while famished hikers ordered plate after plate of greasy eggs and hash browns.

In the main, we were always amused by the hiking style of school-aged hikers. Once we, too, had been carefree, wreckless, and grubby. Now sleep and food mattered more to our psyches. We were twice as old as some of the just-out-of-high-school hikers. Our life styles had mellowed into common sense.

We went inside the post office to mail home our leather hats that doubled in weight when it rained. Two well-dressed men in wool tweed suits talked to the clerk. They flashed identification cards and introduced themselves as private detectives. "You seen a young lady named Sarah Roberts? She could also be going under the alias of Robertson or Lansford."

The clerk shuffled through the register of Trail hikers. "Is she on the Appalachian Trail?" he asked.

"Well, we don't know. She's in these here mountains." One of them turned to us. "How about you? Met anyone named Sarah?"

At Poison Ivy Alley, a few days back, a lone girl had joined up with another couple on the Trail. Her name was Sarah, but we didn't want any involvement with shotgun weddings or jealous lovers.

As usual, it rained the day we ventured back onto the Trail. We stopped to rest in the semblance of a dry patch beneath a conifer. A thru-hiker trounced by, looking like a creature from outer space. He wore a felt hat, which might have been appropriate in the Tyrolean Alps, but which now looked like a damp flapper's cloche. Over his shirt he wore a fishing vest stuffed with gadgets. Two plastic containers around his neck resembled intravenous bottles. A waist snack-pouch bulged around the top of his baggy pants. Heavy rain chaps topped off his bizarre costume. He did not tarry. Like most hikers, he was racing to get to the next shelter before the others.

Right then and there we pitched camp on a roadbed between a thicket and a bank. Roadbeds were number 8 on our descending list of ten preferable campsites.

1. *Dry sphagnum moss*
2. *Pine needles*
3. *Level grass over dirt*
4. *Leaf cover over dirt*
5. *Dirt*
6. *Moss over rock*
7. *Level gravel*
8. *Roadbeds*
9. *Asphalt and cement*
10. *Wood platforms*

If it is raining, there's a possibility the road will flood. No matter how overgrown, the rock base will persevere. We were too tired to go a foot farther.

Soon a big pot of beef stroganoff bubbled on our Primus. Julia poured a little water into the noodles and accidentally knocked against the portable pot handle. The whole pan fell. Mesmerized, we watched as our dinner oozed across the poncho toward the sleeping bags. Suddenly we realized that all wasn't totally lost. Steve grabbed a cup and scooped the gooey mixture back into the pot. He wasn't satisfied until the last dehydrated soy flakes were captured. No calamity could spoil dinner. Grumpy, we looked at each other, then burst out laughing.

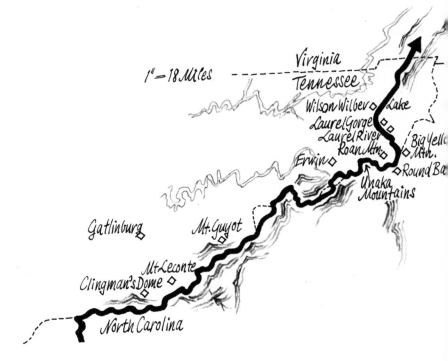

1" – 18 Miles

Virginia
Tennessee
Wilson Wilber ◇ Lake
Laurel Gorge ◇
Laurel River ◇
Roan Mtn. ◇
Erwin ◇
Big Yell◇
Mtn.
◇ Round Ba
Unaka
Mountains

Gatlinburg ◇
Mt. Guyot ◇
Mt. Leconte ◇
Clingman's Dome ◇
North Carolina

Tennessee

113 MILES

Country music and the Grand Ole Opry, backyard stills and moonshine. If ever we expected to see Lil' Abner working his still in a clapboard shack, it was somewhere in back-country Tennessee. Instead, we got a ride into Gatlinburg with two men who could have been models for Steinbeck's *Of Mice and Men*. We stepped hesitantly into the rusted hulk of their Detroit derelict. The driver, small, alert, and steering his friend as well as the car, sheltered a can of beer between his

40

legs. The other man was big-framed and awkward. He gulped three swallows of beer before he said a word. Then he jerked around and offered us a couple of cans. "It'll taste real good," he said, his words stumbling some.

We offered to split one, knowing what a beer could do after hiking on empty stomachs in the sun.

"Ah, come on. Me and my buddy's just out messin' around. We just bought a six-pack. We got plenty." He looked through the back window to see if a police patrol was following before he rolled down the side window and threw his empty can into the Great Smoky Mountains National Park.

The undercurrent of their talk, the way they glanced at each other, put us on guard. The stereotype of this scene switched us out of joint with the woods we were walking thirty minutes before. Suddenly, we were vulnerable to the joy-ride whims of two beer-drinking characters from a novel.

"Here," the man in the passenger seat said over his shoulder, "you want another beer?"

"No, no thanks."

"Come on, it's only friendly to take another beer. Here, take it."

The driver turned to his companion. "Jer, let the folks alone. If they want some, they'll take it." He turned to us. "You'll have to forgive my buddy. I kind of look after him. He's a little slow."

Jer looked sheepishly into the back seat. Both of us shifted uncomfortably, straddling our packs. "Here," he said excitedly, his speech retarded, his child's face misfitting his broad shoulders. A huge hand plunged over the seat with another beer can. "Take it. Won't do no harm."

Angering this man was risky, but drinking was riskier. Then as if the driver were reading our minds, he turned and said, "Don't worry. Nothing's going to happen to you."

They pulled into a gas station–liquor store and got out. "Be back," they said. We wondered aloud if we should get out of the car and hitch another ride. Were these two hill-billies potentially dangerous or just trying to be kind? Why had they both gone into the store? Were they plotting to murder us?

They returned with another six-pack of beer and off we drove again down the highway. A mile later the driver said they had to take a detour because last night the rain caused a landslide on the main highway and the police were moving traffic through the back roads.

The lush countryside rolled by. We kept alert and moved the conversation along with innocent talk. We drove for half an hour and couldn't figure out in which direction we headed. Our map didn't list the road. This was strange country to us. Was it alien, too?

As we neared a dilapidated farmhouse, the car lurched forward a couple times; the driver pulled onto the shoulder. "Back tire is flat, Jer," he said. "Give me a hand, will you?"

The men got out. We grabbed each other's arm. A flat tire? What an obvious ploy. The farmhouse was deserted. Not even a chicken. No car was in sight. We scrambled out of the car in case we had to run for it.

The driver was right. The tire was flat. With relief, we gave them a hand.

Back in the car, Jer persisted in his effort to booze us up. "Ever seen a still? We know of a place up in the hills. They make some moonshine. It's real good stuff. They sell it for forty-seven cents a quart."

"A quart?"

"Real good stuff. You want some?"

"No, thanks, we don't drink much of the hard stuff." The way we drank Southern Comfort on the cold nights in Georgia told a different tale, but we stuck to our northern temperance line, though we were dying of curiosity.

"If you're going to stay in Gatlinburg," Jer said, grinning, "it's a dry county, you know."

They stopped at another gas station and announced, "This is the edge of Gatlinburg. Good luck to you. You all come back sometime." They drove off smiling and waving. Our fears came back at us and made us feel foolish. They meant no harm. The lesson of misjudging others because of stereotypes they resemble was too often forgotten.

As a Trail way station, Gatlinburg was a total disappointment, a penny-ante tourist town where everything cost one dollar minimum. We stocked up all right, but the garish main street with its eye-sore signs and gingerbread motif displaced our sense of woodland balance and quiet. The array of things —just *things*—staggered us. Shop windows were cluttered with gaudy glass bottles and scented candles, totem poles made in Japan, ceramic elephants made in Ohio, pine plaques with homey maxims, Indian moccasins with red-felt tassels, sweat shirts with *Gatlinburg* stenciled in black. The street looked like a carnival sideshow hawking its wares, a thriving waste of time, a sacrilege to the six-thousand-foot peaks of the Smokies an eyelift away.

Out of this city we rushed to follow the Trail that fluctuated between the Pisgah National Forest in North Carolina and the Cherokee National Forest in Tennessee. The timpani blare of Gatlinburg disappeared over the hills. In its place was the staccato of downy woodpeckers beating their strong beaks into tree trunks. In its place were the woodwinds of maples and oaks that softened our thoughts and feelings. The squirrels and chipmunks scampered over the leaves and leaped from limb to limb. The sounds of cities and towns were crude and obstreperous compared to this orchestration. We knew now a new homing instinct was developing in us.

Other times we concentrated, not on our ears, but on our noses. The smells of the woods were varied as those of a gourmet shop. The sweetness of white pine needles mixed with the perfume of wild violets. The musk of wet ground cover moldering under a season of leaves overpowered the frail aroma of wake-robins dressed regally in their velvet petals. Lilies of the valley were in a class by themselves. We picked one for each of us and sniffed them for the next mile as if we were powered only by their enticing bounty of perfume. Fire or Indian pinks broadcast themselves by their petals fanning out in sharp-edged planks, the tips notched into needle points.

We didn't carry pen and ink in the head of a walking staff like philosopher Thomas Hobbes, but we did keep journals, and we did wonder. Yet however much we wrote, we could not touch upon the extravagance of what we were hiking through. The colors of the same trees changed day to day with the sunlight, rain, and fog. Rhododendron leaves, curled like cinnamon sticks, crunched under our boots. Pastures of blowing wild grass issued pollen that sometimes blocked our sinuses but always filled the air with vibrancy. The delicacies of these wonders were impossible to record in our journals, for we were becoming part of them.

We continued over the high peaks, letting the Trail take us down mountainsides, up ravines, along streams. We discovered one king oak ruled nearly every gorge we walked through. These kings prevailed over the other trees in the principality as if the struggle had been waged decades ago. We wrote:

> *Great oaks*
> *are slow pokes*
> *in raising their muscular limbs*
> *but they bully the birches, buckeyes, and beeches*
> *until the competition dims.*
> *These oaks*
> *are no jokes.*

The last shelter we passed before hiking down the mountains to Erwin once again portended the civilized dimension we had to enter to get mail and re-stock our food. The shelter was a dingy indictment of what unbridled freedom in the outdoors can do. Scrap paper, tinfoil, discarded aluminum cups, half-burnt planks of wood, and other junk were scattered inside and out. Undoubtedly, mice, rats, and snakes found refuge there, too.

The story told by a hiker back in Hot Springs, North Carolina, came to mind. "Soon as I get to a shelter," he said, "I set two mouse traps. Carry them in my pack. That way I can clean out the place so they don't crawl all over my face at night and I can get some sleep."

Before Erwin we came to a cluster of a dozen houses and a general store. The sun was hot, our legs were tired, and so we stopped for a quart of milk. Two elderly women marshaled the store from their cushioned armchairs. The shelves were dusty and held equally dusty boxes of rolled oats, soda crackers, spaghetti, and laundry soap. The women drank glasses of water from pitchers tinkling with ice. Two teenage girls played cards on a mattress in the rear of the store. The air was thick and stagnant and sapped whatever energy and spirit they might have had. Neither they nor the women wondered about us. If life was like this on May 10, what must it be like in dead summer?

The temperature clock outside the local bank indicated eighty-four degrees when we arrived in Erwin. Our down sleeping bag was at the post office and we were as happy to see it as a fur coat in Phoenix. A cold beer was more appropriate. In the Lucky Seven a barstooler asked more seriously than he wanted to reveal, "Why do you want to walk two thousand miles with no bar in sight?"

We told him and his three friends that we wanted to confirm our convictions that an unpolluted and beautiful America still exists, and we were discovering that on the whole we were right. The streams we drank from were pure and clear. Animal life was plentiful. The air was clean as the land. The people of the Appalachians were unpretentiously kind and helpful.

Our first beer was on the house, the second on a Korean

War veteran. Our third was bought by a kindly-eyed candy salesman who thought we were doing something memorable but which he would never consider in a thousand moons. "I play poker," he said.

"The hell you do," a friend said. "You couldn't bluff your way out of a circus sideshow."

"Hell, you'd play a sandy for two bits."

In classic barroom banter, the exchange continued for five minutes before detouring to the Korean War, the outdoors, the South, and other unconnected topics. Finally, a half hour later, the climax of all barroom talk was reached—the Meaning of Life.

The bartender set up another beer and brought the conversation back to earth. "Et any ramps yet?"

We heard about ramps and kept an eye out for them on the Trail. Not finding any, we were doubting their existence, like flashlight snipes and Santa Claus. We had sniffed, dug, and tasted every wild vegetable that in any way resembled ramps, a blue-green plant with three leaves similar to the lily of the valley. Often we mistook the unflowering trout lily for this elusive delectable. To have walked through most of North Carolina and Tennessee without having tasted this honored wild bulb was failure.

In the *Asheville* (North Carolina) *Times*, front page headlines announced the most famous of ramp festivals, held in Henderson, North Carolina. Participants ate ramps day and night until the onion odor seeped out the pores of their skins, producing an incalculable aura about their bodies. One ramp eater was odorous enough. A group could burst into flame. Someone recommended last year's politicians be locked in the same room and forced to eat an all-ramp diet.

Our bartender drew us a picture of ramps and assured us that we'd find them sooner or later. After one last beer and hearty farewells, we stumbled out onto the street, passed a sign in front of a Southern Baptist church exhorting us to

Fight Truth Decay, and took our empty stomachs to the Elms Restaurant where we monopolized the waitress with order after order.

Later, the town librarian asked with immediate interest about our adventure. "I'm seriously considering buying the house across the street from me," she said, "as a sort of refuge for hikers." We expressed enthusiasm for her idea and answered more questions about our hike.

By this time we could categorize the questions people asked. Patterns set easily and our answers usually led to other standard questions. To us, however, the most important questions were asked the least.

MOST FREQUENTLY ASKED QUESTIONS

	70%	25%	5%
Where are you from?	X		
How long will the hike take?		X	
Where are you going?	X		
How long is the Trail?		X	
How much do your packs weigh?		X	
How far do you travel daily?		X	
Where did you start?	X		
What do you eat?		X	
See any bear or snakes?	X		
Why are you doing it?			X
What boots do you wear?			X

Roan Mountain (2,565 feet) is covered with Frazier fir on the south side and catawba rhododendron on the north. In June people flock to the summit to enjoy the 1,200-acre Rhododendron Festival. They do not, however, scale the steep southern face. The morning we climbed Roan we had already hiked six miles. Our legs jacked us up the stepping-stone trail as if our tired bodies hardly functioned. In order to maintain balance on some sections, we found Greek dancing steps effective, especially in the mud.

Though the sky darkened and the wind rushed from the southeast, we climbed over a cluster of boulders and beheld a miniature paradise. Hidden on a high plateau, secluded from the noise of the wind, surrounded by a ring of fir and moss-shaggy rocks, appeared an oasis of peace and quiet. Perhaps the mountain heard our groans and made a gesture of encouragement. In any case, this meadowland of wake-robins, spring beauties, trout lilies, and May apples sparked us with hope. What power dwells in serene glades.

We hiked up through the firs and haze. The damp air enveloping the summit penetrated our clothes. We planned to camp on top of Roan, but we would have been the only living creatures. Not even the juncos were hopping through the wind.

The rhododendron at the summit was pregnant, although not about to deliver in thirty-degree weather. Knowing what splendor we were missing, we cursed our fate. Nevertheless, on Roan (re-named Groan) Mountain we discovered ramps and shouted, "Yea!" waving the prized bulbs in the wind. The smell and taste were unmistakable. Ramps indeed. Our bartender was right.

The next few days the Trail took us along the crest of balds. The openness of these treeless summits centered us in one panorama after another. The Unaka Mountain Range we were passing through contained eighty balds. Some, such as Round Bald, above 5,000 feet high, met the sky with nothing except wild grass, scrub brush, outcrops of quartzite, and juncos. On a few, the Forest Service had transplanted a toupee of fir, but the trees were neither spreading nor flourishing on those windblown pates.

What ruled supreme on the balds was the simplicity of the earth, the seductive innocence of nature in its most fundamental form, free, open, and full of light. Too much thinking was prohibited on these slopes; only absorbing what they offered was allowed. This we did with unending fascination at how the expanse of the world could affect the expanse of our spirits. On Big Yellow Bald we sat and let ourselves become enmeshed with where we were, briefly losing our identity to the vastness—and gaining more of ourselves in return.

We passed through bee-loud carpets of spring beauty and flowering spurge, hiking through the woods and over country roads. Suddenly, the blazes vanished. We wound down through an apple orchard to knock on the farmer's door. Mr. Hughs, a friendly, lean man dressed in his Sunday best, answered as if expecting us. "Lot of hikers get lost here," he said. "I think that couple what owns the spring and shed up yonder got scared 'cause so many hikers was coming through their property." Some of the blazes were rubbed out.

He gave us directions back to the Trail. "My family fought off the rebels in the Civil War to keep this land," he said. "Why Little Hump Mountain was bought for a saddle and a pair of ox yokes. You seen any rattlebugs?"

"Rattlebugs?"

"First settlers used to call rattlesnakes rattlebugs. Country's full of 'em. Keep a sharp eye from here to Hampton."

At the springhouse on the trail we met a hiker trying to capture the sunset over the orchard with his camera. We took pictures with our eyes, hung our water bag from the limb of an apple tree, and went to sleep in the darkroom of our tent.

The next morning the going was easy. We covered ten miles from 8:00 until 12:30, for a 2.2-miles-per-hour pace. One barn we hiked by was constructed of chestnut, an eastern tree once plentiful but nearly made extinct by a fungus epidemic in 1904. Lattice work on the top ventilated the hay. The owner slid open the huge door to reveal a shiny Model A Ford coup with sunlight sparking like diamonds on the hood.

"This here barn was built in 1900 for a thousand dollars," he said. "That was a lot of money back then. Chestnut's weathered good. Can't get chestnut anymore, you know. That lattice work's no good in a snowstorm. Looks nice though."

This was pasture country. Over a hill appeared a mule harnessed to a trace and a farmer herding a pair of frisky calves. "Morning," he called. "It's a good one today!"

"Perfect!" we shouted back across the field under a clear, breezy sky.

These were moments we prized. Robert Frost called this gift of peace and harmony with the land "The Gift Outright." The land was not ours, yet we were growing to know the earth with a familiarity and love akin to that of this farmer, someone who lived directly with the extremes of the elements. We walked through extremes both in nature and ourselves. A day of sunshine followed a day of showers. A day of exuberance followed a day of despair. The oscillation kept us alive, kept us moving on, tested the vaults of our persistence and resiliency.

At Laurel Gorge, mountain laurel bloomed in profusion against the backdrop of manganese cliffs. Lavender azaleas blossomed with petals as fragile as Limoges china. The Trail passed along a crevice between chunks of rock. This slab rock canyon roared with the tumble of water over a wide fall; our ears heard the water before our eyes matched the sound. The climb to the canyon floor was steep. As we descended, loose rock rolled downward, gaining momentum as the grade became steeper before sinking into the river below.

At the riverbank the Trail blazes disappeared. Now profanity is out of place in the woods, but our frustration got the best of us. The next blaze that appeared was painted on a rock ledge jutting out over the Laurel River. Rapids thrashed between us and that rock. Carefully, we edged along the rock face, moving with determined care. The white water at our feet stifled our verbal vendetta. We braced ourselves with our knees. We pushed from solid ground, and a moment later dangled over the charging waters. The crash of tons of water sounded from the falls upriver. Here the Trail was definitely not for weekenders in the woods, nor was it a footpath through wilderness. The Trail was five feet under a river that could carry your life away. We sought the lessons of places like Laurel Gorge, yet at the time routing the Trail through such hazards seemed insane and totally unnecessary.

We camped beside the river and lazed the evening away. If we slept with the reassurance that Laurel Gorge was through with us, we were mistaken. In hiking, what goes down must go up. Again the Trail blazes disappeared, but this time the river splashed into a sheer rock wall. The only way out of the gorge was to scramble up a shale bluff to a bridge-like ridge. The loose rock shuffled under our boots with each step. At times it was one step up, two slides down. We grabbed shrubs whose roots clung only to the topsoil. A clump of bleeding hearts poised at a right angle over the river with a tenacious hold onto life. If these tiny plants could do it, so could we.

Farther on, we camped near Wilson Wilbur Lake and took a refreshing swim. Our side of the lake was flat and grassy, the other, a rose limestone cliff where a ribbon waterfall streamed two hundred feet into the lake. A few pines grew through dirt-filled crevices. A mother duck and three ducklings glided along the periphery of the lake, now and then dunking for delectables and flashing their white tail feathers like a chorus line.

By morning the stench of four feet of uncovered mud and vegetation awakened our nostrils. Wilson Wilbur Lake had nearly disappeared. The lake was a reservoir, and the locks were opened during the night in anticipation of more rainfall.

As we broke camp the rain fell. We hiked up to the next crest and there the rain turned to hail. The cold fell over us, and the thick weather grew harsher. Our bodies became overworked maintaining their heat and vitality. All we could do was to keep walking, though the hail continued to pelt us. Our teeth were chattering and we were risking hypothermia, a chronic condition caused by overexposure to the elements.

This time we were glad to see a shelter, even though it was open to the prevailing winds. Our faces were stinging with the cold, our fingers were numb. Even with gloves on we fumbled to light the gas stove for a cup of hot soup. The hail rattled against the tin roof and bounced off the soft earth.

The boiling soup turned lukewarm as soon as we poured it into our cups. To generate body heat we danced, flapped our arms like semaphores, hopped about like rabbits. Our antics must have been mistaken for an Indian sun dance, because as suddenly as the hail started it stopped. Miraculously, the sun burst from behind the rolling black clouds and showed us how sun-centered we were.

After another dance of thanks and shouting cheers, a difference of opinion arose. Steve wanted to make tracks to better shelter before the next turn of the thermometer. Julia wanted to loll about, dangle wet clothes from trees, and sunbathe while she could. Both of us were tense from the constriction of our muscles and nerves against the bitter cold. One had the stove and matches, the other the food; one the guidebook and compass, the other all the medication. Our unwillingness to compromise taught us a lesson.

Lagging behind, Julia lost the blazes at a clearing where another hiker had made a stone arrow pointing toward a rutted muddy road. After walking a quarter-mile down the road without sighting a blaze, she backtracked, all the time blowing three blasts for help on her whistle.

Back at the clearing she felt the anxiety of being lost. Walking miles from any settlement, without means to make a fire, and with night approaching fast, was frightening. Each of us carried water and knew how to find more. Each had a poncho and sleeping bag, and, more important, each other to rely upon. Now each relied upon individual good judgment. After indulging in some mild histrionics that merely sapped her energy, Julia sat down to think. She found the last blaze and walked in the direction she thought the next blaze should be. Meanwhile, Steve backtracked to the clearing.

We met and it was a significant meeting. Through rational action we had solved our problem. We agreed to redistribute the contents of our packs that night so that each of us would be more self-sufficient if we lost each other again.

1" = 50 Miles

West Virginia

Front Royal

Maryland

Potomac River

District of Columbia

Shenandoah Nat'l Park

Big Meadows Campground

Loft Mtn. Campground

George Washington Nat'l Forest

Tinker Mts. Friar Mtn.

ba

Priest Mtn.

Pedlar Lake

Cloverdale

Roanoke

Virginia

452 MILES

Twenty-three per cent of the Appalachian Trail was located in Virginia. The people of Virginia were indeed fortunate. Not only did they have the Trail, but also Mount Rogers State Park, Jefferson National Forest, Shenandoah National Park, George Washington National Forest, and the Blue Ridge Parkway, as well as many other parks not on the Trail.

Every effort was being made in the Jefferson National Forest to accommodate hikers. Since towns for re-provision-

55

ing were outside the Forest boundaries, private concerns were encouraged to build near the Trail and stock camping foods. In the Shenandoah National Park the Trail was so well maintained that the thru-hiker could effortlessly cover twenty miles a day, yet feel relaxed enough to take in his surroundings at leisure. Also in Virginia, the hiker was no longer alone in the woods. Suddenly, he found himself standing next to a trout fisherman, hiking with a Boy Scout troop, or bedding down in a crowded campground.

In the southwest corner of Virginia, the hiker passed through much flatland. In the spring this meant floods and swollen rivers. By the time he reached Front Royal, four hundred miles to the northeast and just outside the Shenandoah National Park, he had probably experienced drought as well. The Trail in Virginia attracted hikers because of these variations.

The elements of the earth were fascinating to study. However, to live with them was to understand them. Walking the mountain woods revealed to us the teeter-totter extremes in nature. The swing of hot days into cold nights, the coming and going of migrating juncos, the flush of spring after winter, were all part of the unrelenting vitality of the earth.

Probably the most blatant extreme we faced was the availability of water. As we walked into a summer of discontent, we discovered that the vulnerability of our existence rested upon the ebb and flow of water. At times too much water threatened our sanity and safety. Other times too little water threatened our health and, to the extreme, our lives. In our Lilliputian membership on planet Earth we seldom found a balance for long.

As the summer progressed we noticed that the average reprieve from rain was three days. After the third day, we could anticipate the gathering of heavy clouds and the inevitable downpour. After the rain, which usually lasted one full day, came another dry spell.

An exception was Damascus, which we reached on May 19. There it rained five straight days. Though Damascus was a frequent hikers' stopover, we were unable to locate a guidebook for Virginia, and had to depend solely on the blazes to find our way through the area. Now the scales had turned and the rainclouds were winning. Inch by inch, then foot by foot, the creeks, streams, and rivers rose to the limits of their banks. What were pleasant meandering rivulets only the day before turned into passionate flooded gulches.

Along one stretch the Trail paralleled a creek. We were forced to blaze our way through thickets and ornery brush on higher ground. The Trail was submerged. We pushed through tree branches that snapped back into our arms and faces, crashed through tangles of growth that hooked onto our packs, slipped down muddy embankments, and grabbed onto wet tree trunks. Each juncture was a flooding tributary, and we groaned at the thought of ricochet hopscotch on rocks across another expanse of water.

At one particular river bend where we had to cross, the creek was so flooded that every rock was submerged. The torrent raced by through a dense cluster of rhododendron, swirling the branches, and pulling the roots every which way. Crossing looked impossible. With resignation we studied the situation. After removing our packs we separated and searched the creek for a way to cross without getting wet feet. We had to crawl over rhododendron roots, crawl under rhododendron roots, hang onto rhododendron roots. They were everywhere, thick as a woven hemp mat. We looked for logs to throw across, but only found them waterlogged and impossible to move.

Subsequent to a conclave, we decided upon building a rock bridge. Furiously, we dug large stones from the banks and heaved them into the water. In theory, this method would be simple and effective. In practice, it was simple-minded and ineffectual. Every time we heaved a five-pound rock into the river, it washed downstream as if it had been a fleck of sand. We tried bigger rocks, aimed them with considered computation at the desired location, and watched as they rolled downstream.

Determined not to be victims, we persisted with another scheme. This time we searched the banks for a rhododendron bush that arched over the flooding water so that we could somehow tightrope across like a circus act. But rhododendron was springy, and would not support us.

The rain continued. The river rushed on. Our fervor waned. We removed our boots and socks and braced ourselves so we wouldn't slip in the mud. With a hearty backswing and a prayer, we threw our boots one at a time over the flooding creek. They plopped in the mire on the far bank. Then we adjusted our packs and carefully mud-skated into the river. The stones on the riverbed cut into our tender feet. The water churned around our legs at the calves. The force of the flow pushed us so that we had to steady ourselves to maintain balance. We could not afford to fall. The water was cold and relentless. We made it to the other side, perfunctorily dried our feet, and put on our socks and boots, wondering if we shouldn't stop to build an ark.

The cycle swung around again when we reached the Tinker Mountain Range just outside of Roanoke. Road tar bubbled underfoot as we walked from the provision town of Catawba. Our first water stop turned out to be a blue-blaze trail that led half a mile back down the mountain. Earlier we had been warned of the scarcity of water in the Tinker Mountains. Our focus now sharpened on collecting water, not escaping it. The teeter-totter once again had swung in the other direction.

Whereas in the deep South we suffered from intense cold, now we almost expired from the oppressive heat of the Virginia mountain crests. Our salt tablets, in a plastic bag like everything else, soon absorbed the moisture in the air and turned into one large, crumbly salt ball. We were sucked up into a vicious circle of taking "salt pinches" to ward off sunstroke, while drinking precious water to ward off the nausea caused by the salt.

When we arrived at Monster Rock Shelter, we found that the water source, a cistern to collect rainwater from the tin roof, was polluted. We walked on without water.

That night we fastidiously scooped cupfuls of rainwater from a leaf-lined puddle on the Trail. We had one canteen with which to cook dehydrated scalloped potatoes and chipped beef. Dessert pudding wouldn't be forthcoming unless it rained. It did. The rainwater, caught in the crevices of our ponchos, was used for the pudding. Our dishes were scrubbed with wet May apple leaves and ferns. With careful rationing we still had enough water to brush our teeth and have a cup of coffee the following morning.

When we did come to a creek, not only did we fill our canteens but also our plastic water jug. This was another piece of equipment for which careful shopping paid off. Unlike the awkward collapsible water jugs, this one, made in England, rolled up on two wooden handles like a scroll. It could be hung from a tree at standing level and turned on like a faucet. Now Steve strapped it to the top of his pack. A canteen of water weighs two pounds. Each of us was carrying about four pounds of water. In the heat the extra weight slowed us down to about twelve miles a day. However, the Tinker Mountains didn't give a tinker's damn about the water situation.

We never knew how important water could be. During these hot June days in the Tinkers we grew to respect this liquid element. Water: 78 per cent of our bodies, and 70 per cent of the surface of the globe. Just as earlier we had cherished the warmth from wood fires, now we valued above all the sound of a flowing stream, the tiniest trickle from under a rock. Occasionally from necessity, such as the time we used the rainwater, we either boiled water or treated it with halo-zone tablets. However, we were spoiled by the sweet, fresh taste of untreated water, and usually preferred not to drink any rather than taste the chlorination left by the tablets, which reminded us of city reservoirs.

By the time we struggled up the final slope of Tinker Mountain, above Roanoke, we had only half a canteen of water. Our thirst was too real to let us enjoy the *bella vista* that the Tinker Mountain ledges offered. A long-haired Sunday hiker sat alone on a rock slab. He volunteered some of his water, but we declined when we found out he still had fourteen miles to truck. A mile and a half later, we heard the beckoning muted sound of water, a primordial mating call that urged us on. We couldn't see the creek for a long time, but only heard its enticing gurgle behind a screen of trees and brush.

When we finally reached the stream, it was low and yellow. This color, we concluded, was due to the sandy bottom. Most water sources on the Trail are not tested, and only once or twice did we see a sign *This Water Is Nonpotable*. Often we thought that since the Appalachian Trail was becoming more and more popular, water sources should be officially tested, especially near shelters and towns. Typhoid and amoebic dysentery can be contracted from drinking bad water.

We reveled in the stream as if we were in a Roman bath. In seconds, as if this simple stream-water were a magic potion, we came to life, resurrected from dangerous dehydration to the spark of ourselves.

The valleys of Virginia culminate in the flourishing Shenandoah River valley. A series of smaller, equally verdant, valleys led up to the Shenandoah. One of these was Taylor's Valley.

At eight in the morning we walked through this serene community cloistered at the foot of four mountain walls. Its residents were already out hoeing their gardens. The rustic houses were spaced for privacy and well maintained with unpretentious pride. Pearl Boone's home was an aged gray slat-board cabin with a red brick chimney on the left and an extra-tall television aerial on the right. A bright green rocking chair rested empty on the front porch, but undoubtedly at any moment would be occupied with a gingham-dressed grandmother snapping beans into her apron. Up ahead an old man with a rake called out, "There's a good creek up the holler, if you-uns want some water."

We stopped at the creek for a drink. When we looked up a russet face eyed us like a cautious backwoodsman. Though we coaxed the hound with outstretched hands, his skeletal long-haired body remained on his side of the creek. He was as skeptical as a stranger. His tail, ears, and hackles were down. It seemed as though he just wanted to get to his business in Taylor's Valley and we blocked his way. Condescendingly, he let us pet him and then passed by, never once looking back, proud and alone.

This must have been the dog trail of Taylor's Valley, because we had gone only a mile when we met a yelping spotted spaniel that couldn't have been three months old. The maternal side of our team wanted to rescue this unmothered pup from the dangers of the wilderness. However, the paternal half argued that this was probably the offspring of the bachelor we'd just seen, and that he would follow his father's scent home. So we left him sitting small and sad in the center of the Trail.

Sinking Creek Valley was another one of those places you wouldn't ordinarily believe existed in modern America. Yet there it was, a fertile stretch of farmland seemingly untouched by the ballyhoo of the world. We passed many abandoned mills with rough-hewn waterwheels, silent after years of slow turning. They easily could have turned a few more centuries. In contrast to the mountain heights, water was plentiful in the valleys. Cows drank from water holes, ponds dotted the farms.

Many of these small communities were being abandoned in

favor of the lure of the big city. We couldn't imagine why. It was too easy to picture ourselves in one of the old houses, our garden blooming, our rocking chairs creaking.

In another languid valley we dutifully followed the Trail blazes through a hoof-printed barnyard and a herd of milling Jerseys. They unnerved us with their walnut-sized eyeballs, their drooling tongues that looked a yard long, their flared nostrils exuding froth. We hurried past the open side of the barn. A huge bull lumbered to his feet. Was it true, what we had heard about red and bulls? What about our bright red packs? The bull stepped toward us. We ran for the high rail fence and vaulted over without the slightest hesitation. Then we admired the brute and his harem.

We walked on down this tight little valley, peaceful and content with some of the most spic-and-span healthy cattle we'd ever seen. The farms and small ranches hugged the foot-hills of the Shenandoah Valley.

An old man in blue denim coveralls came out of his house to talk to us. He asked the usual questions about where we were headed and where we came from, questions he probably asked every hiker who passed. We were the world coming to him. He wasn't in the least surprised that we had started walking in Georgia, though Georgia to him might as well have been Australia.

"I had a brother in Georgia someplace," he said. "I guess there's a lot of places in Georgia though."

"Yes, guess so."

"You seen any rattlers?" he asked. "Lots of them around here. Hot weather brings 'em out. Copperheads, too. Once I killed five rattlers back up in the mountains one day. There was a swarm of them. 'Course, the rattler gives a warning afore he strikes, but a copperhead, now he don't give no warning. He jus' sits by the trail and strikes as you come past. You watch out for them snakes."

By this time we had grown accustomed to snake tales from

locals on the Trail. One out of every two had a special snake story for passing hikers. If we didn't heed their warnings, they assured us, doom would follow. In Damascus even the chief of police gave us an old yarn about how rattlers crawl out of their holes at night and slither into tents to sleep on the chests of unsuspecting maidens. We heard how two copperheads line each side of the Trail to bite hikers as they pass, assuring at least one of the snakes a fangful. We also were told how a rattler always lets the first hiker pass and then strikes the second.

Never once did we come across a hiker who had been bitten. When pressed, the people who told the snake stories admitted that they had never been bitten and, in fact, personally didn't know anyone who had.

Our pre-hike lessons in snake identification included study of pictures of the venomous copperhead, rattler, and cottonmouth moccasin. Thus, we instantly recognized the snake sunning on an avalanche of rocks that we came upon one day in the Shenandoah Valley. This timber rattler, *Crotalus horridus horridus*, did not seem at all horrid. He was a gigantic grandfather coiled in at least four large loops, his rattles inconspicuous against the muscular brown diamond-marked back. We left him in peace, a friend who did nothing to us but fill our eyes with his majesty and ancient wisdom. Perhaps some might have killed him and walked away with the prized rattles, but what balance was there in such an act? Of what use in the cycle of nature was a man's ego?

In spring the woods were populated with frogs. Every puddle was a community of hundreds of tadpoles. If it were not for grandfather snake, the frogs would multiply, and we would certainly grow tired of frogs' legs. Thus we mused as we dreamed of the coiled vision on the rocks.

We met other snakes on the Trail in Virginia. May and June were mating season. We saw many black rat snakes, one a graceful four-foot ripple, forked tongue flickering and head held high as he slithered before us across a hot dusty road. Another was barely visible in the twilight as we dipped into our first valley of the Blue Ridge Mountains.

The whispered word "snake" evoked both fear and veneration. We had reached a mutual understanding that whoever was leader on the Trail must avert danger and at the same time identify the cause of his anxiety with as little commotion as possible. Loud noise was foreign in the woods, and might cause the confronted wildlife to act with hostility. Our warning agreement was just as rewarding when danger did not threaten. Often because of the whispered "bird" or "deer," not only the forerunner, but both of us were able to enjoy the spectacle ahead.

The reaction of man toward creatures of the wild was not half as interesting as the variety of creatures' reactions toward him. Man was intrinsically the same, but a badger is not a newt is not a bear (to slightly rephrase Gertrude Stein).

Whenever we startled a chipmunk, for example, he instantly became nervous and disoriented, and, chattering a mile a minute, dashed from one side of the Trail to the other until he found his hole. Several times we flushed newly born grouse. They would cry with the soulful wailing of a deserted child. We froze until the alarm-clucking mother scolded them safely into the underbrush. The snakes slithered quietly into the grass, every muscle under control, barely threatened by our shadows and footsteps.

The friendly phoebes would perch near by, cocking their heads this way and that as we played music, continuing where we left off. They moved closer and closer, glad, it seemed, of our presence. The frog on a rock at a spring leaped into the water in a graceful dive, and when we looked far back where the water bubbled out, we saw him in his shadowy grotto staring at us like a pop-eyed madonna.

Mosquitoes have no visible fear of man. A raised hand momentarily sent them in flight to another piece of skin that could serve as battleground. What they wanted was blood, and they would fight persistently until the very last. Our reaction to them was just as bloodthirsty. Mosquitoes were not our only insect tormentors. In a pilgrimage across overgrown Friar and Priest Mountains of the George Washington National Forest, we were provoked by swarms of gnats. Had we been aware in advance of the jungle aspect of much of the terrain traversed thus far, we would have dressed like Dr. Livingston in a jungle helmet with mosquito netting around the brim and a white safari suit to cut down the heat. We did the best we could under the circumstances, wearing rubber bands around our pants' legs, generous dabs of Cutter's insect repellent (the spray wasn't as effective as the cream) and wielding tree switches of witch hazel as fly swatters. The farther north we walked into summer, the hotter and muggier it got. In order that these persevering insects not molest us out of our wits, we wore our nylon windbreakers with the hoods up. All it takes is one pernicious mosquito in the ear for a mile, and the hiker is likely to want to commit the hastiest form of suicide.

Another pest to which we had an adverse reaction was a type of short hard worm encountered at several campsites in the Shenandoah region. No matter how careful we were to keep them from the tent, in the morning they would be curled up in our moccasins, under our socks, or in our hair. Fortunately, they did not bite, and displayed little hostility to our brisk whiskings.

A thru-hiker we met in the Shenandoah National Park told us that his brother had been bitten by a poisonous spider and was sent home with a very swollen leg. We often left spiders to build webs in the corners of our tent, the worse evil being the mosquitoes on which the spider would feed.

Whenever birds of prey appeared in the sky, we sensed a silence in other birds, and even ourselves. These hawks and vultures soared with arrogance and daring, though they surely filled frogs, small snakes, and field mice with trepidation. Once, on a long hot stretch of open fire road, we removed our packs and lay flat on our backs to rest. As if this death position had been telegraphed by an elaborate system of communication, a black vulture soon glided into view, then another. The vultures circled, swooped and scouted. More arrived. Perhaps we were not on the Appalachian mountain ridge after all, but lost in the Mohave Desert. Our desiccated bodies were the target of this dive-bombing mob of black scavengers intent upon their meal.

We counted eleven vultures at one time. Actually, we were guilty of baiting them by our cadaverous positions. Undoubtedly we fooled no one, for birds of prey have sight as sharp as binoculars. Nevertheless, the vultures congregated with frightening speed. We were far from alone in these mountains, for the woods and the sky were full of eyes.

Smaller birds appeared as suddenly as the vultures, but were less intimidating. As we wound through the woods mile after mile, and now state after state, our friendliness with the birds turned to familiarity. We saw the differences in their behavior and basic personalities and cast a City of Birds. The squawking, mimicking brown thrasher was mayor; the red-cloaked cardinal, obviously the archbishop; the talkative Carolina junco, the mailman; the melodious song sparrow, the leader of a barbershop quartet. The subtle vireo was the artist of the community, while the black vulture was the Mafia godfather; the flashy scarlet tanager, the scarlet woman; the high-chinned robin, the ambassador to England; and the rose-breasted grosbeak, a kind of Fred Astaire of the alfalfa fields. Amid all this sophistication the American goldfinch, bubbly and frivolous, flitted about like a blond teeny-bopper. Warblers passed us by on their way north. They advanced twenty-three miles a day, a bit faster than we could walk.

Whoever gave common names to flowers must have had fun, too. In the Tinker Mountains we identified turkey's beard. This five-foot plant with spidery leaves in a circle at the base and a white cone-shaped flower, might resemble a hairy scepter, but certainly not a turkey's beard. Nor to us did goat's tongue present a likeness to the tongue of a goat. Indian cucumber root was closer to its name, we found when we tasted it, though our preference remained with ordinary cultivated cucumbers.

In addition to civilized store-bought remedies for snake bites, insect stings and poisonous plants, we were learning invaluable information about certain herbs, such as jewel weed for poison ivy, yarrow and mint leaves for the relief of colds, black snake root or cohosh for snake bite, and so on.

One back-country Virginia storekeeper introduced us to ginseng. The root of this plant is shaped like the human figure, and in Chinese *Sching Seng* means "little man." This root is sold and exported almost exclusively to China and the Far East. As we approached the one-room store, we noticed a new sign among the familiar tobacco and snuff advertisements. *Rawfurs Ginseng*, it said. Under the assumption that this might be the owner's name (like Buffalo Bill or Old Hickory) we entered his humble place of business.

As in many stores in the South, there were few store goods. The standard potbellied stove predominated. An ice cream freezer compartment was squeezed into a corner among antique traps, copper teapots, and iron fry pans. Rawfurs greeted us. In China, he told us, ginseng is valued as a source of longevity and renewed sexual vigor. "It sells for sixty-eight dollars a pound," he said. "The Chinese buy it and can't get enough. These hills used to be full of ginseng. Not anymore. People dug it all up."

We had heard that in the early days of the first Appalachian settlers, ginseng was a sought-after commodity. Second to fur pelts, it was often the leading export. Mountain people would go on "sang forages" into mountain caves from the Shenandoah Valley to the Great Smokies.

Sparked by our interest in this woodland plant, Rawfurs took us to his big yellow house to show us a cultivated patch of ginseng which he had grown from seed. The ginseng plant has three to five compound leaves and produces a single central flower. These particular plants were in their third year. A marketable root takes from five to seven years to grow.

"Ginseng thrives on the north side of the mountain in stands of hardwoods such as ash, beech, alder, linden, and cucumber tree," he told us. "As a rule, it never grows near pine or oak. You have to dry and cure the roots before buyers will take 'em. The ratio is six to one from wet to dry. There's a lot of work in growing ginseng. That's why people dug up the native wild plants."

As we walked the Trail farther into Virginia, we remembered Rawfurs' pointers. But as he said, the ginseng plant is nearly extinct, and we never found one. Nowadays, most people interested in ginseng cultivate the plant from seed. Our desire to find the little man was purely spiritual. Many times we stopped each other to examine a possible specimen. Our most common mistake was to think that wild sarsaparilla was ginseng, for these two plants belong to the same family. The distinction is that the flower stem of the sarsaparilla plant grows from the ground, but that of ginseng grows directly from the center of the diverging stems.

Before the turn of the century herbal medicine was the only medicine. Emulsions, elixirs, specifics, tonics, bitters, syrups, sarsaparillas were sold en masse. Ayer's Sarsaparilla, claimed their preparation

> *Purifies the Blood,*
> *Stimulates the Vital Functions, restores*
> *and preserves Health and infuses New Life*
> *and Vigor throughout the whole System.*

Today most sarsaparilla and root beer extracts are purely chemical. Still, mountain people continue to collect roots for their own personal enjoyment.

The Appalachian Root Woman prepared both sarsaparilla and sassafras roots by scraping them and placing them in the sun at every opportunity. These served as Trail tea.

I am the root woman.
My fingers ply
the deep soil
for my wares.
They are earth crescents.

There is a dark root beer odor
about me.
Root stalks of wild ginger
dangle from my ear lobes,
a trade mark.
For I am the root woman.

In my youth
Indians taught me
to tug edible strings of tubers
from dismal swamps,
to dry spring roots of the woodlands
for winter.

I gnaw on Indian cucumber and milkweed roots.
Sassafras and sarsaparilla
swing from my belt as I walk.
They are poor amulets
for the magic I seek.

One day I will find
the little man, Schin Seng.
When he comes to me, wrinkled and yellow,
I will offer him a jeweled coffer
lined in red Chinese silk.

We will travel over the thresholds
of those plagued with Earth fever.
We will leave the oracle of youth
with the aging.

For only Schin Seng knows the secrets
a root woman is willing to unearth.

On the morning of May 27 the sky blew wild black clouds our way as we headed toward Pearisburg and one of the most unsettling episodes of our two-thousand-mile walk. Since we were guideless, we asked a local fisherman the way. "Go up this road five miles," he said, "and you'll come to Wapiti Shelter where the old Trail begins. On up the mountain it connects with the new section they just blazed. Otherwise, you have to climb that rough mountain over there."

We followed the blazes of the old Trail to the Wapiti (Indian for elk) Shelter. Heavy thunder clouds gathered on the horizon like a bomber force. We were making such good time that we were sure we could reach Pearisburg in a day and a half instead of two.

We followed the blue-blaze trail to a firetower on Flat Top Mountain. Visibility dropped to the nose in front of us. After a sequence of lightning, thunder, fog, and drizzle, rain pelted us as we plodded toward the tower. In the mist the tower complex loomed like an unfinished erector set. The rain continued mercilessly. At any minute we expected a stroke of lightning to zap the tower and us with one colossal bolt.

Then a clearing and a deserted ranger's cabin appeared. We pushed open the warped door and entered a wood-slat utility room the size of a woodshed. To us it was a palace. A broken rusty stovepipe dangled over a fifty-gallon barrel in the corner. The rain dripped from the pipe. A window pane was missing. The other two windows were boarded up. A clothes line was strung across the back wall. We hung up our wet ponchos and sat on a creaking bed spring in the dry center of the room, waiting for the rain to let up. It never did. We left the cabin and moved on.

That day we walked eighteen miles in the rain. By this time our pot cloth, appropriately called the grudge cloth, had acquired a definite mildew odor. Our sleeping bags, though unexposed to the rain, were clammy. Our boots, which we assiduously covered with weatherproofing, even using a toothbrush on the seams, were soaked through. We wished ourselves to the next stopover, Pearisburg, as hastily as our wet wrinkled soles would carry us.

That night a malicious thunderhead parked directly above our tent and rained all night. The next morning we checked our pocket compass a few times to make sure we were headed north. It had momentarily stopped raining, so we could enjoy our surroundings.

We passed several black-and-yellow-madras terrapins slugging through the mud. Our intrusion was not enough to frighten them into their shells. Brilliant orange salamanders swam the puddles. Crawdads scuttled down the sandy banks of rivers. It seemed we were walking on the earth three hundred million years ago when amphibians dominated the evolutionary scale.

We stopped to admire a hobblebush, a miracle of nature that produces whole bridal bouquets, when we spotted the sign

Wapiti Shelter

.5 miles →

We could not believe our eyes. Wapiti Shelter? Wasn't that the same shelter we passed the day before, eighteen strenuous, rainy miles ago? We sat down as if some force had bowled us over. Surely the sign was a prank or an act of vandalism. Five full minutes we stared at the sign. We had no guide. We couldn't backtrack eighteen miles. Finally we regained our senses and moved ahead. Now we had no idea where we were. This time we were lost together.

At the edge of a swampy overflowing stream we saw our savior wearing hip-boots, a canvas hat, and a fishing vest. We started across a sodden log toward our hero. "Hi, we're lost." He reeled in his line. "The Wapiti Shelter isn't near here, is it?"

"Why, yes it is. Right over yonder. Can't see it, but it's there."

What had happened? Agony. Pain. Chagrin. Curses. Horror. With magnificent intensity and perseverance, we had walked in a complete circle. We blamed our embarrassing mistake on the relocation of the Trail and the inadequate markings of that relocation. However, in the final analysis, we had no one to blame but ourselves. After all, hiking in the mountains meant the acceptance of responsibility in the woods, an ability to rely on oneself, and above all, never to presume without checking the information.

Bill Hopkins, our savior, from Salem, Virginia, was trying his luck with trout and wasn't having any. With sympathy he offered us a ride. "Doesn't look like I'm going to get a bite today," he said. "Trout'll never bite after a rain like this. Too much natural food for them to eat. Tell you what. I'm going to Pearisburg, but first I'm going to a restaurant for sugar-cured ham. Why don't you join me?"

If we had been rescued by a knight in shining armor, he wouldn't have been more welcome than Bill Hopkins, a Ph.D. candidate in business administration with a yen to buy land and rake in hay instead of money. Bill drove us to Pearisburg and to the doorstep of a motel.

By now we had learned what was best for us in the way of maintaining our bodies. We knew for a fact that other thru-hikers did not stop every week to ten days for overnight rest. Not only did we need the bed rest, but we also used stopovers to find the produce and protein foods that we were unable to pack because of the extra weight. Each stopover we supplemented our diets with fresh vegetables and dairy products.

Accommodations were not always available. For instance, in Crandon when evening rain threatened far from a campsite, the Crandon Christian Church opened its doors to us. We were extremely thankful for their indoor-outdoor basement carpet. However, we did have misgivings on waking up to a bright-eyed Sunday school class standing over our sleeping bodies.

In Pearisburg, we took a room above a swimming pool

where we sunbathed the day away. Fortunately the noise boomeranged off thick walls. Trucks were routed right through the center of town. Pearisburg was a misnomer. The real name should have been Perishburg.

At the Hollins Motel in Cloverdale, outside of Roanoke, we learned another invaluable lesson. Never cook onions inside the room unless there's a closed-circuit air conditioner. However, Mrs. Hollins was understanding and offered us a picnic table under the magnolia trees. We spread out our flowered ground cloth–table cloth and sat down to a dinner that looked like it had been photographed for *Gourmet* magazine.

A vintage California white wine cooled in an ice bucket beside a long loaf of sourdough French bread. On our tin pie plate–frying pan, we arranged freshly picked heads of wild asparagus that we found along the roadside into town. Around these were artichoke hearts, deviled eggs, and carrot sticks. Our aluminum pot was filled with pepper and potato salad garnished with strips of Danish ham. For dessert we sliced peaches.

Our motel procedure was as follows: First, we never planned a Sunday stopover, a waste of time since stores were closed. Second, we always camped just outside of town so that we could check into the motel early in the morning, leaving over twenty-four hours before checkout time. Third, we learned that although it was a hassle, cooking your own food was less costly and healthier than restaurant eating. Restaurant dishes were usually unpalatable and poorly cooked. What is more, you always went away hungry. We did not want a quarter pound of hamburger with one puny slice of processed cheese. We wanted a pound of each, if possible.

Most hikers frequented laundromats. We didn't. If our room was tub-less, we threw our clothes into the shower stall, added plenty of soap, and stomped on them like Italian peasants during grape harvest. Actually, we were cleaning ourselves and our clothes at the same time. Twenty-four hours goes much too quickly when you have to pick up money, write and mail letters, clean pots, cook meals, wash clothes, wash yourself, read up on Watergate, and relax.

We avoided inns and rooming houses. Despite the belief that they were cheaper, we found they were usually the same price or even more than pleasant motels. Nor did they offer the comfort and privacy we sought. Our precious twenty-four-hour leave of absence was for relaxation, and not for shop talk about how easy Mt. Rogers (5,720 feet) had been, or the pros and cons of freeze-dried foods.

Frequently, in towns like Pearisburg, we headed for the nearest library to read and listen to records. Few countries in the world can boast such a comprehensive library system as ours, which offers people a haven of silence and access to cultural osmosis.

The long descent from the Tinker Mountain region brought us back to the mechanical din of the cities. We heard Roanoke (population 92,115), five miles before we saw it. At first a noise like a seven-story vacuum cleaner reached our eardrums. Then other sounds rose from the valley floor, a snorting bulldozer clawing at a gravel pit, the iron clank of a giant earth scoop, the interstate truck and automobile traffic. Fortunately, we were able to stay in Cloverdale on the periphery.

Two days later the thermometer read ninety-two degrees in the shade. We waited out the afternoon under a spreading oak. By four o'clock the mercury had dropped two degrees.

If anyone saw us hiking that day, our antics must have seemed peculiar. The Trail was routed along a highway, and road walking can be as dangerous as walking across a desert. We always wore our bandanas to keep the sun from our heads. If the road was shadeless, we dashed to the nearest tree. To see someone with a twenty-five-pound pack dashing must be interesting. We rested more frequently, often forcing ourselves to eat snacks. Heat had a way of convincing one that it was better to do nothing. When your goal was two thousand miles, this attitude wouldn't get you too far.

On this particular day we spotted tiny red jewels sparkling in the grass by the roadside. On impulse we both shouted, "Strawberries!" The hot sun virtually disappeared. We threw off our packs and at once were on our hands and knees, pushing the luscious, ripe sweet fruit into our mouths, stems and all. The next half hour was lost to a hand-to-mouth delight. Few berries rival the succulence of wild strawberries. These were our first of the season. Several times one of us commented that it was time to go, that we were foolish to remain in the blazing sun. "Just a few more," we procrastinated. We didn't lick the fingers of our stained hands until sated.

So far we hadn't walked around one lake. Virginia's Pedlar Lake was unique, not only because it was the first small lake on the Trail, but because of its isolation.

What we had to do to reach the shores of Pedlar Lake made a story on its own. At the Appalachian Outfitters in Roanoke, we finally located a Virginia Trail guide. It directed us to the dam below the lake where we'd find a footbridge to the other side. We found half a footbridge, which is as bad as finding half a worm in an apple. Some courageous hiker had forded half the stream and placed a narrow plank (now slippery with moss) to the intact half of the bridge. Only a fool would have walked it.

The outflow from the dam was not deep. What it lacked in depth was compensated for by force. We walked up and down the bank of the charging white water to find a crossing. The bottom was covered with slimy rocks. We removed our boots to try a barefoot traverse, and instantly rejected the idea. The only possible way to get to Pedlar Lake was to wade across in our boots. Even under water, lug soles are tenacious; we plunged through the rushing waters and finally scrambled with squishing socks up the steep riverbank on the other side.

The fish in Pedlar Lake would substantiate any fish story. We saw some grandfather bass more than two feet long. In the shallow pools we spotted several sunfish and lake trout. Julia carried a line and a few hooks in her pack. Cheddar cheese is not the best of bait, but in less than ten minutes she caught a colorful sunfish. Unfortunately, it was too small and had to be thrown back to the fish realm, probably with a life-long fishhook neurosis.

Later we saw this sign posted on someone's property.

> No fishing no time
> Please obey the law
> Don't brake it.
> This is My last warning

Toward the swampy end of Pedlar Lake, where two hundred million years ago we might have seen a brontosaurus bend his long rubbery neck to eat wild swamp grass, we now saw the flight of a great blue heron. He glided, landed, looked our way, and folded his six-foot wings, a gray silhouette frozen on our retinas long after we left him behind.

At Pedlar Lake Road we came to an extremely helpful sign that informed us the footbridge was out and it was advisable to use the road.

Episodes like this happened to other hikers, too. We met Jerry and Alice outside Pearisburg, pouring over a guidebook and looking for something. "This guidebook is just great," Jerry said wryly. "It indicates that the Appalachian Trail Conference is planning to build a shelter here. That was in 1970. Obviously, it still isn't built. It also says there are campsites ahead. I wonder if we should take their word for it?" People who used the shelters relied on the guidebooks even more than we did.

Jerry swung his camera to one side of his shoulder, and he and Alice headed up the power line clearing. We walked on, stopping at a small stream that crossed the Trail. From under some dead stalks we pulled a string of cattail spuds. Our beef stroganoff would have a tuber garnish that night.

Then, suddenly, one of those freak twists of nature occurred. All at once the calm warm air turned cold. Previously, not the faintest breeze was stirring. Now the wind bent tree tops and pushed forcefully against our packs. A Midwesterner, perhaps more than anyone, knows that this is a sign of tornado weather. Terrified, all Julia wanted to do was hit the ground. We rushed on to the campsite Jerry had mentioned and set up the tent as the wind billowed through the nylon and the pull ropes lashed in our faces. We sat under a poncho awning while the rain drilled the ground.

Jerry and Alice came trudging up, looking extremely hard set with the meteorological conditions. Another hiker appeared behind them, muttering blasphemous oaths. The rain poured down on Alice as Jerry tried to establish a rain shield from oversized ponchos; their tent was being waterproofed back home.

We invited Alice over for a swig of sherry from our baby bottle. We wanted to invite her in out of the rain, too, but she declined. Her poncho not only covered herself and her pack but Jerry's pack as well. Often we, too, had suffered injustices from the elements. Soon after dinner the rain stopped, and the lone hiker miraculously produced a fire from wet wood. In the intimacy of fire glow we all finished off the wine. The company was welcome in the starless, thunderfilled night.

Although we didn't socialize much, we discovered that the Trail intensified the individuality in long-distance hikers. The grapevine singles out end-to-enders and tags them with their characteristics. For example, there was Heart Fund Fuzz, the police officer who walked the Trail to promote a charity dollar for every mile; Two–Stick Allen, who raced along with a walking staff in each hand; the X–Guy, a purist extraordinaire, who marked the Trail with an X whenever he left it so that he could return to the exact spot; The Family, an Arizona couple hiking the Trail with their ten-year-old daughter; and Roadrunner Mark, the long-limbed hare who made others feel like tortoises. With a certain amount of curiosity, we wondered what we were nicknamed. Probably The Hermits.

As we walked down Priest Mountain (4,063 feet) we talked to Mike Warren, the first hiker we met who was a member of the Appalachian Trail Conference. The Trail was overgrown beyond recognition, and it took us three hours to descend. Mike drove by as we stood sweltering on the road. We needed supplies. It was June 10, Sunday, and the single country store was closed. Another savior.

Mike is one of those astounding people who has learned to enjoy the best of two worlds. His base is New York City, but on occasion he will call you up in New Hampshire to tell you that he is out for a hike and ask if you would like to come along. He has been an active member of the New York chapter of the Appalachian Trail Conference, and often goes out on his own to mull over relocations of the trail, or make a mileage check with a wheel that he keeps handy in his car trunk. This bicycle-sized wheel is pushed (and occasionally lifted) over the trail, recording mileage as it rolls. In Mike's entire hiking career he must have hiked most of the Trail. On this particular ninety-degree day he was the only other person hiking the Priest. We promised to drop him a card when we reached New York, which actually wasn't far away.

At Harpers Ferry, West Virginia, the Shenandoah and Potomac Rivers meet. Prior to this convergence, the Trail winds above the Shenandoah River Valley, an old but productive tract of farmland that extends the seventy-five miles of the Shenandoah National Park. We found the Trail in the Park well maintained and a joy to walk. Since the Park was only a few hours' drive from Washington, D.C., both road traffic along the Blue Ridge Parkway and heavy use of the

Trail were to be expected. Nevertheless, the lush mountain growth and panoramas into the valleys made up for the often crowded campgrounds.

We passed two sexagenarian couples walking the entire Shenandoah as an appetizer to other hikes. For years they told us it had been their dream to hike the entire Appalachian Trail. Now that their children were in college, they were doing just that. The previous year Hurricane Agnes had postponed their intended hike. Their packs looked uncomfortably heavy.

"How much food are you truckin'?" we asked in Trail lingo.

"Six days each," they answered. "We figured on enough to get through the Park, averaging twelve miles a day."

We didn't comment, but again rejoiced that our packs were super-light.

Through the Park we clipped along at twenty miles a day. Four straight hiking days focused in with an absurd sharpness and clarity. The shadows were honed. A cloudless sky filled in the cracks among the trees with a spotless wash of blue. All the greens of the conifers, the brown grasses and balds, the white-pink mountain laurel, the yellow groundsel were blinding in their full-dress colors. Late spring flowers were in bloom. We passed through knee-high glades of meadow rue. These dainty fringed flowers gave us the feeling we were walking through a Japanese tea garden hung with a thousand tasseled lanterns. The brilliant blue three-leaved spiderworts winked from a ground cover of staghorn moss. Pale yellow evening primroses grew on open embankments.

All through the Shenandoah, deer bounded and abounded. The number of these gentle light-footed creatures seen in the Shenandoah National Park tripled any other section of the Trail. Many times we camped, and before long a doe, maybe two, eased into view. One morning we caught a ten-point buck leaping a four-foot shrub just ahead of us. Another time, a doe nudged her curious fawn from the trail ahead and into the privacy of the bushes. At Loft Mountain Campground the deer grazed at tent sites like contented cows.

All at once, we were walking through weather you could cut with a knife. The last three days in the Shenandoah masked the splendors of both the valleys and ridges. We walked through the rain-shellacked hardwoods to Big Meadows Campground at the northern end of the Park. This campground, jam-packed, noisy, and cluttered like a typical suburb, prepared us for Front Royal and the asphalt roads leading into West Virginia. These "campers" were trading one neighborhood life for another, complete with emptying the camp trash, shouting at the kids, and keeping up with the Joneses' trailer—parked ten feet away. A disquieting scene.

And so we went from the ridiculous to the sublime. We went from a noisy campground to the quiet of a woodland home above Rock Creek Park in Maryland. We spent five days in the company of friends and five nights in a real bed. We went from instant coffee to French champagne, from dehydrated monosodium glutamate, chemical preservatives and artificially colored dinners to fresh soft shelled crabs and veal roast with spinach dressing. And our five-day rest was as natural as our company.

The end of Virginia meant that a psychological, if not a technical, halfway point had been reached.

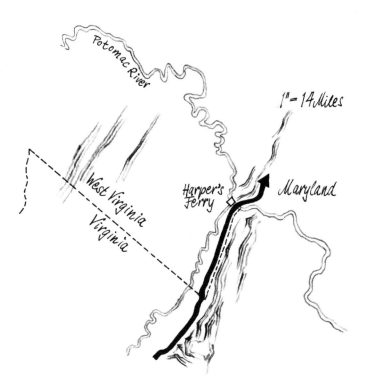

Potomac River

1″ = 14 Miles

West Virginia
Virginia

Harper's
Ferry

Maryland

West Virginia

10 MILES

The halfway point of the Appalachian Trail is located near
Duncannon, Pennsylvania, about a hundred miles north of
West Virginia. For most thru-hikers, however, the halfway
point in spirit is Harpers Ferry, where the headquarters of
the Appalachian Trail Conference (ATC) are located. The
few miles the Trail covers in West Virginia are negligible, but
in walking them hikers can register at the headquarters and

81

talk with staff members as well as walk the streets of this National Historical Park, notorious for John Brown's raid of 1859.

At that time Abolitionist Brown attacked a federal armory in Harpers Ferry, and barricaded himself and seventeen others in the engine house. Colonel Robert E. Lee and Lieutenant J. E. B. Stuart, backed up by a contingent of Marines and townspeople, killed ten men, captured Brown, and put down the insurrection. This was one of the portentous events leading to the outbreak of the Civil War a year and a half later. Both Confederate and Union troops seized and occupied the Harpers Ferry Armory at one time or another.

The destruction wreaked on this strategically placed community took different form in a series of floods beginning in 1870. On many of the remaining old buildings high water marks of these devastating floods were still visible at the time we passed through.

Harpers Ferry was a languid town of old houses and older oaks set amid the ancient Blue Ridge Mountains. We visited the site of the raid and heard the blasting demonstration of flintlock rifles. On our way to the ATC headquarters, we followed the old steps to Jefferson Rock high above the Shenandoah River, and from there walked through Harper's Cemetery. Adjacent this cemetery was Storer College, in 1867 the first institution to offer higher education to the American Negro. The Conference office was next to the College.

No overnight camping facilities were provided at Harpers Ferry, not even by the ATC for long-distance hikers. Since the office was closed on Sundays, and we wanted to visit the headquarters, we remained in town instead of hiking back into the woods. After sunset we picked a spot next to the graveyard. The night air was summery, the grass thick and fragrant. We slept well under the stars.

The next morning we signed in at the Conference office and talked with the staff. The headquarters were situated in an old multi-story home that today could be a mini-mansion, though in the last century it was probably no more than an ordinary home for an ordinary twelve-member family. In these spacious rooms, secretaries trace the two-thousand-mile treks of thru-hikers. Here, also, official ATC guidebooks, the *Appalachian Trailway News,* and related publications are sold.

In 1968 President Johnson signed the National Trails System Act under which the Appalachian and the Pacific Crest were designated national scenic trails. The two-thousand-mile Appalachian Trail was principally the brainchild and dream-come-true of Benton MacKaye, who proposed such a continuous footpath in the *Journal of American Institute of Architects* in 1921. The first mile of the Trail was blazed in New York the following year. Three years later the Appalachian Trail Conference was organized. From this time until 1968, the Trail depended solely upon voluntary support from individuals and organizations. However, under the National Trails System Act, the United States Department of the Interior is responsible for administration of the Trail, in consultation with the Department of Agriculture. The wilderness aspect of the Trail becomes increasingly important as the urban development of America expands.

The Appalachian Trail Conference is a non-profit organization whose goal is to co-ordinate the activities of these governmental bodies as they affect the Trail, promote active planning, and encourage maintenance of the Trail. As the Conference states, "It publishes guidebooks and other descriptive material about its facilities. It keeps much of the Trail cleared and marked. In all its endeavors, the Conference strives to provide a Trail environment of the highest quality."

A Board of Conference officers and three persons from each of the six districts into which the Trail is divided constitute the backbone of the Conference. Parts of the Trail are incorporated into national and state forests, but the remainder is on private land with the consent of landowners. The ATC is involved in many battles to secure land and areas where commercial development threatens the Trail, or where individual property holders are reluctant to give right-of-way. The ATC is making progress toward having the entire Trail on public land. Some roadwalking in Virginia, New York, and other states where the Trail is routed beside main highways shows that many battles remain to be won.

The Trail Conference meets biennially. Individual membership is $12.50 the first year, $10.00 thereafter. Life membership, $200.00. Fifty-seven clubs support the Conference. Of these the Dartmouth Outing Club, the Appalachian Mountain Club, and the Green Mountain Club are very active.

The ATC guidebooks (costing $5.85 to $9.25) are pocket size. The Trail descriptions are arranged in directional sequence from either north–south or south–north, and some are printed in loose-leaf form so unwanted sections can be removed for lighter carrying. Each book in the series is different in style, binding, and emphasis. For instance, the author of the Cherokee National Forest section (North Carolina) is a history buff, and makes the area come alive with his prose. The Maine guidebook author evidently finds information about water and provision stops irrelevant. Some sections of the New York and Pennsylvania guides are little more than factsheets. Other guidebook writers have a penchant for poetry. The Vermont guide was printed in 1968, and relocations have since made much of the information obsolete. The guide to New Jersey and New York is glue-bound so that the weight of unneeded sections must be carried. The book on the Shenandoah National Park is bound by a twisted wire ring, difficult to disassemble. Hikers depend on these guidebooks as much as on the shelters. Unfortunately, the coherence, presentation and updating of the guides often is not commensurate with their cost.

The shelters offer another opportunity for the Conference to improve the lot of hikers. The disgrace of ninety per cent of the more than 230 shelters from Georgia to Maine is not the entire responsibility of the ATC. Hikers who use them must assume the major share of culpability. Nevertheless, as organizer and guardian of the Appalachian Trail, the Conference could do much to improve the disheartening condition of the shelters.

Above all, the Conference stresses that the Appalachian Trail is a wilderness trail. Too many times, however, we found that it was not so much a wilderness trail as wilderness without a trail. The footpath sometimes completely disappeared into unattended overgrowth, as on Priest Mountain in Virginia, and sometimes into flooded rivers and swamps, as in central Maine. At these times, the Trail was certainly not "A joy and satisfaction to follow," as the ATC would have us believe.

We thought it ludicrous to see signs that said *No Motorized Vehicles Allowed* when the Trail was smothered under tangled brush. Once in awhile, we did spot fresh motorcycle tracks ripped into the soft dirt and plant life. A sign means nothing if it is unenforced.

More than 120 million people are within a one-day car journey to the Appalachian Trail. Most of those who use the Trail are little concerned with walking it the entire two thousand miles. Actually, the Conference encourages short-distance hiking. Short-term hikers normally are uninterested in risking life and limb on a submerged trail, such as existed at Laurel Falls, North Carolina, or in bushwhacking through calf-high bogs, as north of Monson, Maine.

The organization and co-ordination of fifty-seven clubs and two governmental agencies is challenging indeed, yet for nearly nine hundred miles in two-and-a-half months, we met only one hiking representative of the ATC. To hike the Trail is to know what must be done.

Pennsylvania

1" = 19 Miles

Maryland

Smithburg ◇

Hagerstown ◇ ◇ South Mtn.

West Virginia

Boonsboro ◇ Washington Monument
◇ State Park

◇ Turner's Gap

◇ Weaverton Shelter
◇ Gathland State Park

Virginia

Potomac River

District
of Colum

Maryland

38 MILES

For two miles the Trail followed the C & O Canal towpath along the northeast bank of the Potomac River. Vines looped from the trees in a thick green canopy that might have been transplanted from the heartland of the Deep South. Water lilies and snapping turtles floated atop the stagnant waters of the 150-year-old Canal. Even though the water was malodor-

86

ous, plants and other wildlife were living the life of Riley on the land between the Canal and the river.

A kingfisher flew by and lighted on a stump rotting in the dense blanket of algae. His shaggy crest was unmistakable, as was his fondness for fish and water. A turtle dove under the viscid layer. Bullfrogs leaped from mossy half-submerged logs and completely disappeared in the murky substance. Clusters of mulberries trailed just beyond our reach.

We stopped to pick a Ziplock bag of day lily buds. Their orange-lemon bells, three and four feet high, flourished among the stingweed. Gathering these dinner vegetables cost us a prickling rash, which fortunately didn't last long.

We dallied along the humid towpath, less than an hour from the Capital. Excavated in 1828–1850, the 185-mile C & O Canal started from Washington, D.C., and connected intervening settlements to Cumberland, Maryland. The Canal was busiest during the 1860's before the railroads appropriated passenger and freight business. Then, in 1924, a flood seriously damaged sections of the Canal, and it was abandoned. Today the Canal is an historical monument under the supervision of the National Park Service, and the flat towpath is a popular bicycle trail.

We passed fishermen pulling in catfish on the smelly banks of the Potomac. This river has taken the lives of a few unlucky fishermen. Knowing how to swim isn't enough if you drink a mouthful of its water, although scavenger fish miraculously have survived.

Near Weaverton Shelter (no water), a loquacious hiker intercepted us, and complained about the invaders who used the Trail shelters. "These flatlanders," he said, "shouldn't be allowed to camp at the shelters. They throw junk all around and take up space. That's all they are, flatlanders." He was dressed in baggy blue bermudas hitched over a beer and bread belly. He wore calf-high Boy Scout socks and boots with the leather grain still shoe-shop clean, and he sported a manicured half-moon beard that was as trim as the pencils he pushed on weekdays.

Immediately after leaving the towpath we crossed the B & O Railroad tracks. In the early nineteenth century, when the Erie Canal attracted traffic and population away from Baltimore, the B & O Railroad was built to rejuvenate the city. Peter Cooper's Tom Thumb Steam Locomotive was the first successful engine used for passenger and freight traffic. The B & O became a vital means of transporting men and equipment during the Civil War, but lapsed into disuse after that. Despite competition with air travel, Amtrak, the national consolidated rail system, was inaugurated in 1971 to "get people back on the trains." Amtrak ran daily from Harpers Ferry, West Virginia, affording hikers an opportunity to visit Washington.

The Trail along the South Mountain Crest above the Potomac was flat as glass. The terrain here was quite different from the lush Shenandoah on the other side of the river. In the last century the iron industry denuded these mountains for charcoal, eroding the land and contributing to the floods that devastated Harpers Ferry in the 1870's.

For two miles we walked a craggy trail and discovered we preferred leaves. We passed many outcrops of quartzite, also known as the White Rocks of Maryland. Although it was six miles to the nearest spring on the Trail, at Gathland State Park, the South Mountain Range has always been famous for spring water, which has been touted by local bottling companies for centuries.

In the late afternoon we barely discerned the outlines of two white animals ahead of us, too small for deer, too large for dogs. What were they? Amazed, we followed their gamboling forms. Goats, a pair of goats with good-sized horns! As we were trying to conjecture why goats would roam the Appalachian Trail, they spotted us and leaped into a rocky retreat. This was one of the strangest encounters of our hike. Most of the Trail was on a wedge between Inter-state Highways 180 and 70. If these were tame goats we doubted they would have bounded away. Certainly the jagged outcrops were suitable for mountain goats. But who-ever heard of such wild creatures so close to civilization? At any rate, this incident livened up our backyard walking for quite a while.

We arrived at Gathland State Park at 8 p.m., on June 25, after ten waterless miles on a hot sunny day. The late hour was a worry. Hikers need two hours to pitch camp, eat, and prepare for bed.

In the 1880's George Alfred Townsend, a former Civil War correspondent, returned to the South Mountain area. At Crampton Gap, the sight of a preliminary battle to Antietam, Townsend built his home and library. Later he constructed a fifty-foot memorial arch to war correspondents. This arch is of terra cotta–colored stone, inscribed with poetry and deco-rated with mythological figures in relief. It overlooks the bat-tlefields of Gettysburg, Antietam, and Winchester, and for all the world looks like it was crafted by an Italian sculptor homesick for the old country.

The 135-acre Gathland State Park, with its alley of trees lined with tables, somehow also smacked of Italy and a scene from "The Godfather." In the dark we finished a dinner dis-covery that added more of a flair than the mediocre macaroni dinners hikers usually fall heir to. While with our friends in Silver Spring, we had bought several instant Chinese dinners. That night the meal was ready in a record three minutes. It consisted of *orotyon*, a packet of dried fish and seaweed, and *misoramen*, a combination of chicken broth, egg yolk, and bean sprouts. Along with this culinary breakthrough, we cooked the day lily buds picked along the Canal. We sautéed the unopened buds in oil and vinegar after boiling them ap-proximately ten minutes. They were as tender and succulent as green beans.

We pitched tent in the dark and, not surprisingly, punctured one of our Girl Scout air pillows. Each hiker has his idiosyncrasies. To us a good night's sleep meant a pillow, and our air pillows were light, cheap, and comfortable. The next morning we administered first aid. First, hold the pillow under water to discover the location of the puncture. Second, dry the wounded area. Third, apply a medicated corn plaster, and to insure healing, a moleskin. Fourth, and finally, burn a match on the outer edges of the wound. Later, when the Girl Scout pillows died, we bought a Japanese inflatable banana and beach ring which were just as comfortable.

North of Gathland State Park the Trail was as level as a Kansas cornfield. We brisked along through the open woods, striving to gain the hiking momentum we had built up previous to our Silver Spring holiday. At times the body was more willing than the spirit to move ahead. We realized this was the normal reaction. The middle third of any long-distance endeavor is the most difficult, the one that challenges persistence and fortitude. It was the middle third that left us searching for the mettle to keep putting one foot before the next, to look ahead for the end that seemed so distant. The middle third lacked the enthusiasm of the beginning as well as the resurgence that anticipated the end.

The blackberries were ripe now, and inordinately delicious. We picked and devoured handfuls, smiling with stained teeth, laughing at each other's wild berry look. The plant life changed dramatically whenever we passed from the woods into power line clearings where the sun completely washed the low growth. In the clearings, the wild roses, fragile whispers of pink, bloomed unintimidated by maples and oaks. So did the cheerful daisies, bull thistles, black-eyed susans, and yellow groundsel, humming with bees and smelling of summer.

The Trail followed a dry creek bed before crossing U.S. Alternate Route 40. A tenth of a mile to the left stood the South Mountain House. This homey tavern, built in 1732, still operated in Turner's Gap, where nineteenth-century

Presidents once traveled. Famous politicians, from Abe Lincoln to Daniel Webster, slept here—and not a few ladies, for at one time the inn was a brothel. Had it not been drizzling we would have eaten our lunch on the terrace under a ceiling of grape leaves.

The couple at the next table in the South Mountain House dining room noticed our clothes and asked where we were hiking from. "Georgia."

"Georgia!" the man said. "Well, you've come a hell of a long way. Where you headed?"

"Maine."

"Maine! Ha! Well you've got a hell of a long way to go. You must be hiking the Appalachian Trail."

"Yep."

The man shook his head. "It takes guts for a woman to start a hike like that."

"It takes more guts to finish it."

The Washington Monument State Park is the sight of the Washington Monument, not the well-known 555-foot one in the Capital, but the 30-foot one. To us the monument, which is supposed to serve as an observatory, looked like a rock beehive (though some imagine it as an old-fashioned cream bottle). Whatever the description, it was an odd monument for the citizens of Boonsboro to have built in 1827. It seems South Mountaineers liked pomp and circumstance (another coincidence between Italy and this region) and dedicated this monument and the one at Gathland several times.

The last of the Trail in Maryland passed through what seemed like the neighborhood vacant lot. Time and again we passed piles of rusted cans, bed springs, and broken bottles. The only joy we gained from these eyesores was that they were also sites for profuse raspberry and blackberry thickets. We discovered clusters of enticing currants, but were reluctant to eat them until we were absolutely sure that's what they were. They looked too tempting to be true.

The closeness of the towns, the noisiness of automobile and

truck traffic, the shouts of children playing kickball and tag, the meeting of local residents using the Trail as a shortcut from market to home, all detracted from the pleasure of hiking.

Once, we passed the remains of a single-engine plane that had crashed years before and was now a tangled weathering wreck. The Trail grazed the shooting range of the South Mountain Rod and Gun Club with its twenty-five bull's-eye targets. (We were glad nobody was shooting.) The weedy dirt range was only ten feet from the Trail, not a distance to instill a sense of safety.

We could tell from the guidebook, the thickening of the air, the knife-scarred trees and painted rocks and tree trunks, that we were close to Interstate Route 70. We often wondered what induced a person to paint his initials in the woods, a feeble attempt at immortality, domination over nature, what? The Indians used to paint deer and elk on the rock faces of caves. They were telling a story. We supposed that a heart and four initials in orange spray paint on a boulder told a story, too. Yet if S.D. really loved P.R. wouldn't the story be told differently?

There were three nice facets to Interstate 70. First, we had a reinforced, sixty-thousand-dollar footbridge over the highway all to ourselves. A sign, *The Appalachian Trail*, alerted drivers so inclined to wave at hikers on the catwalk above the river of racing traffic. Secondly, the embankment on the far side of the highway was blanketed with wood vetch that exuded an intoxicating orange blossom odor in the direct sunlight. Scattered among these were spiffy blue bachelor buttons. We felt as if we had just passed through a picket gate into a country garden. And thirdly, we were only a day's walk from the Pennsylvania state line and our seventh state.

The southern border of Pennsylvania is the famous Mason–Dixon line. In 1765 Charles Mason and Jeremiah Dixon surveyed this boundary, which had been in dispute ever since it was established by William Penn. Mason and Dixon, English astronomers and surveyors, marked this boundary between Lord Baltimore's "Hominey Gentry" and Pennsylvania's "Quaking Cowards." The Appalachian Trail passed near the ninety-first milestone of the Mason–Dixon line, which later became the dividing line between free and slave-holding colonies. Our own memory links to this boundary, however, were neither colonial disputes nor the Civil War, but the discovery of more raspberries, enough to waylay us for an hour.

Nearing Pennsylvania, we met young Mark Henneberger of Smithburg, Maryland. He and his brother were staking a nature trail, their Scout troop project. They had a wagon filled with twenty-four masonite markers: *poison ivy, animal holes, white pine.*

> MARK: *Go on down and get a smaller screwdriver, will you?*
> ALFRED: *Aw, I don't know your tools.*
> MARK: *Well, then get yours.*
> ALFRED: *I don't want to.*

Mark solemnly ran downhill, his stars-and-stripes kneesocks a blotch of color in the somber pines. Alfred turned to us. "You know, I own this. Well, it's on my father's property, but I'm in charge." We asked who was head of the nature trail and Alfred condescendingly admitted Mark was. "You hiking the Appalachian Trail?" he asked. We nodded. "Well, lots of hikers come through here. Will you please sign in?" he asked officiously. "There's a box on the tree here. Name, address, destination and how long you're staying at our campsites. Our troop has these two sites."

"We'd like to camp, but it's too early to stop today," we explained when we saw his disappointed face.

"Well, the rest of the way to Maine is easy," Alfred assured us in a grown-up voice. "You're halfway there, and so it's all downhill."

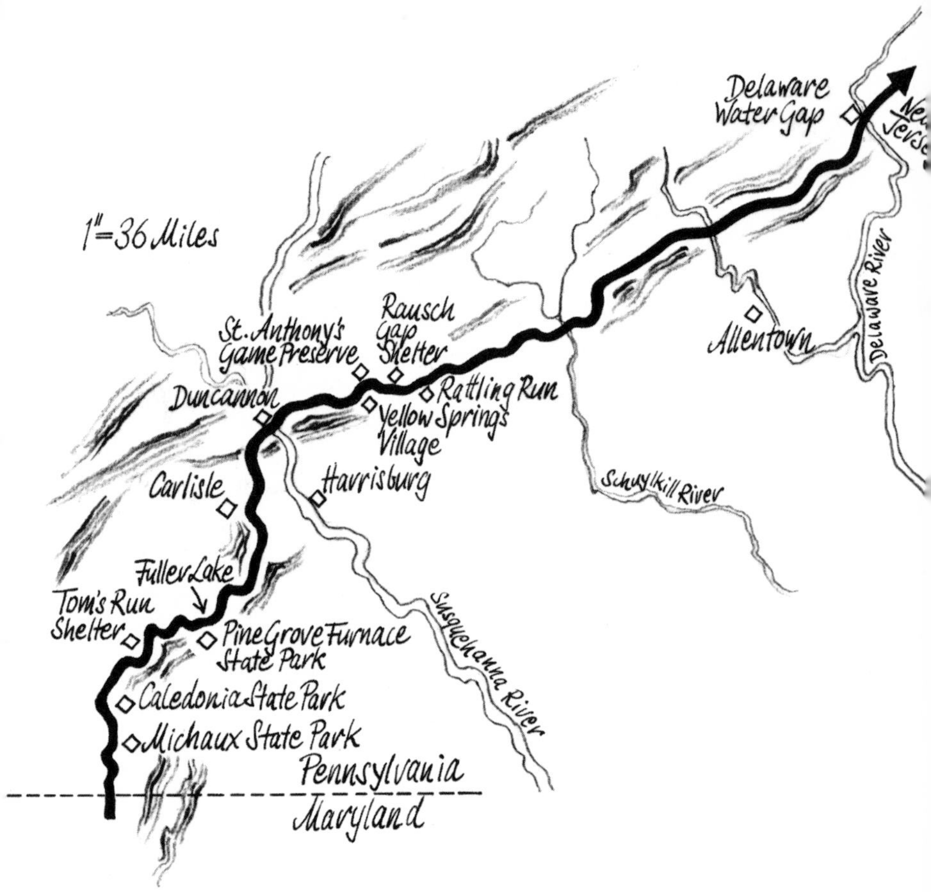

1" = 36 Miles

Delaware Water Gap

New Jersey

Delaware River

Allentown

Schuylkill River

Rausch Gap Shelter

St. Anthony's Game Preserve

Rattling Run

Duncannon

Yellow Springs Village

Carlisle

Harrisburg

Susquehanna River

Fuller Lake

Tom's Run Shelter

Pine Grove Furnace State Park

Caledonia State Park

Michaux State Park

Pennsylvania
Maryland

Pennsylvania

221 MILES

Two thousand miles is a long way to go.
On Clingman's Dome there were inches of snow.
And I nearly took my life in Stekoah Gap.
I think it was a trap, Lord, it must have been a trap.
And you'll never really know what it's like to be bored
'till you've hiked through Pennsylvania, Lord.

In the South Sea Islands the natives have a rite that requires initiates to walk over a bed of live coals, a test performed with no injury or pain to the islanders' feet. We wished we were South Sea islanders walking through stony Pennsylvania. The Trail took us over 221 miles of rocks that might as well have been a bed of hot coals.

Beside the Appalachians stretched the productive lands of the Pennsylvania Dutch, the rolling hills around York and Lancaster where the conveyance often seen was a horse and buggy. Down there was the bread basket of the East, and the soft ground. With such inviting country below, we didn't understand the tortuous route of the Trail along a monotonous, rocky crest with meager views. Perhaps it was a spiritual exercise. Whatever it was, our lug soles might as well have been bedroom slippers. Tender feet returned, and so did blisters.

The weather in Pennsylvania was a mask of drizzle that increased the gloom of gray boulders and ash groves. The muggy air made flying ideal for mosquitoes, and they zeroed in on us. For days on end, we fanned ourselves with witch hazel twigs every hour of the risen sun. The buzzing in our ears and eyes and noses and over every exposed centimeter of skin drove us to outbursts of Rabelaisian obscenity. We could not escape these winged monsters, and too often we lost our blood to the battle. The plague forced us to keep our bodies in motion, forced us early into our tent at night, forced us to hang onto our sanity with conscious endeavor.

Because of constant humidity and lack of sunlight, the forest floor bred this onslaught of gnats and mosquitoes in a growth like that of the underworld. Fungus sprouted in shelves from the trees, each balcony overhanging the next. Vines and ferns intermingled in contortion and anarchy. Indian pipes, their white waxy cylinders hanging shyly, arched low above layers of dark fallen ash leaves. When we wrote home about spotting our first Indian pipes, a reply awaited us at our next mail stop. "When I was a boy, it was said that whoever touched this 'corpse plant' would have bad luck. I heard other tales that if it were picked the plant turned black and died immediately, not to mention its offender." These auguries fell on deaf ears, for we cherished the "ghost flowers," friendly as lanterns in the decaying leaf mold.

Mushrooms grew in numberless shapes, sizes, and colors—vivid saffrons, powdery oranges, drab beiges. Some spread as wide as bread plates, and, sautéed in butter, would have provided an adequate meal. Others were scarcely more than umbrellas for ants. Time and again we saw scarlet saucers nibbled at the edges or with teeth marks at the top, as if a chipmunk had snitched the icing from a cake.

We also saw bandages, gauze pads, adhesive bandages, and moleskins. They became as disconcerting as beer can tabs and chewing gum wrappers. The litter, small as it was, resulted from the tin can–waste paper syndrome endemic in this country. Twice in all the miles we walked, we used canned foods; but we discarded the cans in town where they might be re-cycled and transferred the contents to a re-usable plastic bag, one time even carrying messy corned beef patties. This way we were never tempted to leave the can in the woods or at the source of a bubbling spring. To forget the drudgery of Pennsylvania, we talked for miles about the reason people litter and what could be done to alleviate the waste disease. Our conclusion was that if each individual were fully, totally, and absolutely responsible for the waste, off-scourings, raff, orts he himself generated, the Trail as well as the world would be an easier place to live.

The blazes led us through Michaux State Park, Caledonia State Park, fifteen miles of St. Anthony's Game Preserve, and the Pine Grove Furnace State Park. The Michaux State Park campsites were crowded with two outhouse pit toilets near by. We preferred the woods, but the sky threatened another thunderstorm. We quickly set up camp only a short walk from a summer stock theatre presenting actress Jean Stapleton in a comedy that night. Well-tailored people filled the theatre before a thundershower blustered in to contest with the actors' vocal cords.

The next morning after crossing Pennsylvania Highway 233, we found what we had been looking for all along—Caledonia State Park. Regretfully, we eyed the Olympic–size swimming pool and the more sculptured tent sites. The Park had fourteen hundred acres (and undoubtedly as many picnic tables), fifteen fireplaces, a public eighteen-hole golf course, the mammoth swimming pool, a Thaddeus Stevens Museum, and the ruins of an iron furnace and rolling mill once owned by Stevens, an Abolitionist United States Congressman from Pennsylvania in the 1860's.

The walk through Caledonia perked us up. The Trail was less rocky and we could lift our eyes from the craggy ground. Until then, like unsure musicians, we had kept them buried in our work, constantly watching where we stepped. With more time to look, this park gave us many mind-shots to remember. One was a deer that stared at us from afar and then, to run for cover, explosively leaped in a *grand jeté*, suspended in mid-air like an antlered Nureyev. Another was the aloof, backward glance of a white-tailed fox as he trotted ahead of us before swerving into the brush. At first this fox, with its ears looking like magnolia leaves and its tail hanging behind like a dust broom, stood about a hundred yards away. He stared at us from his end of a corridor of trees while all three of us breathing creatures waited a half minute for the next move.

Had we been hunters we might have given chase to this wily relative of the wolf and coyote, all members of the dog family. Like the raccoon and bear, the fox is a descendant of a tree-climbing mammal that lived fifty million years ago. Extremely versatile, he is cool, analytical, quick, cunning, and unpredictable.

The fox that tolerated us on the Trail was a red fox, perhaps the most familiar and impressive looking of the foxes, especially with his sugar-white breast, russet overcoat, white-tipped tail, long legs with black below the knee joints, and perky white ears. A red fox litter can yield silver, black, platinum, and cross foxes, the last which include shades of yellow and orange. The shoulder height of a fox can reach sixteen inches, its weight up to fifteen pounds.

This small package is a never-ending wonder of strategic brilliance in the field. Stories are reported of foxes bewildering hunting parties by backtracking their own scent, skimming over thin ice, dashing along the tops of fences, hiding in trees, and in general making asses of our species. A favorite trick of foxes pursued by hounds is to charge toward a cliff with the hounds only a jaw-chomp away, and suddenly bolt to a right angle. One fox maneuvered this trick and sent seven hounds over a cliff to their death.

Wondering what anonymous woman left her life behind there, we walked through Dead Woman Hollow to Tom's Run Shelter. As the landscape changed, so did the place names. A gulch was now a hollow, a river now a run. We liked to camp near water sources away from shelters, but on that June 29 we had no choice. Tom's Run Shelter was popular, and most of the flat sites were taken. "Flat" in Pennsylvania merely means not on an incline. Every square foot of ground in the South Mountains is likely to have at least one unmovable protruding rock.

Our dinner at Tom's Run was a novelty—pre-cooked beans. To these we added half an envelope of spaghetti tomato sauce, water, minced onions, garlic, salt and pepper, and chunks of Danish salami, which we carried again after emerging from bear country. We had done without it in Virginia for fear its scent would bring company for dinner. The bean pot tasted as good as if it had come from a Yankee kitchen.

After dinner we hung our food, danced our one-step–two-step to dispel mosquitoes, dashed into the tent, zipped up the netting, and settled down for a long summer's nap.

Ten minutes later an animal was raiding our gear. We shined our flashlights on our packs. Nothing. We searched the food tree and spotlighted the culprit, a raccoon staring our way unblinking, unintimidated. With rounded impudence, he climbed up the tree trunk and gnawed a hole in our bag. A stream of granola sifted through the flashlight beam.

We shouted, shimmied into our jeans, leaped from the tent, and chased the lamp-eyed scalawag from the camp. He disappeared into the black, though not for good. In the moonless dark we cursed and pitched our fifty-foot nylon rope half a dozen times before securing it on an isolated limb farther away from the trunk.

While we struggled to protect our food, the mischievous coon circled the periphery of our camp. Finally we hit upon a method that kept him distant. Arching our arms over our heads and curling our fingers in witchy horror, we bellowed the most ferocious, guttural, heinous roar we could muster, all the time charging the rascal in savage threat. If the coon wasn't frightened, campers in the shelters near by undoubtedly must have been.

We returned to our sleeping bags with the consolation that one raccoon was only a trifle smarter than two of us. Later, we listened to paw steps on the leaves and heavy scratchings in the dirt. Then came a hideous grunt and growl. Thinking the coon had surrendered to a maverick bear, we zipped up the tent flap with so much alacrity that we didn't even verify the conjecture. Merely feet away in the dark each succeeding grunt and growl grew angrier.

One theory was that the horrid sounds were the result of an encounter between a wild boar (we had seen boar tracks in Virginia) and the frustrated coon. Another theory was that the same raccoon had returned and was throwing a tantrum at our changing the food bags to an unreachable location. Still another and far more probable theory was that a unicorn and a winged horse were dueling to the death. We never did discover the truth. Instead, we fell asleep to mystifying sounds outside our tent and wild dreams of monster attacks in the tarry night.

Fortunately, our effort to save the food was rewarded the next morning. Whatever creatures vied for our food left it almost untouched. Another hiker was less fortunate. He lost his entire food supply. Raccoons have paws as nimble as a monkey's, and are known to turn door knobs and open refrigerators as well as pull up a rope to get a food bag.

Our Fearless Fosdick taught us about coonery, namely that these black-masked bandits of the night are crafty, cunning, and incorrigible. We invented, however, coon-proof packs by wrapping and tying the ponchos around them, then emptying a canteen and placing it on top of the packs so that the noise of its clanking on the rocks would awaken us should the pack be disturbed. Finally, we swung the food bags at least three feet, and usually more, away from the tree trunk on a limb too weak to support a raccoon's weight.

Coons are peculiar to the Western Hemisphere and are found nearly everywhere in the United States. If they could survive the coonskin coat era and the craze for coonskin caps ushered in some years ago by the Davy Crockett television series, these lovable rascals can survive anything.

With the passing of the summer solstice, we now coveted cold cereals for breakfast. We still drank hot coffee or cocoa as a liquid fortifier against the loss from perspiration during the night. (The human body can lose half a pint and more of water through nighttime evaporation.) Lunches were still rather uninspired, and finding substitutes for processed Cheddar cheese became the number-one priority. Although package directions on cream cheese advised that it must be refrigerated after opening, food poisoning was a kinder fate than one more round of Cheddar cheese. Cream cheese, we found, not only kept well but was a welcome change. We were also feeling nauseous about Snickers candy bars. Because they seemed to have the most energy pickup, we had eaten them practically every day. Often, we bought individually wrapped brownies in small stores and gas stations along the way.

One of these high-priced stores was at Pine Grove Furnace State Park. Here iron productivity for firearms was at its height during the Civil War. After the war the furnace declined: cheaper products took over the market, and the depleted forests no longer provided enough fuel for the furnace. Finally, when the ore hole flooded, operations were abandoned.

On this particular day, we reached the Pine Furnace General Store hot, tired, and perspiring. The store proprietor, squirting mentholated spray into his mouth, greeted us over the blare of a jukebox on the long sagging porch. We succumbed to his prices, bought a quart of Neapolitan ice cream, sat on the hot stoop, and wished we were running down a beach into a cold lake. Half a mile farther we came to the old ore hole, now Fuller Lake, complete with bathhouse, buoys, lifeguard, and crowded beach. Flinging off twenty-five-pound packs, four-pound boots, and dirty jeans on an eighty-degree blue-sky day and then recklessly plunging into the cool waters was indescribable joy. For two hours we forgot time schedules and miles to cover and surrendered to the summer sun.

Four scuba divers dressed in black rubber wet suits strutted professionally across the sand. A trifle ridiculous in this wee body of water, the divers, perhaps wishing they were under orders of Captain Jacques Cousteau, plunged into the depths of the ore hole. Someone had lost a piece of jewelry. While they were at it, they retrieved a few beer bottles and rusty pots. When the frogmen finished the work, we and the other roasted people were allowed to swim.

By the look of us, no one could have guessed we had been outdoors for two and a half months. Our faces and arms were weathered and tan, but our legs and torsos were ghostly (we preferred jeans to shorts). We came away from Fuller Lake with salamander skins and glazed eyes, a condition ill-advised for hiking but one worth the consequences.

Unexpectedly, Pennsylvania became intriguing for the next section. The soil turned sandy and a scrub pine forest floor covered the mountain crest. Conditions were ideal for ant colonies. The French use the word *dépaysé* for someone who feels out of his element or strange in his surroundings. We walked through this dry, almost coastal, environment with the sense of walking another world.

Aztec-like ant mounds bordered both sides of the Trail for a mile. The mounds rose like miniature temples, perhaps miniature volcanoes recently borne from the depths. One rose in a perfect cone four feet high. The ants built their communities along the Trail for southern exposure to the sun and easy access to sand particles mixed with pine needles for building materials. We were not myrmecologists, but what foot travelers haven't stopped to observe the feverish work of ants? Was the proportion of the ant mounds to the size of individual ants the same as that of the Egyptian pyramids to the human body? We guessed the ants worked harder.

The mounds were inhabited by red and black ants. In some sections, the mounds were spaced ten to fifteen yards apart, like an apartment complex perhaps similar to what futurist architect Paolo Soleri might create in the Arizona desert. Not all the ant hills were inhabited. Some had been evacuated. We learned that often worker ants sense the need for change. Half the ants might stay behind while the others move to build another nest.

Some ants have summer and winter homes. They migrate from one to the other in April and September. We came to discover that ants, belonging to the insect family Formicidae, are among the most remarkable creatures on earth. More than fifteen thousand species are known, and myrmecologists do not doubt more are yet to be classified. The tight-knit social structure of the ant family goes back sixty million years before our own species appeared in its crudest form.

The lone ants that randomly scout for food were once thought to be indicators of a latent capacity for deductive reasoning, since they could successfully return to the colony to report the location of a food source. This "deductive reasoning" was later discovered to be the tracing of a trail of scent the ant exudes from its abdomen as it wanders from the colony. Some myrmecologists think this scent is a vapor rather than a liquid line over the soil. Whatever constitutes it, the scent lasts for about five minutes during which time the ant must report to his fellow workers and have them follow the scent trail to the food. If the group catches the scent in time and moves along the trail, the entire line of ants leaves a stronger scent that lasts longer. If they're not in time, the scent dissipates and the ants go about other chores, such as remodeling the mound, caring for the queen (which can live for fifteen years), or feeding each other by transferring food from mouth to mouth.

The ant mounds we walked past must have reverberated with our boot steps, as indeed they must every time any hiker walked by. Ants rely on sight and sound for detecting objects, but their most vital means of communication is smell. As we paused near a particularly active megalopolis, gun-staple–sized ants crawled up our boots. We stomped them off and took our seasoned scent beyond this community before nightfall.

We saw other examples of members of species working together, like the drama of blue jays one morning. At breakfast in a cove of young ash and beech trees, a chick blue jay wandered from its nest. We took our cups of coffee and left the scene so father and mother could lead the baby back home.

From a nearby camp a German shepherd, playful and curious, trotted over to our site. At once the father blue jay spotted the dog and flew to a branch directly above him. He sat on the branch and squawked like no other blue jay we had ever heard. This ploy was to draw attention away from the baby on the ground. What astounded us was that a passing wood thrush joined the rasping blue jay to double the verbal attack. The dog, momentarily flustered by this harangue, continued sniffing the ground. We interfered with Providence lest the tail-wagging canine gobble up the baby bird.

Finally, mother and father corralled their offspring while we finished our coffee before breaking camp. We walked past the blue jay nest and saw that three chicks were huddled in their grass-lined home on the ground. We gave the dumb parents a few strong words about settling in that neighborhood, and marveled at the play of life forces that interact to shield one's own kind from disaster. This drama with no name was undoubtedly one of millions that occurred each day in the woods.

Had we not eaten in Carlisle, where we bought fuel for our stove, we would have accepted Bill and Betsy Welch's invitation for dinner. Bill picked us up on his way home from work. We talked over a can of beer while their children on our laps eyed us as if we had just popped in from outer space. The Pennsylvania flood of the previous year had devastated the Welches' home. Luckily, they had evacuated the night before the high water struck. A branch of the Susquehanna River overflowed and covered the first floor of their house. They understood our experiences with floods in Virginia, and we theirs.

Although we found the Trail in Pennsylvania exasperating, the people were another matter. Bill and Betsy were the first to invite us into their home. Those who were kindest to us and most understanding were not white collar workers with high income and education, but the middle class construction and factory people. Invariably, the latter gave us rides into towns to re-provision. Rare was the occasion when someone dressed in a business suit picked us up, and although we traveled as a couple, no woman had as yet chanced us and our packs.

Onto the Trail we returned, and reached the thousand-mile mark—Duncannon, with baskets of red and white geraniums on front porches. Blazes on telephone poles led us through town. Mothers called their children in to dinner and smiled and waved to us from their doorsteps. A grandmother rocked her chair on a porch. "Nice day for hiking, isn't it?" she called, her neighborliness sparking a joy in us. The difference from the you-all-come-back-now hospitality of the South was slight, yet the feeling produced was as grand.

We crossed the broad Susquehanna, which lies 450 miles long through the New York and Pennsylvania coal regions. In the early history of our country this mighty river was a magnificent rush of water through rugged land. Now the attractions of the Susquehanna's waters stop at its name, for the river is man-defiled. The crumbly bridge we crossed to the northern bank was heavy with exhaust from cars and freight trucks that nearly bowled us off the sidewalk into the polluted waters.

By the time we climbed the steep embankment to the shelter six hundred feet above the river, we needed the last beer Bill and Betsy had thrust into our hands. The shelter was an earth-floor stall, the ten-degree incline beside it the only possibility for a tent site. We pitched the tent downhill with the door at the top so all our blood wouldn't rush to our heads, cooled our beer in the nearby spring, and thanked Bill and Betsy for their foresight. To practice what we preached, we carried the empty can for three days before depositing it in a trash barrel.

From here on through the heartland of Pennsylvania, we walked the closed, flat ridge tops of the worn-out Appalachian Range. The mountains were laid out in geologically neat rows as if placed by cosmic-size pastry bags. The hiking was monotonous.

Nevertheless, we did find relief and delight in feasting. In Pennsylvania we discovered our first ripe blueberries. Across a power line clearing where low-lying brush was exposed to the sun, blueberries dotted the fields with their purple clusters, skin-popping succulent. We threw off our packs just as we had done for the wild strawberries in Virginia, and for fifteen minutes grabbed two handfuls at a time. We could have sat in one place and filled ourselves, but part of the hypnotism was to roam from one bush to the next, picking the ripest, the easiest, the bluest, the biggest berries in sight. We hardly straightened our backs. Surfeited, we picked two more cupfuls and stored them in a plastic bag for granola the following morning, making any Huckleberry Finn proud and pleased.

Beyond the Susquehanna the Trail traversed fifteen miles of St. Anthony's Wilderness Preserve. In this area were many deserted mining villages, such as Yellow Springs, where mineral spring hotels thrived in the 1880's. Today, the village is little more than a corner of a foundation here and there. Despite the passing of nearly a century, the forest remains distant and respectful.

The creek named Yellow Springs, for its sulphur color, wound through a thick hemlock forest. The greens and browns of the trees mixing with the gray of the rocks switched our everyday scene from the beeches and ashes so sharply that it seemed we moved into a fantasy forest replete with gingerbread boys and mischievous gnus. As we passed through this section, to the right of us a heavy limb creaked, snapped, and crashed through a network of tiny branches, landing on the ground with a shattering of the silence. We were not alone in these dark woods.

A hiker who favored this part of the Trail above all others had attached a white mailbox to an oak. Inside was a scrapbook, Trail register, Bible quotations concerning wildlife, and poems written by the hiker. A haunting note written in ballpoint ink by a shaky hand told hikers that Rausch Gap Shelter, a new lean-to, was being built farther up the Trail. It wasn't yet listed in the guidebook. Perhaps we who read this note might wish to camp there. The ambiance of this deserted village was everywhere. We ate lunch with open eyes.

Crossing Rattling Run we re-entered the Pennsylvania we knew—humid, wet, and rocky. Suddenly, Julia whispered in fearful tones and pointed to the rock Steve, full stride and confident, had just stepped over. Curled in the shadow of the rock in the middle of the trail lazed a snake. Its markings were clear. A rattler. We stood pointing and whispering as if snakes had ears, which they don't, before realizing the rattler buzzed with flies. After a prod with a stick, we pronounced the snake dead. Someone killed it and stole the rattles as a souvenir. The Rausch Gap area is known for its large rattlesnake population.

In a rugged rock-wall canyon with a river and waterfall, we veered a little from the Trail to follow a conifer-lined side path to the new lean-to. In comparison with the other shelters we had seen, Rausch Gap Shelter was a Taj Mahal in a trailer park. Leonard Reed, the shelter committee chairman, designed and supervised the building along with thirty-eight members of the Blue Mountain Eagle Climbing Club. Twenty-five trips during a period of fourteen months were needed for completion of the shelter.

"For a small handful of us," Leonard told us later in a letter, "this was a work of love." The love was apparent as we sat on the plywood bunk space and looked around. Totally unlike any other shelter on the Trail, its simplicity and comfort were an invitation to stay the night, which, given our usual despair at the condition of Trail shelters, was the best praise we could bestow.

The *Appalachian Trailway News* describes the Rausch Gap Shelter. It is "constructed of telephone pole logs with corrugated V-crimp roofing and three spacious skylight areas. It is built on the stone foundations of a building that was once part of the extensive Rausch Gap coal operations that ended around the turn of the century."

The shelter was sunk below ground level. Half a dozen steps led down to a fifteen-foot circular flagstone patio. The grille and fireplace were built in a corner and lowered so that hikers could sit along a ledge half-encircling the chimney. This was a fireplace that withstood rainstorms. Next to it was a carved water trough that channeled runoff from a nearby spring. The water flowed continuously. The trough was designed for easy filling of canteens and cooking pots. It carried the unused water away to drain outside the shelter area.

The space beneath the bunks was sealed with cement. No creatures could build their nests beneath sleeping hikers. The transparent blue-green skylight brightened the sleeping quarters. Gone was the feeling of Siberian prisons. Everything had its place, down to two sharpened pencils secured in holes beside the register. On the back wall hung a sign soliciting members of the club and week-end walkers to relinquish space to thru-hikers. And last but not least, Leonard Reed and his building crew left a ten-inch thick hemlock growing in the middle of the patio and encircled by a huge cable drum that served as a table.

Our campsites had always been home to us because we made them so. We chose locations with care, listened to the wind, were aware of water sources, kept in mind the dawning sun. Rausch Gap Shelter showed us that walking the woods did not necessarily preclude prepared campsites that attracted rather than repelled.

Still, we could not stay at Rausch Gap. It was only noon. Instead, we loitered, drank from the trough, admired, and dreamed. Why weren't there two hundred other shelters like

Rausch Gap? The cost was only three hundred dollars. What of student architects in universities? Wouldn't their designs be welcome to serve as projects toward degrees and experience to incorporate knowledge into real situations?

Brainstorming for a better Trail, we hiked through the hot July sun before coming to a spring with a plastic orange juice glass propped on a stick. St. Anthony's Wilderness was indeed an enchanting forest. We felt like the wanderers lost in the woods who come to a castle where, with no occupants in sight, a banquet is ready for their pleasure.

As we drank a nightcap of wintergreen tea in our camp among beech trees set away from the Trail, a shape limped toward the spring. The sun had set and night poised above us, yet we could distinguish the silhouette as a monstrous Great Dane, a mangy, skinny, four-legged mechanism of skin and bone. It walked as if each step cost an effort to maintain balance. This sad picture of loneliness stopped at the pool and lapped water. The dog was old and nearly blind. It moved on slowly and painfully, a skeleton in the twilight. Then it was gone, an apparition.

We were startled from this ghostly vision by a volley of gunshots. "Hunters," we said. A second and third volley exploded, this time sounding like rockets overhead. We looked up. Clusters of red and white stars spiralled in wagonwheels of light above the trees in the distance. It was the Fourth of July.

1" = 12 Miles

New York

High Point State Park

◇Sawmill Lake

Worthington's Bakery ◇

◇Sunrise Mtn.

◇Brinks Road Lean-to

◇Rattlesnake Mtn.

Vernon

New Jersey

Pennsylvania

Delaware River

◇Kittatinny Mts

◇Sunfish Pond
◇Mt. Tammany

New Jersey

61 MILES

In frontier America, the crossing of a major river was a major event, a landmark of accomplishment as well as an entrance to new territory and adventures. So it was with us when on July 6 we crossed the Delaware River, though the steel and concrete bridge made the event less than arduous. Swamp grass on the islands in the river was pressed flat against the ground as though it had been brushed with hair cream, the result of a twenty-eight-foot flood that had hit the region days earlier. Although it was midsummer, with the air and sun growing hotter each day, the grass would take days before drying out and returning to its upright stand and resiliency.

110

Behind us we left Fred Waring and his Pennsylvanians rehearsing in their workshop in the small town of Delaware Water Gap, and entered the Gap itself, a dramatic ravine chiseled out by the Delaware River. In 1965 Congress authorized the Delaware Water Gap National Recreation Area, a long narrow preserve that will eventually include seventy thousand acres of the river boundary between Pennsylvania and New Jersey.

Crossing into our eighth state, we anticipated a smoke-belching, industrialized New Jersey. The logistics of routing the Trail through this tri-state metropolitan sprawl seemed impossible. Anyone who has driven the New Jersey Turnpike past the sulphurous haze of Newark and the chemical quagmires of Secaucus must be struck with the carelessness of man. New Jersey conjures images of exhaust fumes, noisome oil fields, and littered highways.

We were mistaken. As we walked up into the Kittatinny Mountains of upper New Jersey, we realized this was a different song, and not a protest tune at all.

We were accompanied by Ranger Roy Miller, courteous, knowledgeable, handsome, and strong, a Mark Trail of the real woods. Roy was making his rounds, 4½ miles to Sunfish Pond. "Sometimes I feel this territory is all mine," he said. "I want to keep it in shape. It's like people are walking and camping on my land. You know what I mean?" We did, for we had often felt the same way about the entire Appalachian Trail. It was *our* Trail, and we wanted the best for it.

"Now take that over there," Roy said, and pointed to a charcoal-stained site on the other side of a creek. "That's a restricted area. No one's supposed to camp there anymore because when they do they always leave it messier than when they first come. We'll be coming to Sunfish Pond up ahead. It's a glacial lake and we want to preserve its unique beauty. So we don't allow swimming or camping there."

"Too bad that's the only way to preserve it."

"We allowed camping one summer, and the pond turned into a disaster area," Roy said. "We stressed sanitation and proper waste disposal, but the place was a mess. Beer cans, mildewed sleeping bags, ripped-up tents. The pollution count was incredibly high and a serious health problem for people using the lake for drinking water."

"What about Trail hikers?" we asked, wondering where we'd sleep that night.

"Well, you know," Roy said with a grin. "We rangers give exception to most Trail hikers. Back in there"—he pointed to a faint path disappearing to the left—"is a restricted area, too, but one time I caught somebody there and started over to the tent to give the occupant some words and have him clear out. Well, the guy wasn't in, so I took a look around and knew that this was a person who would leave everything as he found it. He was even drying his tea bags on a string in front of the tent. That's how neat he was. So I let him stay."

Roy, an amateur wrestler when in his prime, taught physical education during the day and tended bar at night. He worked part time explaining nature to the public in the interpretive section of the Forest Service and intended to become a full-time ranger. His job, because of the popularity of the Kittatinny Mountains, and their accessibility to New Yorkers and Philadelphians, was full of incidents. "In fact," he said, "this area is becoming like Central Park."

On the Fourth of July Roy had helped rescue an eighteen-year-old boy from the Mt. Tammany overhang, a sheer-face mountain that juts skyward over Interstate Highway 80 through the Delaware Water Gap. The boy had climbed it twice before but this time had taken a different route. The rock crumbled beneath his grip. He was left on an extremely dangerous ledge he couldn't climb. Roy and other rangers spent three hours for the rescue, finally using ropes to haul the boy up the cliff.

"I was never so exhausted in my life," Roy said. "I love the outdoors, but this was the work of a professional rock climber." The timbre of his voice reflected the excitement of the rescue.

We hiked up the long grade and passed through stands of oak and maple trees clustered as if they survived only by sharing each other's plight. Their leaves, what few dangled from the branches, were shredded like doilies. This thinning of foliage was out of place. The mountains were below tree line, yet the sun tracked us through the sparsely clad treetops, ghostly in July. "Are the leaves dying because of air pollution?" we asked.

Roy shielded his eyes from the sun. "No, that's the gypsy moth," he said, reaching up seven feet of a nearby oak and scraping off a caterpillar.

We learned that in 1868 Leopold Trouvelot, a French scientist living in Massachusetts, planned to hybrid the American silk moth with the European gypsy moth. Such a hybrid caterpillar, which would eat any broadleaf, could generate a thriving silk industry. However, the hybridization turned out to be genetically impossible. After the gypsy moths were brought from France, the caterpillars escaped from Trouvelot's laboratory one stormy night, the beginning of headaches for the United States Forest Service.

Egg masses of the gypsy moth contain from 100 to 700 eggs. Air sacks on the hairs of the larvae make them airborne when small. They have been traced on wind voyages of twenty miles. When Francis Chichester named his famed sailboat that circumnavigated the world *Gipsy Moth*, he must have been aware of the similarity between the namesake and this mobile caterpillar.

The gypsy caterpillar can devour one square foot of leaf surface in a single day. The pupae are hitching south on truck campers and mobile homes. The Great Smoky Mountains National Park is dangerously threatened unless the moth can be checked. Some states inspect vehicles at state lines for this hitchhiking Hun, but such a program is mostly hit and miss. Citizens privately attempt to combat the pest by scraping the egg masses from trees and painting the trunks with creosote. Massachusetts, where the first gypsy moth escaped, loses about three hundred thousand trees each year to the defoliating pest.

Entomologists propose predatory insects such as the calosoma beetle to combat the gypsy moth. This beetle hatches as a voracious grub that eats the gypsy pupae. After its hunger is appeased, the grub crawls into the ground and sleeps for ten months, emerging as a beetle. Then his dinner is served up in the form of gypsy caterpillars. He will eat ten times his weight per diem. In his entire life of two years, the calosoma beetle will eat about 650 gypsy caterpillars. Another natural gypsy moth enemy is the tiny anastatus wasp. This wasp pierces each egg of the gypsy sack and lays its own eggs in the shell. The baby anastatus hatches and takes nourishment from the egg of the gypsy.

With the calosoma beetle and the anastatus wasp, two Japanese wasps have been introduced to fight the gypsy moth. One lays its eggs in the gypsy's egg sack and devours the young caterpillars as they hatch. Another lays its eggs in the body of the caterpillar. Up to one hundred of these eggs hatch and then destroy the caterpillar. Still another parasite is a docile fly that lays eggs in the pupae of the gypsy moth as the pupae hang in their silk-wrapped tent waiting to become moths. The fly eggs hatch and the larvae eat the gypsy pupae. Blackbirds, grackles, cuckoos, and other birds also are natural enemies of gypsy moths and caterpillars.

Though these stories of the predatory life might seem disconcerting, this is the balance nature provides, and these predators are the means of pest control preferred by the Agricultural Research Service, the Animal and Plant Inspection Service, and the Division of Forest Pest Control. Only in extreme cases are pesticides now resorted to, because DDT and Sevin also kill bees and other valuable insects.

Roy Miller told us that New Jersey had an extensive program for breeding gypsy moth parasites which were released in various experimental areas. At present seven parasites were gaining territory in the state.

The most recent hope in the containment of the gypsy moth is a synthesized sex attractant called Disparlure, from the moth's scientific name *Porthetria dispar*. This perfume is used both to attract male moths to traps and to disorient them so that they do not mate.

The moths themselves often contract a streptococcus disease that turns the chemical balance of their digestive tract from basic to acid and causes the caterpillar to hang upside down from its two back legs. Any female caterpillar coming into contact with the diseased body will produce sterile eggs when it later matures into a moth.

In New Jersey the gypsy moth caterpillars were everywhere. One hiker said that he couldn't lean against a tree without squashing one. Actually, they were quite colorful, two or three inches long, and gray with a double row of bright blue spots followed by bright red spots. From the spots protruded tufts of hair. Later on, we saw the large white female moths, sluggish and flightless with their cargo of eggs.

Despite man's research and persistence, it looked as if the gypsy was winning in New Jersey. Now the meaning of defoliation struck home. Lack of protective vegetation was disastrous for hikers. Long sections of the Trail steamed under the July sun. At times we jogged from scrawny tree to scrawny tree and crouched in the make-believe shade of defoliated scrub oaks. One time the exposure to the midday heat and light on a ridge top grew so intense that we had to stop to press our sweltering bodies together under the shade of a half-dead pine tree merely a barber pole wide. The Trail led us over the crests of a ravaged forest and, if we did not hear the anguish of a dying woodland, we certainly saw the deadly legacy of a moth that had robbed the land with impunity.

Despite the gypsy moth, we were delighted by the lush valley farmland and shimmering lakes below the New Jersey mountains. Up top, however, water was scarce and we had to reach it before sundown. Fortunately, New Jersey was a blueberry state and, being ourselves in a blueberry state for miles, we devoured juicy berries like fall-fattening bears. We ate blueberry à la granola, blueberry à la sandwich, blueberry à la hand. The only saving grace for soggy shredded wheat was the half-quart of blueberries we picked one morning before breakfast.

Shortly after the blueberry run, we walked a dirt road through what the guidebook described as the Lake Success housing development. Each house afforded a mountaintop view that home-owners would have fought for. The houses were two-story structures with carports and balconies, some in the last stages of completion. They were all empty. The owners had been bought out for the Delaware Water Gap Recreation Area. We cheered for the additional recreation land, and yet we sympathized with owners; the contractors, no doubt, emerged with the best deal. Signs of vandalism already appeared, as well as the work of the elements, upon these unfinished homes—another instance of more waste that could had been avoided by foresight.

The Lake Success fiasco faded as we later played a lugubrious comedy. The Trail blazes we had followed for miles on the road veered into the scrub and rocks. We climbed over boulders and along a shadeless ledge that revealed the same view as from the road. Then the blazes veered back and half a minute later we were on the road again. A hundred feet farther we rounded a bend and came upon another double blaze, meaning a change in direction. After playing the same charade over rocks and scrub, we reappeared on the road. It was midday, and the sun was at its summer zenith. We did not feel like games. The third set of double blazes we by-passed and stayed on the road. As suspected, the Trail looped back to the road within a few hundred feet. We couldn't laugh at someone's snide prank. It was too hot.

That afternoon we hiked into a shallow valley as gypsy-mothed as the hilltops. A creek lazed through the crevice of this valley, and there we found a few minutes' relief. Our shirts were sopping with sweat. Our wool socks steamed. In thirty seconds we were Brahmins bathing in the Ganges. We sloshed our T-shirts and scrubbed the armpits on a rock, rinsed our bandanas and poured handfuls of water over the baked potatoes of our heads. This runlet was priceless. We enjoyed the water while we could, for in ten minutes the fire would return.

Julia, sitting on a rock by the muddy bank, reached for her boots, but slowly withdrew her hand. A mottled snake stared at her an arm's length away. We eyed the snake as carefully as he eyed us and eliminated copperhead, rattler, cotton-mouth, and coral snake. It was a common garter snake. We retrieved the boots before the snake uncoiled and wound through the blades of grass at the river edge. This encounter warned us to pull ourselves from the drowsiness generated by the heat and maintain our alertness even though the sun and the gypsy moth had diffused our focus of attention.

The climb from the creek led over Rattlesnake Mountain (1,492 feet). Hawk Mountain, Pennsylvania, is called Hawk Mountain for a reason. We gathered that Rattlesnake Moun-tain was no different. Our ascent became a meticulous investi-gation of nearly each rock and handhold.

The landscape that afternoon was surreal. The trees resem-bled those hangers-on that occupy swamps: bleached, pol-ished trunks with stark, honed branches. The mountains were low but their soil was abrasive, almost volcanic. Walking these mountains was like stepping barefoot on used Brillo pads. The comfort of birdsong was absent because of the defoliation and intense heat.

We had one goal that goaded us on—Worthington's Bakery on Highway 206. There, we had learned from other hikers, all wonders of energy-packed goodies awaited the faithful. Visions of blueberry pies, chocolate éclairs, fruit strudels, crusty breads, quivered about our sun-crazed skulls.

At Brinks Road Lean-to we stopped for a drink and respite in the shade of oak trees that had been spared the gypsy moth. The lean-to, though built in 1970, was in the same condition as the older ones: dark, dingy, and messy. Like most, it was built with road access, and thereby invited local Saturday night beer parties. The outhouse was situated uphill from the spring, much too close for drainage and sanitary purposes. A sign warned hikers they were allowed One Nite Only. Would anyone want more?

Worthington's was a combination grocery store and bakery. Five eating hikers, entertaining patrons who entered the store, sat in the shade of the building. They were cross-legged and each was eating his own nine-inch pie smothered with molehills of vanilla ice cream shared from two half-gallon cartons. We joined them with the last cherry pie in the shop and our own quart of vanilla. Whole pie à la mode.

Although afflicted by the same hardships and weather conditions as we were, the other hikers for the most part looked grimier and more tired than we did. We attributed this to their general diet and the loads they carried. One hiker told us he carried an average forty pounds. The others hauled fifty pounds. Many of them stowed cans in their packs, which added dead weight. Several guzzled carbonated drinks, which never really quenched thirst and were short-lived energy-boosters besides. None bought fresh fruit.

As whenever long-distance walkers congregated, discussion

of the Trail and what the Appalachian Trail Conference could do to improve it flowered with invective and hyperbole. One hiker was just as outraged as we were with the erratic blazes all of us had just passed through, as well as with the messy Brinks Road Shelter, and the many mindless locations of the Trail in general.

"Jump-up was fun in Stekoah back in North Carolina," he said. "I liked the challenge, but you'd think that a day of climbing sheer peaks would prove the point. Hell, we aren't rock climbers."

We agreed wholeheartedly. His agitation was contagious.

"I think every official in the Conference should have to hike the whole Trail end to end," he said. "Then they'd know what changes should be made."

"Right," we said, "there isn't enough constructive organization."

"Yeah," he continued, "and they call walking on asphalt for miles on end the Appalachian Trail. That's no trail. That's a highway, and who wants to hike on a highway?"

"Right. Every part of the Trail should be as well maintained as Shenandoah."

He set out for the next lean-to, himself reaching the point where he depended on shelters only for a water source. We found a campsite a short distance from the bakery. At a roadside picnic area the next morning, we wondered why the majority of facilities used by the general public always deteriorated into miniature dump yards. Garbage overflowed literally two times the capacity of the single trash barrel beside our breakfast table. Beer cans, soda bottles, plastic bags, toilet paper, used napkins, orange peels, and other junk were strewn about like the remains of a protest march. Local cars were using the drive-off as a parking lot next to a black, stagnant, foul swamp. Later, we wrote a postcard complaining about the site to the local office of the Stokes State Forest near where the area was located. We received an answer stating that the picnic site had been a source of many complaints, but that the area was owned, maintained, and operated by the New Jersey Department of Transportation, which evidently didn't care about the situation.

Had we reached Sunrise Mountain at sunrise the entire day might have been easier. As it was, the sweat of our brows, the rockiness of the Trail, the lack of ample fresh water in the oppressive heat doubled the burden of our packs. The sunlight fell on our backs like shovelfuls of hot sand.

Our destination was High Point State Park, a mere 13½ miles away. We felt as if we were walking up a down escalator. What water we did cross was murky and so uninviting that we rationed our canteen until the next good source. All the lakes were in the valleys below, bright blue mirages.

The Trail wound over the tops of one false summit after another. Even our snacks failed to cheer us. Toward the end of the day we were covering only a mile to the hour. The unrelenting heat, the exposure from the leafless oaks, the slow hiking over loose, slab rocks dragged our bodies and spirits to a brown-out of enthusiasm.

We passed a few other hikers. One couple, experimenting with the outdoors, probably would turn thumbs down on this and all succeeding attempts in the woods. The overweight girl's overweight pack leaned at a forty-five-degree angle from her spine, increasing the impact of the weight on her drooping shoulders. Several carefree day-hikers passed, bouncy, full-breasted girls and gangly teenage boys out on a picnic. If only we had been picnicking.

At last we reached a rocky crest that overlooked Lake Rutherford. An exhausting mile later, we reached another crest overlooking Sawmill Lake. Then another sweltering mile more and we passed the American Telephone and Telegraph Company microwave installation and dragged down the mountainside to the gate house of High Point State Park. By the time we could see High Point Monument, the 220-foot lookout on the highest New Jersey mountaintop (1,803 feet), we were too weary to care. Julia completely missed it, like missing the World Trade Center on the New York City skyline.

We sank into the red leather cushion seats inside the beam ceiling gate house, thankful to be out of the sapping sunlight. By a stroke of fortune, we applied for the last campsite. The next man in line was turned away and had to drive to another park.

"You look pretty tired," Ranger Rick Strain said. "You ought to be. It was ninety-five degrees in the shade down here. Probably hotter up there on the Trail. I'm off work in about fifteen minutes. Like a ride up to the campsite? It's about two miles."

As we were waiting for him, we read this newspaper clipping posted to the gate house bulletin board.

Camping in High Rise

Campsites, Incorporated, has announced plans to construct a twenty story campground in downtown New Orleans and is seeking financing for the project. "This will be unique," said Wesley Hurley of Hi-Rise. "It is designed for today's different brand of camping. People don't want the woodsy bit now; they want to camp in comfort near the city."

Plans for the four million dollar project call for eight lower floors of parking and twelve upper stories with 240 individual sites equipped with utility hook-ups for campers and carpeted with artificial turf. The campground will include a rooftop pool.

Ranger Rick, as they called him, drove us to one of the attractive sites adjacent Sawmill Lake. These campsites were a far cry from the high-rise concept of outdoor living. All sites were hidden in the trees far enough away from the lake to preserve a serene unpeopled shore. Water was available at easy walking distance. A clean beach awaited us. Our particular spot was a ground tent site with a small, clear stream that flowed under a plank-wood footbridge. Before leaving, Ranger Rick warned us that High Point had several bear families with young rapscallion cubs.

Our pre-dinner swim awakened our souls, the warm water embracing our tired bodies and spirits. A little boy stood up and rubbed his small fist into his eyes. "Hey, wait a minute, you guys," he called to his companions, "I got salt in my eyes."

In the morning Ranger Rick drove by in his pickup and took us on a tour of the High Point Lodge and the Monument. The restaurant of the Lodge now served as an entomological station for studies of the gypsy moth. The primary attraction, however, was a mascot black bear, affectionately called Mischa.

"Mischa became the mother of two cubs," he told us. "She tried to commit infanticide and the cubs were separated. Then one day the father became unnerved and attacked a small girl trying to feed them. The girl lost an arm and the bear was destroyed. Finally, the mother bear displayed such a hatred for one of the cubs that a decree went forth that the cub should also be shot."

Ranger Rick gave us a smile and a wink. "The night before the firing squad both cubs somehow got loose," he said. "Just don't know how that could have happened."

The Trail crossed the New York state line into Unionville, and then returned to New Jersey, a section entailing about eight miles of asphalt walking. Truckin' mile after mile in sparse shade during a summer heat wave was bad enough. Hiking the full glare of the sun along paved road was masochistic.

> *Too hot,*
> *even too hot for God, Jesus and Mary.*

Too hot in the Methodist Church.
Too hot in the public library.
Parking lot's bare.
Too hot in a car.
Too hot to cross the street without shoes.
Too hot to read the Vernon News.
Shades drawn
since dawn.

So touch me not, brother.
It's too damned hot.

We took asylum from the heat in the Vernon Public Library just off the Trail. Our propensity for libraries was boosted by the treatment we were given that day. For three hours we stayed inside. The librarian sent out an assistant who returned with ice-cold soda. Though we usually didn't imbibe soft drinks while hiking, in this heat we had no intention of exerting any of our 603 muscles. We would walk at twilight after the library closed. The soda was followed by glasses of ice water and then an offer to use the bathroom to freshen up. In this haven of kindness, we waited out the sun and wondered if Jesus, while walking the hills of Galilee, took salt tablets and postponed parables until dark.

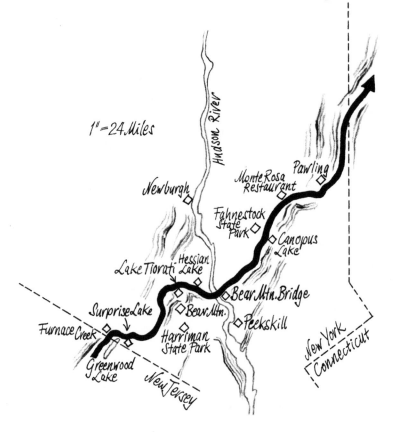

1"=24 Miles

Hudson River

Pawling

Newburgh

Monte Rosa Restaurant

Fahnestock State Park

Canopus Lake

Lake Tiorati   Hessian Lake

Bear Mtn. Bridge

Surprise Lake   Bear Mtn.

Peekskill

Furnace Creek

New York / Connecticut

Harriman State Park

Greenwood Lake   New Jersey

New York

97 MILES

We entered New York on a dump truck. It was 7:30 that hot, smudgy morning, July 10. The Trail blazes were nowhere in sight and so, searching and cursing, we continued on a gravel road nearly half a mile, the time wasted looking for blazes more than an irritation. We were losing ground to the heat of the day that would inevitably leaden our pace by ten o'clock.

A huge yellow dump truck driven by a smiling, toothless, plump captain of a road maintenance crew, pulled up. "Are you looking for the Appalachian Trail?"

"We've been looking for twenty minutes," we answered, trying to curb our impatience.

"Throw your packs in the back and I'll drive you to it," he said leaning out the window. "It's only a short way back."

He pulled a lever and the mammoth load-bed of the truck strained upward with a whine as if this mechanical dinosaur was about to receive eighteen tons of solid boulder. We dumped our twenty-five-pound packs into the yawning loader, climbed into the high cab of the truck, and the driver cranked down the light cargo.

"Hikers lose their way here," he said, thoroughly enjoying his incongruous role. "I guess they don't keep the Trail cleared very well. The blazes are nearly grown in."

A minute later we climbed down from the cab while the captain raised the loader. The bed angled down so we could reach our packs.

New York awaited us with an array of extreme experiences. It was the first state so far in which we had crossed a slurried creek. Water. H_2O. We depended on it and were beginning to realize that there were not merely two kinds of water—salt and fresh. Some was sweet, some bitter. One spring's water would have enough minerals that you could chew it, another's would be light and clear. The brands of water were as plentiful as brands of cigarettes—a faulty analogy, given the healthful properties of water.

At Furnace Creek the water was smirched a deep root beer color and frothed and foamed at the rock traps and small dams of branches and dead wood. We met only one hiker that day in the mountains over Greenwood Lake. He knew the area, and told us the water was brown because of its humic acid and mineral content. Nonetheless, to assuage our fears, he offered us some fresh water he had with him.

Stream after stream consisted of this unappetizing froth and dark water. In Maine, we had been told, the water was naturally yellow-brown as a result of the swamps and bogs. Pond and lake waters are often green or yellow because of abundant floating algae whose pigments reflect these and other colors of the spectrum. The only harmful effect of this coloration in Maine is that it makes it impossible for sunlight to penetrate the water deep enough for the production of underwater plant and animal life.

In New York, however, we couldn't take chances. At times we were no farther than fifty miles from the largest city in the country. We knew that in low concentration detergents produce foam. In isolated cases we had heard that this foam may rise to heights of several feet. Some detergent clouds have been identified as vehicles from other planets.

Fortunately, the water problem was alleviated by the number of towns on the Trail in New York. We hiked a long boulder ridge above Surprise and Greenwood lakes. The yielding vistas with geometrically lined mountain ranges steamed in the background and looked as we felt—hot, top-heavy, and humbled by the oppressing sun.

We held the words "Greenwood Lake Village" in front of us as if they were carrots and we the mules. The name sounded so restful and comforting. Surely an oasis in this stuffy woodland desert awaited us so that we could cool ourselves "Under the Greenwood Tree."

The side trail to Greenwood Lake Village led three-quarters of a mile down the mountain. Traffic blare and shouts from summer crowds filtered through the trees. As we descended, the noise grew louder. We passed discarded beer cans and counted five abandoned frying pans that campers had left along the way.

The beat poet Ferlinghetti once wrote a poem called "New York Is a Summer Festival." As we walked down into the town of Greenwood Lake, we rode the very axis of the festivity. Manhattan had moved to Greenwood Lake and brought with it delicatessens, Midtown accents, the Mafia in shirt sleeves and bathing trunks, mamas in sunglasses, pale, bookish newlyweds, baby strollers, rude, pushy shoppers from Macy's, and still ruder sales clerks—it was the garment district, complete with soot and car horns.

Greenwood Lake Village was a back-alley Gatlinburg, Tennessee. The invasion of the billboards, flashing business signs, posters and price signs—the general visual pollution— attacked our eyes without letup. The jumbled advertising current charged both sides of the village street. The shock of this anarchy heightened our disappointment. All we wanted was to escape the commercial war as soon as possible. We wondered how the smothering atmosphere of this tourist town could in any way refresh the spirits of those who came to visit it. Indeed, what must be the home living conditions of the vacationers when they traveled to this hell to get away from it all?

Somehow an exception always blooms in the midst of frenzy. We met one man who ran a small market where we dashed for a grapefruit, a quart of milk, and a hard roll lunch. The man invited us to sit on a bench he provided in front of his store and to tell him about our hike. "You hikers that come through here," he said, "really are something. I try to talk to all of you."

Every now and then he hurried inside to wait on a customer before hurrying back to our story. We were his ticket to adventure, the one he probably never cashed.

"One time a hiker came into the store," he said, "and I was keeping an eye on him. He looked in bad shape. In fact, I saw him weave back and forth like he was going to faint. I guess he wasn't eating very good food. Anyway, I took him back home and fed him for three days and wouldn't let him hike until he promised to eat a proper diet."

"It's either that, or you fall over your feet," we said.

"Well, if you two want to rest here awhile, you're welcome to camp right behind my house." He gave us his address but all we could think of was our exodus.

During the days to come, we became increasingly homesick. As we plowed through the heat, crossing the interstate highways, hearing the inescapable mew of traffic, shuffling through the people in towns, our thoughts bound us to good ol' New England. We had heard that the central states of the Trail would tax our stamina. What we heard was correct. We also reasoned that the contrast would be pronounced once we did step from New York into the more wooded states of Connecticut, Massachusetts, Vermont, New Hampshire, and Maine. Reaching New England had evolved from a goal, to a need, to a longing.

Nevertheless, we did enjoy sections of the Harriman State Park in New York. One night the fireflies gave us a royal fireworks display before we went to bed. We hadn't seen them in the higher elevations. Lightning bugs aren't climbers. Scientists still don't know the purpose of their illumination, although they believe it has to do with the mating of the sexes. That night the twinkling in the glade offered us Christmas in July.

In the morning the mist drifted up from the lakes and curtained parts of the landscape. Despite the proximity of a highway, a family of deer—doe, fawn and buck—nibbled the dewy morning grass along the fence. The mist hid us, but even when we walked toward them for a closer view, they didn't start.

The Trail through Harriman State Park was worn, but few people were in sight. Perhaps they had anticipated the dump of rain that day and waited inside their campers until it was dry. If they did, they missed rushing to a giant mountain hemlock and huddling under its umbrella of needles. On the downhill side of the tree, we stayed out the shower and remained completely dry.

We sat and listened to the rain and watched the watering of the world from ringside seats. The shower was warm, and it soon stopped as suddenly as it had started. We waited a couple more minutes until the edge of our hemlock umbrella drip-dried, and then stood, adjusted our packs, strapped our hip belts, and continued on downhill.

We walked over gentle bald rocks the size of Paleozoic turtles. By noon we were sunbathing at Lake Tiorati, not more than an hour's drive from New York City. As we lazed on the beach at the far end of the lake, we wondered why so few people shared our sun worship. The surrounding wooded areas, thick with pines and darker still with the recent rain, held secrets alien to the casual vacationer.

In New York the hardwood leaf cover was still intact, as opposed to New Jersey's moth-eaten canopy. The exception to our easy climbing days was Bear Mountain (1,314 feet), which was not high but was composed of sandstone and shale that slid underfoot and broke off in chunks when we tried to hold onto it. On the south side, this stampeding rock was the only climbing surface. Lug soles were miraculous, but not on crumbly mountain faces. In the tumbling loose shale that plummeted through the air on a fast downward journey, we envisioned our own bodies rolling, crashing, and settling at the bottom.

The zigzag route up the cliff got us to the summit without a mishap. We removed our packs and sat on a rock slope that fell toward the valley. The morning sharp greens, blues, silvers, and browns spread outward, a crystalline reward for the harrying climb. The air was crisp and invigorating.

Although we were proximate to nearly eight million people, we had not met many hikers. One we did meet introduced himself as Warren Doyle. He was a thru-hiker, and so we were expecting a long conversation, but he kept checking his watch as though he had an important appointment on Madison Avenue. Finally, he explained his preoccupation with time.

"I'm trying to set a record," he said. "The current one for hiking the whole Trail is seventy days, but I'm trying to make it in sixty-eight. This is my forty-fourth day."

"You're going exactly twice as fast as we are. This is our eighty-eighth."

"I've got some help," Warren said. "My father meets me at the crossroads so I can get food and sleep right away. I'm walking every step, even road walking."

"You on schedule?"

"I'm a little behind. I have to make thirty miles a day, but today it's thirty-five. Sometimes I get up at two or three in the morning."

Within three minutes he was off again, leaving us sprawled in our Valhalla beneath a flowering shadbush. We thought of him after that as the rabbit in *Alice in Wonderland:* "I'm late, I'm late for a very important date. No time to say hello–goodbye, I'm late, I'm late, I'm late, I'm late."

The danger of Warren's adventure to us seemed a risk of life and limb. In broad daylight (or daylighted fog) the Trail presented nerve-wracking situations. At night? Personally, we didn't go for it, but understood the challenge. The frontiers are gone for people like Warren Doyle. To tackle the land and elements with speed is a modern American concept. We preferred to set up a campground and explore the radius of our tent site. On occasional luxurious three-day vacations, we still observed different plants and animals. One afternoon we chose an arbitrary patch of vegetation, and in this space no larger than a throw-rug, we counted twenty-eight different plants and flowers.

It turned out that Warren beat the goal by four days. Many hikers quashed jealous reactions toward his endeavor. The Appalachian Trail Conference protested in these terms: "We do not recognize stunts!" One man, the Conference informed us, took twenty years of vacation time to complete the Trail. A family from Ohio drove 91,000 miles over 185 weekends and one two-week vacation, to walk the Trail in four years.

The youngest was nine years old when she finished. These are records, too, and just as risky for a nine-year-old girl as Warren Doyle's marathon.

To us the Trail was. Time is relative. How long you took to walk it was your own business.

We met several other loners on the Trail. One of them was an older man, tanned and trim, carrying a Shell Scott paperback mystery. We passed each other frequently, each time exchanging a few words about hiking. The last time, the hiker was picking and eating high bush blueberries. We discovered the reason he took solace in the woods. He had recently lost his wife and hiking companion to cancer. Now every Sunday afternoon he walked the Appalachian Trail through Harriman State Park. The woods gave him comfort, a time to be with himself and his memories. He was not a happy man, but the Trail helped him not to be a defeated one.

A few miles later we passed a young long-haired singleton under a red tarp tied to two small pines. He said he was out for a couple of days and had set up early (it was only four) in case the threat of rain turned real. His camp was situated on a ledge overlooking the Hudson River and the surrounding mountains to the east. This young man would be eyewitness to a glorious full moon as it rose over the mountaintops just as the sun dropped away for the night. He would become more of himself when the morning blazed forth after a quiet night of alertness and wonder.

As we descended the far side of Bear Mountain, we heard a swish of wings and saw a flash of black through the trees. Then another. At first we paid little attention to the three crows sailing through the dense woods. Then we noticed their bright red crests. We had been on the lookout for pileated woodpeckers ever since we spotted the first one in Pennsylvania. Ornithologists admit it is rare to see one of these cackling, red-crested birds whose beaks serve as automatic drills.

We stopped and stared at the three musketeers, who were

now vying for positions around a tree trunk. The woodpeckers flew down the mountain and disappeared as suddenly and magically as they had appeared. Their wing span reaches thirty inches. From a distance their white shafts of feathers and red heads differentiate pileated woodpeckers from common crows. At the other end of the family totem pole are the downy woodpeckers, not much bigger than a sparrow.

To know that pileated woodpeckers inhabited the mountains above the interstate highways and grounds of the Bear Mountain Inn relieved some of the despair we felt about the encroachment of cityscapes and escapees. In fact, we marveled at the solitude of the Bear Mountain Inn that morning. Scarcely a soul was visible. The pond was unrippled, the raked paths empty.

The Bear Mountain Inn was a mansion-sized lodge of wood and stone with expansive views of the mountains. We lounged in the bucket chairs and the hewn-log furniture upholstered in red vinyl. King Arthur would have found the mammoth stone fireplace and andirons to his liking.

Perhaps a feeling of repose was compatible with the proximity of a giant metropolis. We left the Inn lest our reverie be shattered by the arrival of a buzzing tourist bus. The complex of grounds at the Inn included Hessian Lake with paddleboats, a spring-fed Olympic swimming pool, and across the highway, a trailside zoo and nature museum. This museum was the site of Fort Clinton, captured by the British during the American Revolution.

We stood before a statue of Walt Whitman and read the inscription:

Afoot and light-hearted I take to the open road,
Healthy, free, the world before me,
The long brown path before me leading wherever I choose.

Henceforth I ask not good-fortune, I myself am good-fortune.

Henceforth I whimper no more, postpone no more, need nothing,

Done with indoor complaints, libraries, querulous criticisms,

Strong and content I travel the open road.

This was our song, too, and we felt the impact of its truth as we walked toward the Hudson River and the Bear Mountain Bridge.

Once again a major river, this time the Hudson, marked a major passage in our long journey. This was our closest point to New York City, thirty miles away. Here the Appalachian Trail turned away from the crazy-quilt nerve center and steered us directly to New England where the woods and mountains predominated. We were prepared to pay the twenty-cent bridge toll. For some reason, the fact that hikers were required to pay a toll only added to the mystique of crossing the Hudson.

It was a fine, clothes-whipping, sunshiny day, and we imagined the New York skyline. That is, we craned so far over the silver grilled platform of the bridge that we were sure we spotted the George Washington Bridge, thirty miles downstream. Low with their cargoes, barges moved slowly below us. Painters were giving the bridge a new coat, and their faces and arms were splattered with silver. Their solitary scaffoldings swayed with the gusts of wind. Some jimmied up the tension cables. We dreamed of taking a riverboat up the Hudson and on to the Great Lakes, an American Rhine journey. It is no wonder that landscape artists continue to paint the palisades along the Hudson. Even today there is a feeling of serenity and peaceful living among these high river cliffs.

In New Jersey the sun and lack of water were advantageous in one respect: they made for absence of mosquitoes. We learned that if you could sit in the sun long enough, you would be rid of the noxious aircraft. New York was wooded, dark and deep, not to mention damp. Mosquitoes proliferated. We swished them away with twigs. They froze in formation an inch or two out of range. We smashed them dead and they seemed to resurrect in greater numbers.

Mosquitoes are apt to turn hikers into buffoons. We met John, another thru-hiker, on the Trail one morning. He wore shorts and a light T-shirt. Every second of our conversation John was slapping one thigh, then the other, then his neck, then his forearm, his thigh again, then his forehead, the other forearm. He never stood still. He was the most animated hiker we had seen. The man was a mechanical wonder, Don Quixote fighting a windmill.

"I almost skipped this part of the Trail," he said. "These mosquitoes are driving me crazy. Almost skipped to Vermont, up to the high mountains where they don't bite you to death."

He was swishing them with a red bandana when he wasn't slapping them with his hands. We showed him the Witch Hazel Technique, which was easier and more effective than the Red Bandana Technique.

"Hey, I never thought of that," he said, and rushed to snap off a nearby branch.

We had just about had it one day with mosquitoes, so we stopped in a meadow under the glaring sun. A few butterflies flittered through the grass. Just over the hill we could see the top of a stone silo and the mansard roof of an old farmhouse. The silence was broken by a farmer coming toward us in a jeep, bouncing up and down as the tires hit the meadow ruts.

"You seen any cows come this way? Put 'em to pasture, but they're likely to wander."

We said that we'd stepped over some hints on the Trail.

"Hiking the Trail, eh?"

We nodded noncommittally. Somehow the pasture scene

was too peaceful to clutter with speech. The farmer drove off, and we shook our bones back into a facsimile of an upright position.

Selecting a campsite was more difficult in New York. Property owners were conscientious sign-posters. Everywhere we went along the Trail were No Trespassing signs. We were beginning to have that feeling we weren't wanted. The freedom of our walk in the South had taken a turn toward civilization. Part of the way through Harriman State Park, we had to avoid entanglement in utility guy wires, sometimes at eye level (but not necessarily visible in the thick brush), and often in a snaky mess at our feet. The No Trespassing signs were interspersed with No Hunting or Fishing, Keep Out, Beware of Dog, and other advertisements.

At Fahnestock State Park Campground we picked a site as far from the madding crowd as possible. The park was ill planned with no cleared sites, simply large parking lots for whatever equipment you happened to have. What most people happened to have were mobile homes, tent trailers, transistor radios, portable televisions, portable stoves, motorcycles, speedboats, and boisterous kids. The smell of sizzling steaks nauseated our dehydrated food–oriented stomachs. People trod past our tent set up on a knoll overlooking the lake in which swimming was prohibited. As Julia played her flute, screaming children shouted, "Shut up, or I'll blow your brains out!"

In the morning a thick condensation clung to the vegetation as if it had rained. As we climbed above Canopus Lake, the undergrowth became so thick we had to use our arms as scythes to sweep the weeds away from our perspiring faces. We could see virtually nothing but high trees and sumac bushes, and, underfoot, a slight hint of trampled grass. Fahnestock State Park had accepted the Appalachian Trail, but that was the end of the commitment. Maintenance? Sure, all those hikers would keep the Trail cleared.

By midmorning we could wring out all of our clothes, and it wasn't even raining. Monte Rosa Inn was right off the Trail, and Mama Rosa, in black rustling taffeta, greeted us. She was a plump cheerful Italian from Venice. We sat at a marble coffee table on the terrazzo porch while she scrambled some eggs for us. She was expecting a large dinner crowd, and smells of garlic, basil, and oregano drifted from the kitchen. Her sister-in-law tore home-grown lettuce into a giant colander. Our table was too small for the breakfast Mama Rosa prepared, a platter of half a dozen eggs, eight pieces of toast, an entire pot of steaming coffee, a jar of strawberry jam, and a plate of butter. If she didn't know, she guessed—all hikers had Italian appetites.

We left Monte Rosa, walked down Knapp Road, crossed the Taconic Parkway, continued along back-country roads with tree-shrouded houses, walked down Mountaintop Road, crossed the Interstate 84 bridge, and continued through wooded residential areas. Roadwalking again. No Trespassing signs and fences nagged at us. Tired, and ready to pitch camp for the night, we rested under a maple. Equestrians are very much aware that asphalt and concrete are taboo for horses' hoofs. We were finding that the same applied to human feet.

The fifteen hours that followed—our last night in New York—seemed like a comedy. In fairy tales the knight rides up on a white steed to rescue the maiden. In this case, we were both rescued by a teenager riding bareback on the one-horse-town horse. "Hi," she said. "You hiking the Appalachian Trail?" We answered this mounted upstate Annie Oakley, and asked if there was a campground nearby. "Sure," she said, her eyes lighting up. She backed the fidgety horse to get a better look at us. "You can camp right behind our house. My mother won't mind. Last year we invited twenty Boy Scouts to camp there. On my honor." She placed her hand over her heart. "Just follow me, I'm Bonnie."

Bonnie's mother was talking to the landlord. The septic tank had just overflowed, not a propitious time to ask anyone a favor. But Bonnie, fourteen, and her eleven-year-old sister Carol, had latched onto us as if we were their best and only friends. Their mother told us Bonnie brought home everyone and everything. This was especially evident from the number of cats and dogs in the backyard.

"You're welcome to set up your tent and use the water in here," she offered. The harried woman stifled a miniature riot between the sisters as we made our way through the tall grass at the back of the house. Naturally, Bonnie on her horse, Carol, and the dogs followed. Later the horse, Ladybug, skitted, pawed the earth, and plopped a pile of fresh manure right on the tent site. Unabashed, Bonnie decided to play the Lone Ranger, performing "Hi-Hos" over our sleeping quarters. Anxiously, we watched as the horse reared and landed inches from our tent.

The next event in this rodeo was a race between Carol and Bonnie. (Carol was at a slight disadvantage, being on foot.) From in front of the house we heard screams and threats. We imagined the worst, the stampeding of Carol's small body, Ladybug at a standstill, her head lowered, sniffing the corpse. But youth is strong. Carol returned, dry-eyed and exuberant, just as we were blowing up our Girl Scout pillows. Calmly she reported, "Ladybug knocked me down." Then as if this crisis were a week old, in an adult voice she said, "Boy, you guys sure know how to live."

After we finished dinner, Bonnie returned with two cups of tea. She confided to us, "I was going to commit suicide last month by drinking Clorox. My mother grounded me and I couldn't go out with Tom. He's my boyfriend." Her petulance was that of a typical rebellious teenager desiring freedom.

"She told Mom a lie," Carol said.

"Well, you would, too," Bonnie answered angrily. We

sympathized with her and at the same time tried to make her see the wisdom in her mother's discipline.

That night we gave ourselves to these children's fantasies. Bonnie scrawled letters on our backs, which we had to guess, and Carol made us play the Helen Keller game of guessing objects with our eyes closed. They tried to pressure us into watching television, but we insisted we needed our sleep. We expected them back. Fortunately, you can't short-sheet a sleeping bag. As suspected, Bonnie climbed a tree to spy on us and then couldn't get down.

We both took a long time to fall asleep. The dogs sniffed around the tent and the resounding three hours of chatter we had had with the girls filled our heads with nervous excitement. Carol promised us she'd be up before we left at six o'clock. She was a little imp, quick and bright. Sure enough, the next morning as we were brushing our teeth she appeared, drowsy and barefoot, draped in an orange cotton bedspread. We placed a poncho on the wet ground and offered her some coffee. Already she was wide awake.

She asked our ages and then commented, "Wow, I didn't think anybody over thirty years old could hike." Then as we were eating, in an admirable British accent she said, "I always do exciting things like this."

We all tromped out the driveway together. With exuberant youngness that was innocent and charming, Carol affectionately hugged us both. "I hate farewells," she said.

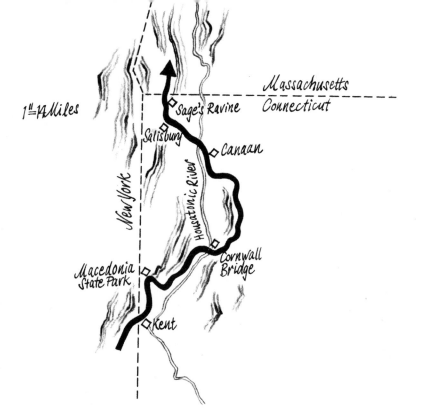

Connecticut

56 MILES

To connect means to join, and so Connecticut linked the Central and New England States. This linchpin of the Eastern Seaboard re-introduced us to the plentiful paper birch, the white courier of the northeast that stands in such starched elegance. Aspen and white pines, along with the other hardwoods and hemlocks, transformed the light of summer into a new spring. Shadows cast were loose, spottled, and light, a touch of Monet.

139

The change in territory was subtle. The change in the towns was more noticeable. A short distance into Connecticut the Trail passed close to Kent, where we bought fresh peaches. Kent was New England, all right. Its tree-shaded streets, its low-storied white houses, its picket fences and country flavor were combined with the established and the monied. The cleanliness of the town, its casual, almost studied charm, marked Kent as Yankee, as did a squad of teenagers strutting to soccer practice on the clipped fields of private schools.

The easy walking in Connecticut is recommended to acquaint hikers with both the Trail and New England. Macedonia Brook State Park could provide an ideal base camp. Arriving at the Park on July 16, we found good sweet spring water, the kind of tongue-tinkling nectar we remembered from the South. The park contains 2,294 acres and, though the mountains' peaks are only around fourteen hundred feet high, they command a view of both the Catskills and Taconics. (During the Revolutionary War, one hundred volunteer Scatacook Indians devised a signal system along these peaks that could transmit a message from Long Island Sound to Stockbridge, Massachusetts, about a hundred miles away, in two hours.)

We camped in a hidden tenting area off the main gravel road that traversed the park. Green, yellow, orange, red blazes marked a system of trails that explored every corner of the park. The white blazes of the Appalachian Trail circumscribed the park's periphery.

The following morning we walked through elegant woods on a well-maintained connecting trail that did away with the memory of the many No Trespassing signs a few days before. Even the birds matched our revived humor.

We descended a steep staircase route a quarter-mile to the broad Housatonic River. The Trail followed a dirt road that paralleled this 111-mile-long river, its source at Pittsfield, Massachusetts, its mouth at Long Island Sound. The walk along the riverbank was as flat as the Potomac towpath, but considerably less offensive to the nose.

For five miles we walked a leisurely morning beside the young sound of old water. The Trail took us through pine farms as well as uncultured stands of hardwoods. At noon we parked under a company of hemlocks edging the river to eat ham and swiss cheese on rye, almonds, gumdrops and jelly beans. We practiced Bach's Fourth Brandenburg Concerto for flute and recorder, watched two boys downriver fish like Mark Twain characters, and spotted a gaggle of geese resting on sandbars.

More leisurely walking along the Housatonic filled the afternoon, including a detour through a cornfield as high as an elephant's eye. The hot sun that fell on the heads of corn also fell on ours. A few yards away from the arch of trees we concluded that corn fields, though hardy and proud, were not a hiker's paradise. The return to shade cooled us immediately and, although the zenith of the day took its toll in perspiration and gulps of water, we still relished the walk through such friendly woods. And yet, the Trail was taking us farther away from the Housatonic we had enjoyed earlier in the day. In committee we outvoted the Trail and descended the mountainside to the Housatonic Meadows Campground near Cornwall Bridge on U.S. Highway 7.

Walking indeed has its advantages, since few people pay attention to hikers, while cars mean tolls, gate fees, registrations, parking spaces. On foot we avoided these demands and selected the choice spots in parks and campgrounds. We cooked our dinner on a flat table rock beside the river. In the cooling twilight, at five feet elevation above the water, an arrowhead of geese shot past us as if these masters of flight formation were speeding to the Canadian north before moonrise. The geese were probably the same we had spotted on a sandbar resting out the noonday sun miles back. They followed the river as strictly as if they were reading a map, and disappeared in a dazzling veer to the left around the river-bend. The sighting was one of those quick everlasting surprises that cannot be forgotten, a reminder of ancient instincts.

By the following morning the water level of the river had dropped one foot. The changed scene jarred our sleepy eyes. We performed our ablutions from the table rock and watched the sunrise through the mist. The birds were up, and so were two fly fishermen in rubber hipboots standing in midstream. For ten minutes we admired the delicate S's of their lines over the water. The artful way in which these fly-casting fishermen brought back their arms once, twice, and then into the final stroke forward, was as natural as hiking had grown to us. With the backdrop of the river and the curve of muted trees along the banks, the sight of these graceful movements across the vaporing stream entranced us. One of the men snagged a fish and reeled it in, the glint of its tail flipping and bobbing through the current. The man was both dancer and hunter. By the time we finished our coffee, his line was full of trout.

We lingered on the river rocks. The sun had yet to rise fully. Water bugs skated the pools. Oak leaves dangled in the sun shafts and easy breezes. The flow of river eddies trembled soft base harmonies. These hot days were worth such mornings.

Later, we met a young couple bike-hiking from New Haven to Lenox, Massachusetts, where the Trail passed close to the famous Tanglewood summer music workshop and festival. The cyclists gave us a concert program and asked if we could make it by the following weekend. Since the Trail to Lenox included a lot of roadwalking, we thought we'd probably see them there.

The previous year the couple had walked the Appalachian Trail near Mt. Katahdin in Maine. We found their description of Maine less than encouraging.

"We hiked in June," they said, "and weren't prepared for

all those swamps. We heard that Maine was wet, but didn't imagine it was *that* wet."

Shortly afterward we met Richard, a lone thru-hiker heading south, the first hiker we intercepted going from Mt. Katahdin, the northern terminus, to Springer Mountain in Georgia. "When did you leave?" we asked him.

"June third," he said, "and I want to tell you it was like something out of a science fiction horror story. Maine was so full of blackflies you could hardly see the Trail. It was really bad, really bad."

Richard was from the South, and was as unaware of the annual blackfly scourge of New England as we had been of the cold in Georgia. "But you made it this far."

"New England is great," he said, brightening up. "The best part is up ahead. You've got a lot to look forward to."

As usual, we exchanged hiking ideas and asked each other what foods we carried.

"Last week," Richard said, "I called my mother and she said, 'What's the matter, you sound funny.' I said, 'Nothing's the matter,' and then when I hung up the phone I fainted, keeled right over. It was pretty bad. Some people said I probably wasn't eating enough good food."

"Like what?"

"Well, I've been eating a lot of instant rice."

We resisted the temptation to preach nutrition to this young hiker, but couldn't help giving him parting advice. We were in the same money-less state as other hikers, yet we realized that a diet of non-food such as instant rice welcomed disaster. We had seen and heard many similar tales along the Trail. If the same amount of attention given to equipment were paid to understanding nutrition, fainting and long-term general fatigue could be avoided. Unfortunately, most people hiking the outdoors know extremely little about the need for proper intake of protein foods for rebuilding muscles and carbohydrates for increased energy output.

We bade Richard good luck, and hoped he would at least buy some brown rice, if not chipped beef, brazil nuts, raisins, and a Snickers candy bar or two.

Down a conifer-covered mountain we walked into Salisbury, a classic New England town settled in the Taconic Mountains in 1720. As in our home base of Hancock, New Hampshire, nothing much seemed to have changed in Salisbury in nearly three centuries. The bookshop on the main street caught our eye. We spent an hour browsing the walls of books, and left only because it was five o'clock and closing time. Ever since we finished T. H. White's *The Sword in the Stone* we had been thinking of what to read besides the guidebook. Evenings were longer now and we missed reading. Mike McCabe, the bookseller, found us copies of Whitman, Jefferson, and Thoreau, but they were all hardback and too heavy for the Trail. In a scramble to find the right book, we hit upon Robinson Jeffers' *Selected Poems*, weighing in at four ounces.

As in many New England towns, a bell chimed the hours. At six o'clock we spread a bag of groceries on our ponchos in front of the creek that flowed past the public library. A few minutes later in the warm, quiet sunset, we had devoured a summer salad of tuna, green pepper, two tomatoes, a bottle of artichoke hearts and a cucumber, all mixed with olive oil and lemon juice. For dessert we served succulent cantaloupe, a quart of peach ice cream, two yellow delicious apples, and a quart of grapefruit juice.

Before leaving Salisbury we bent our faces over the rim of a weathered white marble fountain bowl and let the water spray into our throats. Near by, a dozen teenagers brooded on the steps of the town hall. Dressed in the modern idiom, and fitting the town like a sandlot baseball team on a polo field, they smoked cigarettes and drank soda pop. Not one laughed or smiled. Bored stiff. How they could be so spirit-less on such a day in such a town was beyond us. Probably the one pressing thought of these jaded juveniles was how to escape Salisbury. We could have lived there for years, each day looking to the whale weathervane on the church tower, to nearby Bear Mountain, to the shelves of the bookshop and library, to ourselves. How little is needed to set the mind at peace.

Outside town and into the woods we shared grounds for the night with a four-member family of skunks. The birches and scrub brush camouflaged these nocturnal members of the weasel family. Fortunately the docile, unaggressive creatures bushytailed away into another cluster of birches. Skunks have only one weapon of defense, and the oily spray they exude from the vents under their tails is one of the most persistent noxious odors of nature.

In the morning Mike McCabe met us at the apple orchard where the Trail crossed his own property and led toward Massachusetts. He gave us a United States Geological Survey quadrangle map of the area. "You'll be climbing these four mountains today," he said, holding the map. He pointed to the horizon. "There they are. You'll have some good views, too, but it might get hot later on. You'll be going into Sages Ravine. You'll like that." We could tell that he'd rather be hiking that day than selling books.

The climb over Lion's Head, Bear Mountain, Race Mountain, and Mt. Everett (2,603 feet) favored us with sweeping views, as Mike said. The summits, with scrub pine and oak, cooled us, and the vantage points revealed the gradual but certain change of Connecticut hills turning into Massachusetts mountains.

The hot, steep climb down Bear Mountain into Sages Ravine led us to a raw aquamarine river slashing through a conduit of rocky cliffs and thick-trunked trees. Pools glistened like molten glass, one of them pulsing so irresistibly that a glance was hypnotism enough to compel us to throw off boots, packs, and clothes and plunge into the paradise of its icy waters. Seconds later we leaped from the pool, boomeranged by the iciness, hoping that the shock was as therapeutic as it was welcome.

On a boulder in the center of the river, with green hemlocks, yellow birches, and jade ferns lining the edges, we ate lunch between waterfalls. The narcotic of rushing water washed away our cares. The USGS map told us we were already one thousand feet into Massachusetts. What do maps know?

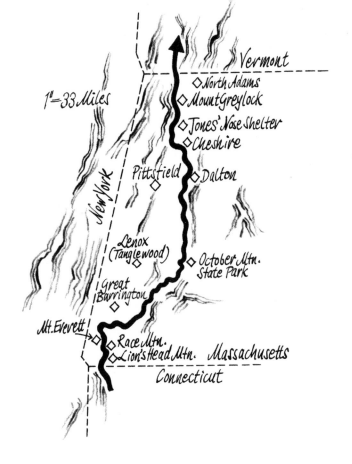

1"=33 Miles

Vermont

North Adams

Mount Greylock

Jones' Nose Shelter

Cheshire

Pittsfield

Dalton

New York

Lenox
(Tanglewood)

October Mtn.
State Park

Great
Barrington

Mt. Everett

Race Mtn.

Lion's Head Mtn.

Massachusetts

Connecticut

Massachusetts

134 MILES

In the woods all you have to do is pick a spot and watch the world perform. At the bottom of Mt. Everett we watched the adagio of changing sunlight, the tumble of leaves, the shimmer of wind, the time-ticking of a creek. It seemed the performance was orchestrated for us alone.

The Massachusetts woods were full of performances, the cities and towns, too. We were so used to the calm of the

Trail that we completely forgot summer is vacation time. We looked forward to attending the Berkshire Music Festival at Tanglewood, and taking a motel room in Lenox, as an epicurean weekend. We approached the event like the priest in Daudet's short story, "Three Low Masses." Envisioning the roast duck prepared for the customary Christmas midnight supper, the priest recites each Mass faster and faster, until his words are gibberish. So we hurried to Lenox, stumbling over our feet, keyed up for comfort and culture. How were we to know July 20–22 was a sell-out Beethoven weekend, the most popular of the festival?

At first we had planned to get a room in nearby Great Barrington, but the town was a bedlam. In and around Great Barrington people were attending the dance festival at Jacob's Pillow, the Shaker community, Tanglewood, plays, concerts, art exhibits, antique shows, museums, lectures, film festivals. The list was endless, and so was the stream of cars into town. We even had to abide by stoplights to cross the streets, a disconcerting experience when the most we had to watch out for in other states were rattlesnakes.

No room was available in Great Barrington. The town was a madhouse, a midsummer nightmare. Cars lined up in the horseshoe drives in front of hotels. One after another, their frazzled drivers returned to hot, car-trapped families shaking their heads.

One inn clerk told us we were lucky. Since they had so many calls, they were prematurely opening a new building. An hour later we stepped into the run-down lobby of a main street locale. The building was a paint-chipped derelict from the last century that was being hustled into instant use for the emergency overflow. The young, ambitious manager was waylaid at the switchboard by a message that the plumbing in room such and such wasn't working. In the stuffy four-person padded freight elevator, we asked the cost of the fourth story room: $19.95. When we saw the room, our suspicions that the management was profiting by crisis were confirmed. It was colorless and dingy, smelling of disinfectant and senility. No tub, only a shower stall. The window filtered noise from the traffic below, no air conditioning or swimming pool, and we were still ten miles from the Tanglewood grounds. As tired as we were, the energy we would have expended battling the cockroaches and noise wasn't worth the effort.

Now there is no denying that Ludwig Van Beethoven was a great composer, but we began to resent his popularity. Even the October Mountain State Park near Lenox was filled to capacity, with two tents to every site.

We hitched to Lenox, bought food, and made it to the back gates of Tanglewood with our three-dollar lawn tickets. When the gates opened we headed straight for a butternut tree at center front on the lawn just outside the pavilion chairs (and about a block-and-a-half away from the concert stage). The white walnut with its myriad leaflets was a haven of comfort that July evening. We rested our backs against the broad trunk. Corn on the cob and hamburgers cooked on our Primus stove. Performances were going on all around us, including the one we gave. Never had we been so conspicuous. It must have been our catchy red packs against the lawn, or perhaps the stove was sending up smell signals.

We weren't the only picnickers, although we were the only ones actually cooking. Others brought picnic lunches. Some tossed green salads in large wooden bowls, some ate French bread and cheese. Wine corks popped, candles flickered. In the relaxed atmosphere the worry about where we would stay for the night vanished.

A woman walked up and asked, "What kind of stove is that? It's fascinating. We've been watching you and we've never seen one before."

We told her it was a standard backpackers' white gas stove.

"I use white gas to make jewelry." She pointed to her husband on a lawn chair ten yards away. He waved. "My husband is a chemist. He timed your stove to see how long it took to boil the corn. Exactly seven minutes," she exulted as if it were a NASA countdown.

Later, a tall, John Wayne–type squatted down to talk. "I hike all around these hills," he said. "I love the Great Outdoors. That's why I come to these concerts. The wife, well, she's not too keen on camping out. Once we were in the woods and it was freezing, I mean freezing. She complained the whole time and said we should pack up and go back home. Where you hiking?"

"The Appalachian Trail."

"Coming down from Maine, huh?"

"Up from Georgia."

"*Whheeeewww.* Georgia. Well, I hiked some of the Trail, but not that much. Once I stayed at the shelter at Greylock. In fact, I think I'll stay there tonight. Not going to pay good money to stay in a motel. You want a ride up there? I'll be coming back tomorrow."

We told him we were going to spend the night in Lenox, and added doubtfully, someplace.

Another man ambled over, natty in a beige summer suit. He looked disdainfully at our frying hamburgers. We hadn't eaten meat or eggs for nearly two weeks and were attempting to re-nourish.

"I never eat meat," he announced. "The fat isn't good for your system. I eat whole-grain cereal, cream, and bananas most of the time." We turned over our excessively greasy burgers. "You should try it. Brown rice and lentils are good for you. I always eat whole wheat bread and beans, even for breakfast. And a pot of legumes is always soaking or simmering on the stove. You can buy better food at health food stores."

"We haven't been able to find too many health food stores along the Trail," we said, smiling at each other. We tried to explain that we had to buy what we could get at the small general stores along the way. Now that we were in New England, bulgar wheat and lentils were stocked even in the smaller stores. The man looked down his nose at our dinner and walked off through the disgusting, unhealthy picnickers.

In an article on raw foods in the magazine *Let's Live*, we had read about a couple that climbed Mt. Whitney (14,494 feet) in California. They boasted that their intake had consisted of three oranges, one avocado, and a few dates. (They did not mention what they had for dinner after they came down.) Their conclusion was that hikers can live on raw foods, that is, if you leave out of consideration long-distance hikes and weight factors. We saw few oranges in the South, let alone avocados or dates. Whenever we did find fresh produce, we ate it on the spot. Occasionally, after a stopover we carried an orange out of town, a special treat. Often we boiled eggs and carried one or two, but usually ate them right away. Three oranges can weigh up to 1½ pounds. To maintain our vitamin C level, each morning we took a 100-mg tablet. These we kept in a plastic container with a moisture absorption packet.

Other entertainment came to our butternut tree under the accumulating rain clouds. A long-haired young man living in a van for the summer borrowed one of our tickets so he could leave the grounds and re-enter. Evidently, he had found a hole in the wall before the gates opened. Two blankets away, a woman drank herself blotto and wagged her tongue at her husband so loud, long, and incessantly that he took their blanket and stomped away from her threats. A man to the right of us looked at girls through his binoculars. Citronella candles appeared along with twilight mosquitoes. People slapped their bare legs.

We withdrew into our windbreakers and listened to what seemed an interminable number of Beethoven variations on a theme, played by pianist Andre Watts. Tanglewood felt like a family reunion. We spotted our bike-hiking friends from Connecticut and went to say hello. Peter and Maureen invited us to share their campsite at October Mountain State Park. We preferred being on our own to a raucous stacked campground.

The principal concert began at eight o'clock. The Emperor Piano Concerto and Beethoven's Fifth Symphony are old warhorses that might do better out to pasture. The public at Tanglewood had traveled miles to hear Beethoven, and no doubt their enjoyment was heightened because they knew the program by heart. Nearly six thousand people were intent and silent and paid respectful homage to the Boston Symphony Orchestra and pianist Phillipe Entremont.

As the applause rained down on Eugene Ormandy and the artists, rain rained down on us. Drunk with dinner music and half a bottle of Portuguese wine given to us by departing music lovers (who overheard the story of our hike four times) we waited for the crowd to disperse so we could escape into the bushes. Wearing our packs among the summer concertgoers, we were anything but inconspicuous. However, the rain and traffic distracted ushers, ticket-takers, and policemen.

We waited for a break in the stream of headlights and then jogged directly into a field that slanted away from the gates down into the dark. The trail of lights guided us to a cluster of trees in a field not too far from Nathaniel Hawthorne's house. As we struggled with the tent in the knee-high wet grass, reeling under the influence of the wine, which had contained more than the normal amount of alcohol, we fashioned some of our own "Tanglewood Tales" to rival those of Hawthorne.

We woke to the mellow whispers of rehearsing cellos. The muted sounds were ghostly in the morning drizzle. We hitched a ride back to Lenox and waited out the rain in the public library, a stately, carpeted mansion with deep easy chairs, mahogany tables, and reading desks. The singly lighted oil portraits and table lamps added to the cozy atmosphere on such a gloomy day. We removed our boots. If only the library furnished its patrons with a deep, hot bath.

Lenox had the air of heartland New England. The people were bright and fast, even in a heavy morning rain. The very graffiti in the gas station lavatories were scholarly, compared to the body mania of other regions' graffitists:

> *To be is to do*—KANT
>
> *To do is to be*—HEGEL
>
> *Do be do be do*—SINATRA
>
> *To be or to ba*—JOHN PHILLIP SOUSA

We headed for the Trail connection in October Mountain State Park about two miles from Lenox. Hitching a ride never seemed to be a problem. We figured that mobile Americans seldom have an opportunity to invite strangers into their homes in the old fashioned tradition of American hospitality. Instead, their automobiles have become surrogate homes, and by picking up hitchhikers, the drivers are really inviting strangers into homes on wheels. We noticed, too, as we had all along our route, that those who did pick us up belonged to the less monied classes, people less insulated, more open and trusting. We grew fond of the drivers of pickups, construction workers on their way home, and the bake-your-own-bread Volkswagen drivers who stopped when the Lincoln set breezed by.

When we reached Dalton we were soggy and depressed. Dr. Steve Namrehs practically carried Julia, who—overnight, it seemed—had acquired a persistent side-ache. Only a motel room would appease us. Finally, a friendly motel-keeper without a vacancy called a widow who often opened her doors to overnight guests during the Beethoven weekend. At last, a hot bath, and rest.

The Berkshires are gently rolling green hills that were made from a smaller mold than the Green Mountains of Vermont.

Hardwoods fight for light among dense pine forests. A tree we especially liked, and one abundant in New England, was the striped maple or moosewood. It is a tree of about twenty feet with a slender, smooth, green trunk with white zebra stripes. In New Hampshire it is often called the goosefoot maple because of the shape of its leaf.

Anyone who thinks all tree trunks are brown or gray is mistaken. There are the white and yellow birches, the metallic gold of the latter resplendent and shiny in the sun. The striped maple is green and white. Then there is the red-maroon satiny bark of the sugar birch and cherry trunks, not to mention the yellow-green of young swamp willows or the black of the walnut. Tree trunks naturally were close to us. We leaned against them, held onto them when slipping downhill, gripped them when climbing, observed them when resting. Their skeletal shapes peopled our world, and in the intimacy of their knots and curves we took mental and physical repose.

We walked down into Cheshire, untouched by tourism. Bicyclists and front porch swingers rode out the late afternoon sun. A man drove by in his car, stopped, and asked, "You expecting mail here?"

"Nope."

"Well, since you're hiking the Appalachian Trail and it's Sunday I thought if you were expecting some I'd open the post office. I'm the postmaster."

The United States Postal Service, steadfast, tolerant friend of thru-hikers. Not once did we have anything but bend-over-backward help from postmasters and postmistresses. They realized the importance of food packages, letters, and money forwarded to thru-hikers. Some of the popular post offices, such as Harpers Ferry (West Virginia), Damascus (Virginia), Hot Springs (North Carolina), or Monson (Maine) had overflowing stacks of mail set aside in corners just for Trail hikers.

We sat at the foot of a life-size statue of a cheese press.

The big cheese in Cheshire turned out to be John Leland (1754–1841), the town hero. Leland was a Baptist clergyman who in 1789 proposed the abolition of slavery, was active in both political and religious liberalism, composed popular hymns, and in 1811 was elected on the Republican ticket to the Massachusetts Legislature. Leland lived in Cheshire for fifty years. In 1801 he went to Washington, D.C., to present President Thomas Jefferson with a 1,200-pound wheel of Cheddar cheese made by the women of Cheshire. Thereafter, he was referred to as the "Mammoth Priest."

July 23, the day after we arrived in Cheshire, was a milestone of our trip—our Hundredth Day on the Trail. At sunrise we were off to the distant hills and Mt. Greylock (3,491 feet), the highest point in Massachusetts. The day was cellophane clear with unlimited visibility. Halfway up the mountain we spotted a bird twenty-five feet ahead of us on a straight stretch of the Trail. At first we couldn't identify it because the bird kept hopping along at a distance from us as we progressed. Our hiking companion was a woodcock. This squat fat bird with its long needle-nose bill and camouflage feathers led us up the Trail for five minutes before it tired of our company.

The sharpness of every outline held us in awe. On a rock projecting into the Trail the sun spotlighted a jewel, a crystallized amethyst. The royal prisms danced in our eyes. Slowly we lowered our heads to examine the gem. Perhaps we could chip it off and carry the treasure with us. Steve's head jerked up in disillusionment. He identified our precious gemstone: "Guano!"

Shortly after, we came to a shelter on the mountain called Jones' Nose. Just before rounding a bend, the irresistible smell of bacon filled our nostrils. A group of teenagers was cooking breakfast. Dan Emerson, the leader, explained that he was in charge of the boys, who were part of the Homeward Bound program sponsored by the Massachusetts Department of

Youth of Human Services. Homeward Bound is based on the
Outward Bound program for young people to develop self-
reliance in the outdoors.

Each summer about one hundred miles of the Trail were
selected for the teenagers to walk in five days. We noticed
that all the hikers had new packs and boots. The government
footed the bill so that these youngsters, delinquent fourteen-
to seventeen-year-olds, could enjoy the woods. They were
given the choice between this and other more institutional
programs such as the YMCA or remedial houses. The boys
were court referrals.

"It's a great challenge for them and me," Dan said. "You
see, they have learned a different type of survival in the city.
A lot of them don't know how to respond to the outdoors.
It's more hostile to them than the city streets."

One of the group called their leader. Breakfast was ready.
Even if they didn't like the idea of hiking the woods, it
seemed to us that these teenagers were involved in what they
were doing.

"Any disciplinary problems?" we asked.

"Oh, sure," Dan said. "They side for each other and can
make hell for me. Last year I took a group on this same
stretch. It was miserable. Rained the whole damn time. The
boys didn't understand that once we started we were bound
to finish. But long after the trip was over, they still talked
about it."

The program started in 1965. "So far, studies show that
recidivism is twenty per cent," Dan said, "as opposed to forty
per cent in other programs. So it's working."

On the way to Jones' Nose we were distracted a couple of
times. First, by two farm girls wandering down the side of
the road looking into every pasture for a cow that was due to
calve. They were as worried as if the cow were their own kin.
"She was due, all right," one of them said. "If you find her
along the Trail, would you tell one of the farmers?"

We promised, but soon our minds were on the red raspberry patches. Just one of these delectable fruits hanging like a jewel in the morning sun was enough to savor all the way up the mountain. Red raspberries were twice as precious as black because of their scarcity and, most important, their lush concentrated flavor. We were ambushed for several minutes.

Whoever Jones was, he had a big nose, aquiline and proud, and he held it skyward, an eagle's beak, a great de Bergerac appendage which we climbed until we were above the forehead on the bald. The sky was cloudless, bright, and clear. We were giddy with the fragrance of the pines and the spongy sphagnum moss that bounced underfoot. Wood sorrel grew in thick carpets. The pupils of our eyes turned green.

> *Am I green?*
> *Do I have a sun green on my shoulders?*
> *Are my fingers deep lobed*
> *with alternate veins?*
> *Is my blood the color of moss*
> *ridden by a summer stream?*
> *Are my eyes green and papery*
> *the way the sunlight*
> *falls through leaves, my eyes—*
> *the color of my mind?*
> *A hemlock moored in shadow.*

Just short of the top, we paused to rest. The boys, who started at least half an hour after us, passed by whistling, smiling, and maintaining a pace that looked like a fast-motion film. The entire troop of these energetic peripatetics flashed by.

"Come on, move it," one of them said, bumping into the one in front. "Lunch at the top, idiot. Hurry."

The leader brought up the rear and gave us a wan smile. Conspiracy, mutiny on the Trail. By stepping up their pace they were leaving him behind and slighting the authority he represented.

We followed them toward the summit of Mount Greylock. At the top we towered over seventy to eighty miles of the surrounding territory, scanning a sprawling, mountain-bumpy spread of earth as far as the horizon allowed. When the buildings and fields of North Adams directly below were overlooked, nothing but green mountain peaks filled the scene, a fitting tableau to close theatrical Massachusetts.

Mount Greylock played a two-part invention in our repertoire of firsts. For lunch, instead of the monotonous Cheddar cheese, we spread honey butter on rolls. Whipped honey did not melt, and provided a novel energy source to our hackneyed diet. Secondly, off in the distance some sixty miles was Mt. Monadnock, the mountain we conditioned on before embarking on our hike over three months ago.

We distinctly saw Monadnock's peak rising above the surrounding eroded peneplain. The discovery that we were so close to New Hampshire excited us. Monadnock is not the region's highest mountain, its most famous, or its most difficult to climb. One woman of the area, in fact, has climbed it no less than 250 times. To us, however, this mountain, nearly two states away, represented the Alpha and Omega of our two-thousand-mile odyssey. We were homeward bound.

Long Trail
Norwich
Sherburne
Woodstock
Pico Camp
White River Junction
Killington Peak
Rutland
1" = 23 Miles
Mill River
Gov. Clement Shelter
New Hampshire
Griffith Lake
Baker Peak
Mad Tom Notch Shelter
Bromley Mtn.
Story Spring Shelter
Stratton Pond
New York
Arlington
Kid Gore Shelter
Connecticut River
Glastenbury Mtn.
Bennington
Bolles Brook
Sucker Pond
Vermont
Massachusetts

Vermont

134 MILES

No other words but the French *vert* and *mont* would be accurate in describing this state, for the Green Mountain Range runs a verdant chain up Vermont all the way to

Canada. The Connecticut River is the eastern boundary of the state, Lake Champlain the western. Envied empire of maple sugar and Cheddar cheese, paradise for skiers, hideaway for artists and writers, home of the 260-mile Long Trail, Vermont represents freedom from congestion, a forested peace.

The Long Trail is a source of pride to Vermonters. This footpath through the wilderness affirms their commitment to man's need of the outdoors. Established in 1910 by the Green Mountain Club, it extends the entire length of the state from the Massachusetts border to Canada. One hundred miles of the Appalachian Trail coincide with the Long Trail; the two trails part at Sherburne Pass, where the Appalachian turns to the east.

As soon as we crossed into Vermont we noticed the difference between the two trails. The Long Trail had many more mileage markers and indicated water sources. It was cleared of overhanging brush. Directional signs were frequent, clear and attractive, on shellacked brown boards with engraved yellow lettering. Constantly we were reminded to pack out what we packed in. Split log walkways were provided in low soggy areas. Thoughtfully placed ladders and stepping-stones helped hikers climb cliffs and cross swamps. One of the Green Mountain Boys with Ogden Nash humor placed this sign in the mud:

Walking on this bridge of rocks
keeps the water from my socks.

BURMA SHAVE

The Trail led us through stands of American beech that covered entire mountainsides. The smooth gray trunks somehow had that institutional feeling: they looked like painted porch poles, or better yet, water pipes in a high school basement.

Since the Long Trail and the Appalachian Trail coincided,

we met more hikers, and quite a number of backpacking dogs. These canines were usually amiable and well mannered, pleased to be unleashed in the wild. On one mountaintop, however, we met a lone hiker and his dog walking south. The dog growled and remained close to his master. "She won't bite," the man said. "It's just that some hiker beat her with a staff once and ever since she's been afraid. Before that happened she was as friendly as any dog. Now every time she meets someone with a backpack, she growls."

More north-to-southers straggled by, and we wondered what was in store for us up ahead. They were bedraggled and grubby, their boots cracked and muddy. As we skidded along some split log planks, we realized the reason. Entire sections of the Trail had been washed out by floods that summer. The state was declared a disaster area, but luckily by the time we arrived most of the lowlands were dry.

Despite the hot sun, the shore line of Sucker Pond south of Bennington was still muddy. We found a fairly dry site adjacent the limpid water and camped. Later, we read Robinson Jeffers' poems by twilight, moonlight, and then flashlight. The mist crept over the pond and bats flew from the woods to swoop after insects flitting over the water. Bats, the only mammals capable of true flight, are nocturnal, and although they do have limited vision, they rely primarily on a system of high frequency blips for navigation. Above the range of the human ear, these sounds ricochet from objects back to the bats' ears, much like sonar blips. The silent, jagged flight of these bats overhead was mesmeric in the night, like blackjack oak leaves thrashed about in a windstorm.

Our reverie was broken by campers on the far side of the pond. "Hey, come on over and get high!" they shouted, dispelling all illusion of privacy. Their shouting continued into the early hours, and in the morning we woke to the sound of motor bikes hot-rodding the trails. We opened our eyes, raised our heads, and watched the blue chiffon lift from the pond as the sun rose over the ridge. A kingfisher skimmed the lake and landed on a log adrift near the shore. He scolded us as if we were making the racket. We apologized for the tomfoolery of our fellow man.

A moment later we saw a different bird shoot across the lake. Both of us gasped at the strong, streamlined silhouette. It flew with the determination of a hunter, perhaps a maverick of an exotic species. Perhaps we had hit upon a reportable sighting. As we scrutinized the strange bird's shape and color, our eyes shaded from the dawning sun, we realized our mistake. What held us spellbound was a common *Turdus migratorius*. A robin. Our enchantment with the wonders we saw every day gave the commonplace a new dimension.

By the time we reached Bennington on July 25, we were so pleased with the Long Trail that we headed straight for the editorial office of *The Banner* and arranged with the editor to write an article about it.

Later, in a restaurant, we met John Paulson, a standing member of the Green Mountain Club. He told us of the Trail ahead and about his boyhood hiking experiences in the Green Mountains. Even today he still hiked with the old-style frameless pack, and carried two pairs of boots, a light pair for nimble-footed climbing and a heavy set for solid downhill footing.

John thanked his father for his Swedish endurance and stamina. Every winter when John was a boy the family hiked to Sucker Pond to chop down a Christmas tree. Somehow the entire day was spent searching for the perfect tree and somehow the perfect tree was always found a scarce few minutes before it was time to go home.

His father and relatives carried the packs, with food and camping equipment. In those days they made their own pack frames from ash branches. Since he was small, John didn't have to carry anything. One winter, right after they selected the finest fir of all, a freak blizzard stormed in. John could hardly walk through the deep snow, but his father, already laden with two packs, prodded him on and ordered him not to stop. We pictured this strawberry-blond Swede sitting before us as a small boy, and protested when he said his father kept him going with a switch. "I was forever thankful to my father for his discipline," he told us. "He saved all our lives during one of the worst snowstorms Vermont has ever seen."

John told us we might find the shelters ahead an eyesore. "The Green Mountain Club has a caretaker system," he said, "and primitive tent sites at most of the lakes to cut down on shelter use. The town objects to the shelters. In fact, there was a proposal to blaze a trail through here to North Dakota. Bennington vetoed it. We got more hikers through here now than anywhere, I bet. Trouble is, not all of them are good-mannered like you." He gave us a parting Swedish wink.

Our ride back to the Trail was offered by a teenager who said he was going in our direction; but after he let us out he turned around and headed back to town—free taxi service. Help from strangers never ceased to amaze us.

Outside Bennington we walked the four miles up the abandoned railroad bed that paralleled Bolles Brook, a water source for the town. The clear pools of this brook magnified the pebbles at the bottom and strung out their colors in liquid mosaic. Though the New England blackfly season was officially over, a few stragglers hadn't received notice. In camp Steve stirred a dash or two of these pests into the fried rice while Julia fought them with her flute near the creek. Black-flies were never intimidated by movement. In fact, we never quite figured what they wanted, since they did not siphon blood like mosquitoes or land and feed like honest flies. When Julia executed a military about-face, only milliseconds elapsed before the blackflies' gnatty bodies again plunged into her eyes or, even more jolting, dived into a deep mouthed breath to explore the cavities of her *embouchure*. The hazards of woodland fluting.

Two months earlier we had celebrated Julia's birthday on the Trail. Now Steve climbed Glastenbury Mountain (3,764 feet) with a bouquet of birthday flowers fastened to his pack. As we reached the top, the wildflowers drooped, and so did we. After rounding several false summits and then finally scaling the real one, all we got for the climb was an enclosure of more conifers. We had seen our share of forest-thick mountain peaks. Openness was what we now sought.

At Kid Gore Shelter we sat at a makeshift table in the fog. Eating at a place named Kid Gore was less than cheery, as was passing through Mad Tom Notch. Two boys already occupied the shelter, so we stayed outside to light our stove for hot soup. The air was clammy and cold. Fine birthday.

The shelter overlooked a declivity between peaks. The split pea soup warmed us along with creamed cheese on sprouted wheat bread, one of our favorite lunches. A few bites of food perked up humorless minds. Even a gray sky revealed some color. The valley was a natural aviary. Downy woodpeckers tapped at stunted limbs. Tinier birds flew in and out of hazy foliage. One we'd never seen, a messenger with white breast and gold and black along the sides of his head. Later, in an environmental library in Woodstock, Vermont, we identified him as a Blackburnian warbler.

The boys came over to light their Primus stove from ours. If we heated the bottom, they told us, the stove would ignite without our going through the laborious procedure of filling the circular well with gas. We used an eye dropper for this purpose. Although lighting the stove was now a habit, the nuisance of opening the bottom tank to fill the eye dropper, propping the eye dropper while closing the tank, replacing the key that controlled the gas-feed to diffuse the gas, igniting the eye dropper fuel in the shallow well, and finally lighting the gas released by the key, often proved exasperating, especially in the rain. Nonetheless, the stove weighed only eighteen ounces and, except for a few temperamental occasions, worked efficiently and fast. We now added a new bit of information to the Primus Club: you could save yourself a few steps by slightly heating the bottom of the stove, as our neighbors successfully did.

The boys told us that the Trail register in the shelter contained an account by a man who stayed the night with his dog and spent the entire following morning using a pair of tweezers to pull porcupine quills from the dog's body. Some people falsely believe that angered porcupines eject their quills long distances. Actually, the quills must be violently shaken in order to be released. The extraction of porcupine quills from man or beast can be painful indeed. An experienced person should perform the job.

One time we witnessed the damage of an enraged porcupine on two dogs. One pup, a high-strung Alaskan husky, had to be taken to a veterinarian and drugged. The barbed quills were embedded in her muzzle, jaw, and tongue. The other dog, a good-natured mongrel, was more cautious, and so was struck by only a few of the three-inch spines. Close examination of the quills revealed why the porcupine's privacy is considered with deference by old-timer canines. The barbs were as tenacious as fishhooks. If deeply embedded, they would be impossible to extract except by a jerk with a pair of pliers.

After lunch at Kid Gore Shelter we continued our claustrophobic walk among the thick evergreen forests of the mountains, our boots hitting roots and snags with nearly every step. Although we were reaching the higher peaks, our anticipation of lofty views didn't come with the Green Mountains. Colin Turnbull in his book *Forest People* tells of a pygmy tribal chief. One day the author took the chief out of the dense jungle and onto the plains where animals roamed. When the author remarked on a distant herd of elephants, the chief laughed and told him that he was mistaken. Those were ants.

Only when they drove closer to the herd would the pygmy believe the distance between himself and the elephants.

In Vermont we felt somewhat like the pygmy chief, whose field of vision was accustomed to being confined by the surrounding trees. The pine forests were friendly, green, and peaceful, yet we longed for a sweep of the entire range we had been walking hour after hour, day after day.

We were also coming to realize how popular the Long Trail was. We passed sixteen hikers one day. On another day we passed seventy-six. When we came to Story Shelter in the early afternoon, the tent and shelter space already were occupied. A hiker put up his fifteen-stake tent and separate rain fly. Fortunately, our tent had eight stakes and the rain fly was sewn onto it, making it a unit. Most hikers are hooked on equipment, and our neighbor was no exception. Gadgets meant comfort. His Swiss knife had everything from scissors to saw. His stove was fueled by pressurized propane. His food was arranged in plastic canisters and bottles on the table. When we left the site he was still struggling with the tent. With the weight he was carrying, he wouldn't have made it through Georgia on the Appalachian Trail.

On the other hand, there was Jimi of Virginny hiking to Katahdin. He had little money to spend on equipment so he bought the cheapest of everything, including boots. As a result, he had to re-sole them. Now his pack (an inexpensive make) was ripping a second time. When he passed us we were sitting beneath a sign that read:

Springer Mountain 1,463 miles

Mt. Katahdin 537 miles

Jimi had planned for five years to hike the Trail, at a time when it wasn't a popular idea. This summer he finally made it.

"I like hiking alone," he said, " 'cause whenever I hook up with somebody else, it's all right for the first couple days. Then the other guy starts getting finicky and all that, so I go on by myself. I started out with another guy. After awhile he was complaining, so one night I plain up and asked him why he was doing it if he didn't like it. And he told me he didn't know. After that he went home."

Jimi had spirit and he was smiling. Not many thru-hikers smiled. "What are you eating?"

"I don't know about you two," he said, "but my appetite is just unsatisfiable. Man, I don't know what I'm going to do when I finish hiking. Put a stopper in my mouth, I guess. You know, when I get into town I eat whole pies and drink a quart of 7-Up. And I don't gain any weight either. It just goes right out the bottom of my shoes. You know what I mean?"

We nodded.

"I tried eating some of those trailburgers, you know, those dehydrated concoctions? One time I took that stuff out and then I said to myself, 'Hell, I ain't going to put my hands into that stuff.' So I just dumped it into the frying pan, and would you believe that stuff wouldn't even *fry!*"

Jimi of Virginny headed for Stratton Pond alone, in case we got too finicky. We didn't know if we'd make it that far. We'd already covered fifteen miles. Later, we found out that the Trail had been re-routed after the floods hit the area to avoid further inundation. Consequently, all the water sources we depended on were gone. The 3.7-mile hike to Stratton Pond, the nearest water supply, was a forced march.

By the time we reached Stratton Pond, only Steve acknowledged Jimi. Julia gave the Virginian a fix-eyed stare as if she had never seen him before. The hard hiking inflamed the pain in her side, which had started at Dalton, Massachusetts, and was still taking its toll. "Wow, she really looks tired," Jimi said, offering us a piece of bread. "She doesn't even recognize me."

Hikers sometimes succumb to this hypnotized state. Exhausted beyond physical endurance and afflicted with unexpected pains, for their own protection they retreat into the world of the spirit, light-headed with hunger, weak-kneed with a series of lackluster mountains left behind. When the campsite really does appear, they can't believe it. In this case, we found one of the last available sites in this restricted area.

At once we came to our senses. One does not dillydally when less than an hour of daylight is left to cook dinner and pitch the tent. And what of Steve's birthday, still uncelebrated? Two boxes of birthday candles were in Julia's pack, but would they be a surprise? Of all evenings, this was the one for brown rice, which took forty-five minutes to cook. Then the caretaker came visiting. Yes, yes, the cook nods, pushing handfuls of candles into two slices of bread as the caretaker explains that seventy-five cents is asked for on a voluntary basis for the site. "Yes, we'll pay, but the breadwinner is getting water. Why don't you see him at the stream?"

The caretaker likes female company. "And we have twenty-two caretakers in seventeen locations. We're paid just $150 a summer. I picked Stratton Pond because when I hiked the Long Trail I thought it was the worst site of all. I wanted to improve it."

"Interesting. Oh, no, here he comes with the water. Where can I hide the candles?"

The caretaker chatted with the water carrier while unnoticed activity took place behind a tree. "I just got word that a caretaker's been missing for four days now," he said. "He was up at Griffith Lake. There are a lot of weird people who come out around here. Anything could have happened."

Finally, the Green Mountain Club left. "Happy Birthday to you! Happy Birthday to you . . . !"

We tied the blown-out candles together so we could eat the brown rice and birthday bread by candlelight.

The following morning we met our caretaker again. No new word had arrived on the missing caretaker. "Nope, I just don't know what happened to him," he said. "We've had a fairly heavy season in this camp so far, eight hundred overnighters in all. One Friday we had fifty-nine tenters. But that other caretaker. I don't think anyone would just desert like that and leave all his belongings."

"You mean you suspect foul play?"

"Maybe. Some people get pretty upset about fees and care-takers telling them where to camp and all that. If we don't charge fees, these places'll be all torn up. Most people don't know how to camp anymore. They come out here for a weekend and think all they have to do is chop down any old tree for a big monstrous fire, and dig up the ground to pitch their tents, and dump trash and garbage anywhere they want to, even in the pond. So I don't know what happened over there at Griffith Lake. Maybe he was out hiking and fell down and broke a leg. There are a lot of swamps over there, too. Who knows? Maybe some weirdo did something to him." We never did find out what became of him.

Later on near Griffith Lake, Bill MacArthur, a member of the Trails and Shelters and Long Trail Guidebook commit-tees of the Green Mountain Club, further explained the care-taker system. "We plan to build more primitive campsites near the shelters," he said, "but we don't plan to build any new shelters because of the misuse of many of them. The U.S. Forest Service suggested their removal, but the Green Moun-tain Club definitely opposes that plan. They're the only pro-tection a hiker has in inclement weather. One winter a group of twenty hikers snowshoed into a blizzard and escaped a real disaster by huddling in a shelter until they were rescued.

"By the way, what do you think of the Long Trail south of here?"

We liked the Long Trail and told Bill that it was a tribute to members of the Green Mountain Club.

While picking chamomile blossoms in the wind-swept grasses under the lookout tower on Bromley Mountain (3,300 feet), we again met the two boys from Kid Gore Shelter. They were from Michigan and hadn't yet graduated from high school. As ever, they were alert and curious. "Hey, what are you picking? What are you going to do with it? Make tea? You thru-hikers? We were thru-hikers. Started in Georgia and were doing twenty miles a day so we could finish before school started, but by the time we got to the Smokies we were tired and not having any fun. Now we just do twelve to fifteen miles. Sometimes we just stop at a shelter and stay."

"What do your parents say?"

"Oh, they think it's a great idea, provided we stay together. It's safer in twos, don't you think so?"

We agreed, both remembering a seventeen-year-old hiker who started at Katahdin and was going to meet his brother at mid-Trail toward the end of summer. If he had been walking with his brother, he might have had some help when he reached Vermont during the recent flood. Bill MacArthur told us of the extent of the flood. It had swollen creeks and knocked out bridges. One of these was a nine-thousand-dollar suspension bridge built by the Green Mountain Club fifteen years ago across the Mill River. The flood rose thirty-two feet and washed out the bridge pilings. The young lone hiker lost his life when he tried to cross the river on a slippery log, and fell off. He was wearing his pack, which dragged him under water. He came to the surface and grabbed a branch hanging out from shore, but the branch yanked free from his weight. The current took him. No one could help. It happened three days after the flood washed away the riverbanks and was the first death on the Appalachian Trail, a tragedy that made us hike with extra caution. We detoured around this now bridgeless river crossing. Talk of this death reached all sections of the Trail.

Farther on, one of our best views of Vermont came unexpectedly. We started up a rock pinnacle called Baker Peak (2,800 feet). The final three-hundred-foot climb up slabs of granite was steep, sometimes requiring an extra-solid grip by both boot and hand, so we could not turn around to see what the guidebook described as "views unfolding with each step." What we did see when we reached the top was the first unobstructed mountain view since Mt. Greylock, in Massachusetts. We removed our packs, sat down, and enjoyed the jumbled array of Green Mountains that spread around us in the hot five o'clock afternoon. The visible heat combined with the anarchy of the green pyramids and, if we had not known better, we would have thought we were somewhere in the Amazon River Valley. The shimmering of the sun and the fever of the wind enveloped us.

The Green Mountains were an anomaly in mountain ranges. None of the mountains followed that rank-and-file order of the Smokies or the Shenandoah. Each mountain was an individual. We looked down on Otter Creek Valley, askew as the mountains, and wondered what erratic upheaval caused such a helter-skelter range.

One morning we walked a corridor of spruce trees on a hogback between two loud unseen river branches. We might as well have been walking blindfolded on a plank over angry rapids. We broke into a clearing and followed the main stream. Like transparent mercury, the Cold River creamed around huge rocks. We stopped often for a drink.

> *River, O River, I wash my eyes*
> *with your mirrored surface.*
> *My hair flows as grass*
> *from your peaceful banks.*
> *Your musical rhapsody gurgles*
> *in my loosened throat,*
> *and the tiny seashell stays of my feet*
> *sink clear and strong*
> *to your sandy floor.*
> *The siphon of my nostrils*
> *creates whirlpools of scents*

from the animals that have forded your shallows
and dropped graceful necks,
as mine, O River, to restore life
to their green and simple days.

At noon we reached the Governor Clement Shelter (built in 1929) and ate lunch. Although the shelter was as old as most, the gloomy atmosphere of other lean-tos was absent. What we especially liked was the open sunny clearing and the overhang that provided living room space in front of it. A sign on the back wall read: *One of the most remarkable Governors Vermont ever had.* Later research divulged little more than the fact that Percival Wood Clement was governor from 1919 to 1920, undoubtedly a vintage year.

The three-mile climb up Mt. Killington (4,241 feet) was slow and steep. Julia developed stomach cramps and laid down while Dr. Namrehs brewed a tea of chamomile buttons, a natural calmant. The combination of sun, drinking ice-cold river water, and the long steady climb had, we thought, caused her side ache to return. This time it was the doubling over kind. Fortunately, the chamomile and some aspirin relieved the pain.

Three hours later we reached Cooper Lodge just short of the summit. This lodge, built by the U.S. Forest Service to accommodate sixteen hikers, had a wood-burning stove and a table, and was completely enclosed. A steep trail directly behind the building led $\frac{2}{10}$ mile to the top of Killington.

We left our packs and climbed to the summit. We were a bit shocked in topping the mountain peak to look down upon a huge orange restaurant (closed) and a red ski tow operating for summer tourists. The views from Killington were spectacular, the best we had seen all along the Trail so far. Wayah Bald, Clingman's Dome, Mt. Greylock, none had provided us with views like this, yet we enjoyed them more when the whine of the giant cables and the slamming of aluminum doors from the ski tow stopped for the night. Skiers and hikers looked to the mountaintops from different perspectives.

As soon as we were alone on top of Killington, we lingered and seemed to float on an island in the sky above all other mountaintops. The distances urged us on, drawing us beyond the intervening peaks to the last gray-green summit at the edge of the horizon. Never before had we seen so many pines in one eye-scope. Their individuality at close hand was lost to the merging of one mammoth field of trees.

Back down to our packs we went, and from 6:30 until 7:50 we bolted the three miles to Pico Camp with the hope of finding flat ground. We sped over the root-and-rock-infested Trail, parts of which were newly routed and yet to be worn down. The surprise of such a reserve of energy at the end of a long, hard day, especially with the pain in Julia's side, once again underscored the lessons we had learned, namely, that the human body, under the impetus of a determined will, can generate startling displays of stamina and power. We virtually trotted those three miles. Our packs became merely extensions of our skeletons and sinews.

On that race to Pico Camp, we beat the darkness by a shadow or two but lost the hope of finding a flat square of ground for our tent. The meaning of "primitive" tent sites was left to the discretion of the Green Mountain Club. Some native tribes are referred to as "primitive," yet we couldn't for one minute imagine their camping on sloping ground or raising a dwelling on a fifteen-degree angle.

At Sherburne Pass on U.S. Highway 103, we veered east off the Long Trail and back onto the Appalachian Trail. Most of this section was maintained by the Dartmouth Outing Club headquartered in Hanover, New Hampshire. Now the Trail crosscut the foothills and took on a more pastoral ambiance. For many miles until the Connecticut River, back roads were followed. The evergreens gave way to the hardwoods of the lower altitudes. Besides this, the metamorphosis from the Long Trail to the Appalachian Trail was not only directional. On the Long Trail we had indeed felt we were on a "Footpath through the Wilderness," despite the number of hikers encountered. Now, although we met fewer hikers, we were back on dirt roads and following orange and black paint blazes that looked like Halloween vandalism.

We noticed, too, that the Appalachian Trail took hikers over the more strenuous areas no matter what, while the routers of the Long Trail followed more sensible paths and inclines, attempting to make the hike as enjoyable as possible. What was more, in all the fifteen hundred miles of the Appalachian Trail we had walked so far, we saw only one Appalachian Trail Conference official and only one club member actually working to clear the Trail of overhanging brush. In the mere one hundred miles of the Long Trail, by contrast, we met nine members of the Green Mountain Club out hiking, working, surveying, and enjoying.

On the Appalachian Trail we passed one shelter after another with open trash pits, aluminum foil, and soda bottles strewn about. Nowhere on the Appalachian Trail had we seen a sign similar to the one on the Long Trail at Sherburne Pass:

> Since dumps draw flies, porkies and other
> varmints, the next six shelters are dumpless.
> Please burn what will and take the rest home
> with you or to the next road crossing trash
> can.

While traveling a country road down a mountainside one afternoon, we passed between a barn and a large white clapboard New England farmhouse. A dog ran up with a stick in his mouth. While we threw the stick, his mistress talked about Grandma Gatewood, whom she invited to stay overnight during a thunderstorm some time back. We heard many tales about Grandma Gatewood, who was sixty-seven years old when she first hiked the Trail from Georgia to Maine. The story was that she wore tennis shoes and curled up on the ground at night to sleep.

"I invited her in that night," the woman said, "because it was raining cats and dogs. Her sneakers were all wet and the water had ruined the watch she was wearing. I hunted around the house to find an old Timex to give her. When she left, she asked me for my address. As she was leaving, she told me I didn't dot my *i*'s, and winked."

The Dartmouth Outing Club maintained several locked cabins along this stretch of Trail. We persisted in tenting every night, since the cabins were in the same state of negligence as the shelters. One drizzly morning we awoke and uncovered our packs to get the stove. We had purposely leaned the packs against a pine as a protection from the rain. Under our ponchos was a woven nest of needles and grass. Some industrious creature spent a cozy night out of the rain. Such little worlds around us.

Man is not always so inventive. As we approached the Connecticut River early the following morning, we passed a lone hiker rolling up his sleeping bag under the cacophony of an Interstate highway overpass. The hiker, on his way down from Katahdin, said he couldn't figure out where to camp that night to get out of the rain. " 'Course, I didn't sleep much here," he said over the din of truck and car traffic.

Hanover was immediately across the Connecticut River, the longest body of water in New England. As we crossed the open girder bridge from Vermont, we gave little thought of the river's length. "Yea!" we shouted, waving our arms like revolutionaries.

Then, two blocks into our thirteenth state, Julia doubled over in pain.

The map shows the Appalachian Trail through New Hampshire with the following labeled locations: Gorham, Madison Hut, Tuckerman Ravine, Lakes of the Clouds Hut, Mt. Washington, Galehead Hut, Zealand Falls Hut, Mizpah Hut, Mt. Lafayette, Mt. Garfield, Crawford Notch, Franconia Notch, Great Bear Cabin, Mt. Moosilauke, Wachipaauka Pond, Glencliff, Woodstock, Hanover. Also labeled: Vermont, Connecticut River, Maine, New Hampshire. Scale: 1"=22 Miles.

New Hampshire

154 MILES

The interlock of time and place could not have been more fortunate: we had planned to stay in Hanover anyway, but not at the hospital. Julia's system was malfunctioning, and the doctor recommended bed rest and further exploration into the matter. On the morning of August 2, we had the doctor's promise that in six days we would be back on the Trail.

177

The life of a woman on the Appalachian Trail is no Miss America Pageant. We were to learn that of 179 thru-hikers since the initiation of the Trail in the 1920's only 24 were women. Our experience had attested to the scarcity of women hikers. Believers in the equality of the sexes, nevertheless we had to admit that physical differences were important on the trail, and affected our hiking.

The jolt of strenuous sections, such as Priest Mountain in Virginia, combined with oppressive heat, complicated menstrual cycles. On some occasions we would have to make quick plans for a stopover to reach a drugstore. These incidents were minor, that is, until the first appearances of severe cramping. Now we were waylaid by an unforeseen emergency. Fortunately, we had come to the right town at the right time. The Mary Hitchcock Hospital in Hanover was well equipped, and the doctors competent and professional. We were no longer merely administering to blisters, and we were thankful that we reached Hanover when we did. Had these undiagnosed pains occurred in the White Mountains, Julia's life could very well have been at stake.

Many times we envisioned ourselves in circumstances that could have been extremely dangerous. The isolation of many parts of the Trail set a grim stage for broken arms, sprained ankles, concussions. All that was needed to trigger the danger was a misplaced step, a loose rock, the eating or drinking of contaminated food or water. The risks of being remote from expert medical help were none too slight. Now that we were approaching the White Mountains, especially the Presidential Range above tree line where the weather could wreak havoc upon unsuspecting hikers, we were doubly aware of the hazard involved.

The Mary Hitchcock Hospital was one of the best in New England. With minimum bother and form-filling, we made an appointment, had Julia's pain diagnosed and treated. She was released in three days, and ordered to convalesce another three.

We had heard from several sources that the Thayer Hall cafeteria on the Dartmouth College campus was a bonanza for Appalachian Trail hikers. The meals were served on an all-you-can-eat basis, an Eldorado mother lode. Lunch and dinner were reasonably priced. Breakfast at one dollar probably put the cafeteria in the red.

The extra days we spent in Hanover were an investment in ourselves. The rest reinvigorated our bodies, deterred apprehension about further emergencies, and reinforced our determination to continue the Trail. We regained strength and confidence.

Under the doctor's strict orders, we forfeited two small mountains directly outside Hanover for flatter terrain. Nonetheless, the strain of carrying even a half-empty pack was an ordeal for the ex-patient after five days of bed rest. We sent quite a few articles home in preparation for the steep White Mountains ahead. Among these items were a spatula, Boy Scout signal mirror, plastic bottles, flower and tree books, sun lotion, and large Band-Aids. Most of these, except for the books, we rarely used. This "fall cleaning" lightened our packs noticeably.

The Trail was as we had left it, muggy, muddy, and mosquitoey. We passed more hikers from Maine. Along with their stories of fresh trout and moose, they told of unrelenting rainstorms. Two hikers said they had eliminated a forty-mile stretch before Monson, Maine, because the bogs were so bad. Steve suggested we concentrate on the immediate White Mountains and face the bogs when we came to them.

One particularly hot afternoon we broke clear of the woods and sat on an open bank of a gravel road away from the irritation of the mosquitoes. Julia found one four-leaf clover, gave it to Steve, then found another. All was right with the world.

A mile up the road, our four-leaf clovers went into action. Late in the afternoon we were uncertain of a campsite for the night. We turned into a side road with a sign: Camp Walt

Whitman. All we wanted was some water and a flat patch of grass to set up our tent. Instead, we were invited to a spaghetti dinner.

Ten minutes later, we were seated at a table of eight in a dining room of a hundred animated youngsters, all eyeing us as if we were movie stars. The camp director introduced us as "Two superhikers hiking all the way from Georgia to Maine." Applause filled the dining room. The counselor at our table informed us there hadn't been so much excitement since a man came to show slides on Red China.

To us this exuberant response was a great tribute, and we long remembered the recognition of these campers and their leaders. Each summer a group from this camp hiked Moosilauke, our next mountain peak. The children were backpackers, so we knew they appreciated the efforts of our hike. Many people along the way commented about our trek. Yet, after our initial explanation we were usually left with that empty feeling that they really didn't know what we were doing and what it meant to us.

That night the camp director introduced us to George, a geology professor from the University of North Carolina. George was renting a farmhouse at Camp Walt Whitman as a base for independent study of the surrounding mountains. He invited us to stay overnight. The house was pre–Civil War, and it had settled quite a lot since it was built. Ceilings were low, and the floors had long since buckled under. The house was surrounded by weeds and foliage. A damp wood odor greeted us as we stepped over missing floorboards. Inside were three cast iron stoves, a pump organ, a chest of exquisite goblets, and an antique mirror with silhouettes of Washington and Lincoln in bas relief on the copper frame. Cold beers and showers were gratefully received, since it had been unbearably mucky all day.

George hiked a lot himself, and told us that in the back of his mind he had always wanted to walk the Appalachian

Trail. He worked in the White Mountains in 1939 when Joe Dodge was the hutmaster at Porky Gulch. In commemoration of Joe Dodge's long service with the Appalachian Mountain Club, a new lodge was built at Pinkham Notch where he used to have his old cabin. "Yep, Joe was a great fellow," George reminisced. "I was up there again just a while ago. Things have really changed. Now you know what they call Lakes-of-the-Clouds Hut? Lakes-of-the-Crowds. And the hutboys are so different. When I was a hutboy, we used to really welcome the hikers and sit around and talk about the outdoors. Everybody was friendly then. They don't seem to care too much about the hiker now."

The next morning we dawdled to Wachipauka Pond. The heat was increasing with each August day, and we planned to jump in the pond the moment we reached it. No sooner were we standing ankle deep than we were under attack. Julia got it first. A pincer grabbed her big toe and hung on tenaciously. Steve retreated shoreward. Crawdads. In the shadow of each rock was a pair of claws.

By noon we reached Glencliff, a half-dozen houses two miles from the base of Mt. Moosilauke (4,810 feet). The sky was so besmirched with humidity that the upper mountainsides were hidden behind thick, heavy, hot air. The views from the top were heralded as some of the best ever. Our four-leaf clovers wilted. We sat under a giant black locust tree and dozed away the sticky afternoon. A hiker with a head-to-hip pack passed us. The heat seemed to buckle his knees as he plodded head down toward the Glencliff post office, a window at the rear of a private home.

From his long shaggy beard and khaki clothes we later recognized the same tired hiker in a newspaper photograph. He was Ed Kuni, the sixty-year-old outdoor conservation editor of the *Sunday–Independent* in Wilkes–Barre, Pennsylvania, and a director of the Appalachian Trail Conference. Ed was attempting to hike the entire Trail. An earlier attempt had been cut short when he was called back to Pennsylvania because his home had been destroyed by floods. We heard that this second time he suffered frostbite in the mountains of the South and had to be treated medically before continuing. The day we saw him, these setbacks showed clearly in his dogged hunched figure. He was heading home.

During this time we still followed the garish Dartmouth Outing Club Trail blazes. Just up the first slope of Moosilauke we stopped for the night at Great Bear Cabin. Permission to stay in the locked cabins is granted by the Outing Club at Robinson Hall in Hanover. We regretted not having asked for the key, since this cabin dominated an ideal setting and was well maintained. We decided that since a thunderstorm threatened, we wouldn't pitch the tent, but instead camp on the cabin porch.

That night we had two guests. The first was a hiker we met earlier in the day. He was out for a ten-day trip and was feeling the need for company. Consequently, he invited himself to share his dinner with us. Julia was suffering from over-exertion too soon after her illness, but our guest was bent on man-to-man talk with Steve. His name was Earl, and he was out soul-searching. He had changed from hiking khaki to civilian sweat pants. We both took one look at them and mentally calculated at least three pounds for this luxury change of clothing. "My father wants me to be . . . but I want to be . . . ." He went on and on as the steam from our stove filled the twilight air. What was wrong with us? Were we so aloof we couldn't speak to this jumbled soul? Perhaps we did not understand his purpose in hiking. He had wanted to get away from the city and solve some problems, to think. We could understand that. What we didn't understand was why he was talking. Over the porch rail was an incomparable evening, all rose and golden, the mountains a summer haze, in the distance the soothing burble of a brook. Yet this hiker would not be quiet and listen. Finally, our guest ambled off into the dark.

No sooner were we sweltering in our sleeping bags than the second uninvited guest jumped up. Brazenly, he climbed onto the porch and scratched at the packs. Our flashlights, always ready for emergencies, searched out the intruder. Once more we were faced with a bandit, the ever-hungry, ever-curious coon, this time the size of a bear cub.

Immediately, we realized we wouldn't have a moment's peace until we were zippered into our tent with our packs poncho-wrapped and Boy Scout secure. We had been through this scene before in Pennsylvania, and were aware of the odds. First, we heard the coon on the porch, no doubt surveying the situation. Next, he inspected the tree that held our food bag. Fortunately, we had enough experience to know that our food was coon-proof. Finally, he scampered to our tent. The packs were in front of the netting so we could keep an eye on them, but by this time we were so tired we left their fate to our four-leaf clovers. In the morning we discovered the coon had dropped his calling card a foot away from the packs. Coon Pu.

Moosilauke was our first significant mountain since Hanover. The climb was steep and slow over rocks and boulders. The doctors at Hanover had advised us to take it easy for the next couple of weeks. What we wanted to know was how to take it easy on a mountain peak of 5,000 feet. The air thinned and opened up the country for the ridge walk above tree line on the breezy summit. We were better able to see from the sheer ledges of Jim and Blue Mountains, secondary peaks of Moosilauke. The scene was reminiscent of Chinese landscape paintings. Mountains, cascades, sky, in tones of silver, dark blues and greens, imparted a misty Oriental feeling.

The descent of Moosilauke was the longest and most demanding of our hike thus far. A series of streams washed down rock and shale flumes. The Trail followed these thin ribbons of water. Our knees quivered. The guidebook mentioned we would be climbing down log ladders that might be slippery from the runoff. It failed to mention that most of these ladders were useless because three out of four rungs were missing. At times guy cable, strung like a clothes line, provided the only security from a fall. We inched down the mountainside. No wonder the kids from Camp Walt Whitman were awed by our trip.

Halfway down we succumbed to the sheets of water that slid down the blue-gray rock and sat under the ice-cold waterfalls that fell in terraced insouciance to rock bottom. At times like these we gave little thought to propriety, having only one thing in mind—relief from the tension and sweat of climbing. We streaked in and out of the waterfalls, able to stand only a few seconds of their invigorating pulse and flow.

At Lost River tourist attraction on Highway 12, the same river flows half a mile through a series of subterranean caves and potholes. From here we thumbed a ride into Woodstock for supplies. Greenwood Lake, New York, and Woodstock, New Hampshire, had a lot in common. They were both noisy, hot, congested tourist traps. We walked from the hundred-degree street at seven in the evening into the air-conditioned supermarket. Perhaps the manager would let us cook dinner in some out-of-the-way corner near the frozen vegetables. Instead, we sat on the baked asphalt and quickly ate our ice cream, scooping the melted corners before the entire brick was a creamy glob.

The nearest campground was private, expensive, and out of town. By this time Julia was feeling the strain of the climb and suffering from her weak condition. We decided to cross the street and camp in the school playground after dark. By nightfall one of us was hysterical and the other nearly so. First, we couldn't get the tent pegs into the soil, which was hard as rock. One peg after the other bent. The tent collapsed as the pegs sponged from the ground. Julia wept uncontrollably as Steve calmly did all the work. "Sit down," he commanded. "Take two aspirin and rest."

By ten we were inside the tent and suffocating from the heat. The down sleeping bags proved invaluable in the higher altitudes, but we were in the valley. It was still a hundred degrees, or felt like it, humid, and breezeless. We were finally in control of the situation when a bright beam flashed through the netting. Startled, we pulled the bags over us and peered out, on hearing the voice of The Law.

"You planning to stay the night?"

"Yes," we answered, as civilly as we could.

"Well, I guess I'll let you stay, but be out of here real early before anyone sees you."

We bade Justice good night and awoke in the morning to the sound of nearby bulldozers. As we left we passed a parade of wide-awake construction workers moving into the school grounds.

In the days to come our drive to reach the granite mountains of the Granite State propelled us onward. The twelve hundred square miles of the White Mountains Range make up the White Mountains National Forest under the jurisdiction of the United States Forest Service. The White Mountains are divided by Franconia Notch. South of the Notch rise the Franconia Mountains with Mt. Lafayette (5,249 feet) as the star. On the north side of the Notch rises the Presidential Range with Mt. Washington (6,288 feet) as superstar—the highest point in New Hampshire and the highest point on the Appalachian Trail north of Tennessee.

Lafayette Campground in Franconia Notch was overrun with vacationers. The only reason we were rewarded with a site was that we had no vehicle. Everyone else compensated for our deficiency. Most vehicles carried other vehicles— motorcycles, motorboats, bicycles, trailbikes. That night it rained so hard that even those with house trailers packed up and returned home the next morning. At times rain was an advantage. In this case, it deadened the constant truck and car traffic on Highway 3, a short, ill-planned distance away from the campground.

From this popular place we called ahead to Pinkham Notch

to make reservations for the huts at Lakes-of-the-Clouds, Madison and Carter Notch.

The four-mile Bridle Path led us up toward Greenleaf Hut at the foot of Mt. Lafayette. This path was not only the shortest, but since the hutboys—who did the work of maintaining the White Mountain way stations—used it to pack in supplies, it was also very well maintained. Loose soil was braced by pine and step-sized split logs. Most hutboys carried loads of eighty to a hundred pounds. Some carried more. These back-breaking records were regarded in the hut fraternity with obvious pride. We passed one of these American sherpas coming down from the hut. He wore a ladder-type wooden rack to which the supply boxes were lashed. Many hutboys referred to the sherpas of Nepal, often bragging that they carried more weight than these high-altitude porters, commonly known as "tigers," who carried supplies for Himalayan expeditions. What the hutboys failed to mention was that, even though the sherpas carried a mere sixty pounds, they were doing so at altitudes four times as great as that of Mt. Washington. Nonetheless, one hundred pounds is no small cargo, and the hutboys had a right to be proud.

Julia, who was feeling on top of the situation after a rest at Franconia Notch, passed two young male hikers huffing and puffing. They frowned and five minutes later, exerting themselves so as not to be out-hiked by a woman, passed us.

For us the White Mountains began with Mt. Lafayette. The morning we reached Greenleaf Hut forty-four people milled about. We were indeed in the heart of the most celebrated mountains in the northeast. Nevertheless, we heard so much about the grandeur of these peaks that we hoped the crowds would be inconsequential.

Sam, cook for that week at Greenleaf Hut, gave us a peanut butter and jam sandwich on freshly baked raisin bread. Hot chocolate and tea were provided for Presidential Range hikers at every hut for a dime. "We're supposed to help thru-hikers all we can," Sam said. "I'll even give you two sandwiches just so you don't tell me you left Georgia June 30. You know that Warren Doyle, who was trying to set a speed record? He made it to Katahdin. But what did he see?" It was the first we heard of Warren's success since we met him in New York.

The Appalachian Mountain Club operates eight huts of varying sizes in these mountains. These huts provide dinner and breakfast for overnighters at $15.25 ($1.50 extra if a trail lunch is included). Some huts are located in the more remote regions of the mountains, others, in the spotlight of popular demand. Greenleaf was an in-betweener. The stone hut was close to Highway 3, yet a stiff climb up the mountainside.

"The strenuous climb up the Old Bridle Path is a good sieve for eliminating the crummies of the world," Sam commented.

The starting hutboys were paid about $30 a week, and they were able to live the summer on the mountaintops away from the turbulence of big city life.

As we talked, the weather rolled in, covering the bare-boulder shoulders of Mt. Lafayette. Sam offered us a table to sleep on and dinner at a reduced rate. "We're making ice cream tonight," he said, but we declined the invitation, anxious to reach Garfield Pond by nightfall.

By the time we were back on the Trail, the swing of fickle weather once again wrapped Lafayette in a thick swirl of fog. The clouds wisped by, sometimes so dense we couldn't see the rock cairns which marked the trail. Often we confused the rocky landscape with the Trail. The cairns rose like lost Indian temples in the mist. The wind blew billows of clouds away from the mountain so that we could see the gulfs below and tiny Greenleaf Hut squatting beside a pocket mirror pond. Then the wind blew the clouds back again, opening and closing the scene faster than in a Shakespearean tragedy. In the distance lightning ignited the horizon. Ten seconds later the thunder rumbled up and over the boulders like a hurtling unseen roller coaster.

We began to doubt our decision to continue our climb as we met several people heading back down. Among them were the two male chauvinists who passed us on our way to the hut. "It's cold up there," they said, with apprehension in their eyes. "We're not taking any chances. It's started to rain, and you could get hypothermia."

We took careful notice of these two hikers retreating to the warmth of Greenleaf Hut, but with experienced eyes we looked to the weather and ourselves. We climbed on.

At the top of Lafayette the clouds suddenly cleared and the break filled with age-old crumbling mountains, stately and grand. The vision was unearthly. We were literally the only inhabitants of our earth. We turned onto the Garfield Trail along the top ridge, a wild lichen-green existence blown to smithereens by the wind, our windbreakers drawn tight around our faces, the sun dancing through the clouds. We met other hikers coming south. They were mountain people, scampering over the rocks, drunk with the fresh gulps of wind.

When we reached Garfield Pond, the shelter and tent sites were abandoned. The Appalachian Mountain Club (AMC) maintained twenty shelters and campsites in the White Mountains. Explicit information was published that listed tenting areas where fires could be built. The Forest Service acted as a bodyguard in enforcing these regulations. We had grown accustomed to finding our own water sources and tent sites all the way from Georgia. But not wanting to incur a twenty-five-dollar fine, we moved on. The sign that indicated the relocation of the shelter gave no mileage to the next tenting area. We dragged on, worried that darkness might envelop us in the mountains without water or a place to sleep. The area was too densely forested to allow us to break from the Trail, let alone find a clearing for our tent.

We climbed Garfield Mountain, pausing momentarily at an open spot on top of an old building foundation for the expansive view. In ten hours of hiking we had covered nine miles. In despair that the next sites were too far to make before nightfall, we came to a spring—and were relieved to find the trail leading to the tent platforms.

The caretaker showed us to a platform and collected a four-dollar fee. The receipt entitled us to stay at two other sites. This was the first tent platform we had slept on, and it was not to be the last. Instead of pegs, the tent was tied to eyescrews at the side of the raised structure. However, the platform was built to accommodate two small tents. Thus, a lot of rope was needed to secure the tent to the far side.

No matter how high and dry such a structure might seem, the ground is ninety per cent softer to sleep on than boards. Also, if you have to get up at night, you're likely to climb out the door and fall two feet to the ground. This particular platform was a delight to chipmunks, who made their home underneath and gathered leftover chow by the light of the silvery moon. Platform camping and the 109 people we counted on the Trail that day were ill omens.

The next day, while we were eating a piece of cold chicken and warm baked bread at Galehead Hut, the hutboy told us some of the reasons for the relocation of the shelter and platforms at Garfield Pond. The water was beginning to be polluted by overuse. Also, someone actually built a campfire on one platform and, naturally, it burned down.

Galehead overnighters were in for a good dinner that night. The kitchen help was preparing a large pork roast, a loaf of Greek bread, and some bottles of Chateauneuf du Pape. We dumped our chicken bones into the garbage barrel. "How do you dispose of this?"

"Compost," the hutboy said, "but we're trying different methods. At the Zealand Falls Hut they have trouble with bear, so they have a mechanical compost shredder. First, it was built into a pine case. Well, one morning they came out and the thing had been ripped to pieces. Bear. So the AMC built a fiberglass casing. Do you know that in three days that too was ripped to shreds?" Hut waste posed a crucial problem, especially with the number of people who walked the White Mountains.

"Any cats here?"

"Oh, sure, bobcat and lynx," the hutboy said. "What we've been seeing lately is called a coydog. It's getting more and more common. People bring their dogs up here. They get lost and mate with coyotes."

The walk to Mt. Guyot (4,589 feet) opened another splay of the White Mountains, and still another squadron of rough cumulus lumbering across the sky. Winds prevailed and the clouds sped at fantastic rates above us. We wished we were making their time. Farther on, the Trail edged Zeacliff Ridge. We sat on a slide of granite to marvel at the wondrous peaks, valleys and gorges of the Appalachians. No less than thirty mountains jagged the horizon.

We were not yet above the tree line. To get there we would have to come down into Crawford Notch, and then ascend into the Presidentials. Still, from the outset at Mt. Lafayette, we had noticed a change, not only in the flora and fauna, but the geological structure of the mountains. During the Ice Age, several of these peaks were so high that the glaciers which covered the region passed beneath them. Certain plant species that grow in unglaciated Alpine and subarctic conditions are found on these New Hampshire peaks.

Bunch berries were profuse, along with diapensia, a relative of the galax we walked through in the Smokies. Most of the bunch berries were at the flowering stage, for early summer just reached these mountains now in August. Three-toothed cinquefoil also was common. These alpine plants were low, and hugged the ground, like the juncos that accompanied us. Everywhere, the pines were twisted and pushed flat by the wind. No dunce pine caps here. "Get down, here comes another blast!" So year after year the pines crouched lower.

Perhaps our stiffest adversary, apart from the crowds in the White Mountains, was the unrelenting wind. Cooking became a challenge. Hiking hour after hour in a wind crossfire sapped our energy. Most of the time we wore our nylon hoods, gloves and sunglasses, which enabled us to see better, not because of the sun, but because they protected our eyes from the wind.

Invariably, we were befriended by a junco or two. These birds have to be the hardiest mountaineers in the world. They are found at elevations of six thousand feet in weather conditions intolerable to man. They hop along the ground, plucking a seed from a crowberry here, eating a kernel of mountain sedge there, quite cheerfully at home in a gale. Their bodies might be said to resemble the yin-yang circle, their white breasts looping around the slate gray body.

Zeacliff Ridge rose above a ravine and a large pond covered with lily pads. We speculated about the possibility of leaving the Trail and completely losing ourselves in the White Mountains. They seemed endless, barren, and wild. That pond looked completely isolated and inaccessible. In fifteen minutes we clambered off the ridge and came to a sign: *Water*. Some hikers had scratched in the paint with their knives: "Don't believe it. Don't trouble." We were low on water, however, and followed the sign. Besides, could you seriously trust graffiti?

After ten minutes of downhill climbing on a blue-blaze trail, we ended up at the stagnant lily pond we had thought was so inaccessible. True, it was water, but potable water it was not. Exhausted, we dragged back up the ridge and tromped on, roused by the thoughtless antics of hiking clubs and administrative bodies—no mileage posted, no identification of the condition of the water. Even a moose wouldn't have drunk from that pond.

The yellow and turquoise snake coiled on a boulder in the

rays of setting sunlight wasn't upset by the water situation. Taking his advice, we enjoyed the Zeacliff Ridge, which bordered the canyon.

Across the mighty chasm parallel to our course, a speck of red moved in the line of trees. A backpacker made his way along an abandoned railroad bed to Crawford Notch. That pinpoint of red, that nearly invisible ion of hiker color, served notice that man's physical stature against the tableau of a magnificent canyon, let alone against the entire cosmos, might very well be more a thought than a thing. Here we stood on high, feeling spunky with the power of looking down on nature. Tomorrow we, too, would be ionized inside that great ravine.

We came down from the mountains, and on Route 302 hitched a ride to Bartlett for supplies. Our driver was a thru-hiker who had dropped out in Pennsylvania. We didn't blame him. That state was enough to put anyone out of commission. "I was really going to stop in Pennsylvania and start from the other end in Maine," he said. "But I just never made it. I'm sorry now I didn't get back on the Trail." We wondered how many like him had started and then dropped out. With equal awe we were amazed at what kept us going.

For us, the most difficult climb of the Presidential Mountain Range was the two-thousand-foot ascent from Crawford Notch to the summit of Mt. Webster (3,910 feet). On the way up we passed several hikers sprawled by the Trail. One trio, two boys and a girl, had persevered to the jagged stone cliffs jutting out above tree line. One boy gave the girl a hand while the other pushed. She was complaining bitterly and expressed regret for having undertaken the endeavor.

One of the boys took out his U.S. Geological Survey map and said that according to his calculations we had passed the summit of Mt. Webster and were nearing Mt. Jackson (4,052 feet). Only a mile later did we reach the Mt. Webster summit cairn and marker. We were savvy to the perils of hiking and hoped the kids we passed had the sense either to backtrack or speed up.

Thirteen miles of the Presidentials were in that no-man's land of the "tension zone," a term ecologists use to define growth above tree line. What we commonly referred to as "weather" was given free rein on these unprotected peaks. On Mt. Washington the wind exceeded hurricane force (75 miles per hour) 104 days of the year. Scientists atop Mt. Washington have clocked wind velocity at an assaulting 231 miles per hour. The summit is in the clouds 60 percent of the time. We were lucky because August is the month when Mt. Washington's temperatures are most favorable, a balmy 16 to 55 degrees.

Once on the ridge, we sped up our mile-an-hour pace. Unfortunately, we passed over Webster and Jackson Mountains in the clouds. We arrived at Mizpah Hut at six o'clock, just as thirty-five overnighters awaited the dinner bell. Mizpah Hut was the only restricted area that provided tent platforms for hikers in the Presidential Range. We signed up for the last platform and the caretaker led us outside through a sparse pine break to our accommodations. One brilliant orange tent was already set up on the platform. Its occupants looked up at us with as much distaste for our intrusion as we felt for theirs. "Last one," the hutboy said, expecting us to show enthusiasm for being so lucky.

"But we aren't supposed to set up our tent with theirs on the same platform?"

"This is all that's left. Sometimes we have to put three tents on one platform. That's the procedure."

"There must be some spot on the ground around here."

"The Forest Service permits tenting only in designated areas, and the platforms were built for this purpose."

"All right," we acquiesced. The hutboy left, satisfied that we'd share the site. The platforms were squashed into the spruce growth so tightly that, literally, only one foot was free for walking the ground between the platform and the trees. The site was intolerable.

Not for one moment did we go along with such camaraderie. Quietly, we packed up our gear and walked back to a site someone else had used off the trail. It was tight, but soon our tent and a makeshift awning were up. It threatened rain, not an extraordinary event. Our stroganoff was cooking and orange tapioca jelled in our insulated cups.

Suddenly, the caretaker popped through the branches into the clearing. "I'm sorry to tell you that you really can't do this. I'm warning you for your own protection. A forest ranger makes his rounds after dinner and he can fine you twenty-five dollars."

We then explored the quagmire of uncertainty and lack of planning by both the U.S. Forest Service and the Appalachian Mountain Club. In the need to protect the Presidential Range from the onslaught of people and misuse of the land, no alternatives were provided for experienced hikers not wishing, or not wealthy enough, to stay at the huts. Only four tent platforms were available from Crawford Notch to Pinkham Notch, a popular section of mountains, and one that invites an overnight under the stars.

"I must admit," the caretaker told us, "that the hutboys are prejudiced against tenters. Some people just aren't educated enough to live in the woods."

"Why build platforms?" we asked. "They take up as much space as ground sites."

"They're much better adapted to preserving the plant life," the caretaker said, authoritatively.

Our dander was up. Nevertheless, we bowed to authority and returned to the platform. But, we wondered, what if those three inexperienced hikers from Mt. Webster were to come along and couldn't afford nearly fifty dollars for the hut? Where would they sleep? Would they be sent on to Pinkham Notch because there were no more platforms?

Back at the tent platform, the other occupants had left temporarily. They returned laughing and talkative. The light from their flashlight landed on our tent and they mumbled, "Oh, Jesus, we got company." Our exact sentiments.

In our journals that day we wrote: "We have never been refused or evicted from any campsite in over 1,700 miles. The AMC of the White Mountains was first to have this honor. We are pissed." Even the police officer in Woodstock let us stay in the school yard when he saw that our tent was up and we were disturbing no one.

On the other hand, we recognized that the concept of recreation management needed to be implemented. The White Mountains National Forest was unique in that most of the Presidentials were above tree line. Again, unlike most of the other national parks and forests, the White Mountains had multiple, uncontrolled access points. The increased use and abuse of this area forced the AMC and the Forest Service to plan public use of this mountain country according to principles similar to those of urban planners.

However, we tried to put these contentions behind us. The hiking was engrossing enough to take our minds from the problems of environmentalists. Perhaps nowhere else had the modern world affected our hike more than in these mountains.

Once past Mizpah Hut, we followed the ridge above tree line. The sign posted at the beginning of this section indicated the danger:

STOP

The area ahead has the worst
weather in America. Many have died
there from exposure even in the summer.
Turn back *now* if the weather is bad.

U.S. Forest Service
Dept. of Agriculture

We seriously considered the sign and attempted to evaluate the elements. It was foggy, rainy, cold, windy, and damp. Visibility was less than twenty feet. Nevertheless, the weather was not the worst we had seen, and the Lakes-of-the-Clouds Hut was only four miles away. We didn't meet one hiker (or any other moving object) until we arrived at Mt. Monroe, when a single file of long-legged maidens came gamboling down the mountainside. Their bare legs and joyous spirits cheered us up in such foul weather. Soon we were inside the Lakes-of-the-Clouds Hut sipping hot chocolate.

"You sure don't look like typical AT-ers," Bruce the hutmaster observed. "They're always so grubby and never look healthy. Most of them come in here bedraggled and complaining about the White Mountains."

It must have been a matter of degree, because we felt draggle-tailed ourselves (but kept our complaints in reserve). One by one other hikers straggled in, shivering and wet, and went off to find the perfect bunk in the segregated sleeping quarters. They quickly returned to the dining room where it was warmer. On such a gloomy day we at least expected a fire in the hut's potbellied stove. Our clothes were soaked.

The din became louder, and we retreated into a corner.

> *Well, I've walked the Green Mountains*
> *and I've walked the White*
> *with not a thing in mind, Lord,*
> *except their height.*
> *And I met a hundred people in a single day.*
> *Would you believe I took this hike to get away?*

Later the hutmaster talked with us. (He wore a bright red construction hat for cooking and a golf cap for serving.) "This is one of the nicer days," he said as if we were in Florida. "Might even clear up by tomorrow." A group from a boys' camp arrived, adding to the general pre-dinner commotion. We paged through the register to pass time. It read like a high school yearbook. "Gee, I really think this place is swell." "The hutboys are dreamy—Susan." "Fred Smith was Here." We were looking for the familiar $\wedge$ sign used by thru-hikers, but in the scribbles only spotted one or two.

Dinner consisted of spicy oregano homemade soup, chicken, potatoes, rolls, tossed salad, and gingerbread. We raced to each side of the server and unashamedly cleaned our plates twice.

Lakes-of-the-Clouds Hut was the largest and most used of the White Mountains huts. It was situated 1¼ miles from the summit of Mt. Washington, the prime attraction of the Presidentials. The weather that whipped over Washington was the most severe in the continental United States. The jeopardy of climbing to the summit amid the vagaries of the weather still does not deter hikers. Many of them, either ill-prepared or unknowledgeable, fall victim to the erratic climate. Hundreds have suffered frostbite and worse. From 1849 to 1976 eighty-three people have died on Mt. Washington.

At 6:40 A.M. a band of pots, pans, and harmonica woke us up. Nearly everybody was energetic and gung-ho to climb the mountain. We had climbed so many that even Mt. Everest would not have seemed out of the ordinary.

Breakfast was comparable to what we ourselves would have cooked, and a come-down after dinner: lots of starch, no bacon or eggs. A speech on folding the cot blankets was imposed on us along with a demonstration. "First, shake out all crawling matter. The blanket will weigh eight pounds lighter. Next, make one fold, like this. If you're a daring type, you can do it like this. [Laughs, as the hutboy gives the blanket an expert flip.] Now you should have four pretty folds on one side and raggedy edges on the other. Place the raggedy edges away from the door. After all, how would you like to see a ratty old blanket the first time you stepped in the door?"

Waiting for the swirls of clouds to sweep away from the rugged summit, and hoping that the famed peak would perform a striptease, kept the people inside Lakes-of-the-Clouds Hut dashing to the windows. A youngster would shout, "Hey, I can see it!" But the clouds would pour over the top faster than we could run. An hour later, the rumor spread that the latest weather report indicated clear skies. The hope shattered when someone surmised this meant the valley floor, and certainly not whimsical Mt. Washington.

Julia had promised the crew a morning flute concert. In order to be inconspicuous she scrunched into a corner and played among the hubbub of dishes and departing hikers. Immediately, an ominous silence descended on the hut. Dishes stopped clanking. People stopped putting on their packs. Hutboys quit joking. After nearly twenty-four hours of constant noise, the resounding echo of flute-song filled the silence.

The clouds evaporated over Mt. Washington. The flute player seemed to be enticing the mountain away from its shroud and out into the sunshine. When the concert was over, a little boy walked up and, enraptured by the music, in a high voice said distinctly, "That was very good."

In three minutes the Lakes-of-the-Clouds Hut was evacuated. We joined the rush to the top, knowing the temperamental nature of these mountains. We climbed the boulder nose-cone in sunshine that opened up the yawning valleys like the bomb-bay doors in B–59s. As expected, the clouds moved in when we reached the summit Tip Top House. Among the records established by the nearby meteorological station, which is anchored to the mountain with heavy cables, was the deepest snowfall for the peak. It occurred in the 1968–69 season and totaled 556.4 inches. The highest temperature recorded on the summit was 71 degrees. The day we were there, August 16, Mt. Washington's summit was a warm 55 degrees, with winds west to northwest at 18 miles per hour.

A pack shelter (like a hitching post for backpacks) ranged one wall of the summit lodge. We walked across the Mt. Washington Cog Railroad tracks and, peering over the edge,

saw very little. The cog railroad puffed to the top, climbing
one foot for every four forward (at one point it angles 37
degrees), and unloaded passengers.

To us the passengers were incomprehensible. Dressed in
city duds, they immediately entered the Tip Top House,
bought post cards, and headed for the restaurant, without
taking a single whiff of mountain air before their ride down.
They would miss the crowberries and friendly juncos with
their gray and white paneled square-dance skirts. Perhaps the
passengers would catch the panorama of Mts. Clay and Jefferson, which had come from the shadow box and into the sun.
However, would they experience that ancient, timeless pilgrimage, walking away from the observatory and looking
back to find the hot coffee, post cards, and chichi tourist
attractions transformed by the fog into a Machu Picchu tem-
ple of the Andes? The cairns were lichen-covered pyramids
built by the faithful tribes of Asia. All right, perhaps this was
just the Appalachian Trail through the White Mountains of
New Hampshire, but that was enough.

We had made reservations to stay overnight at Madison
Hut, but decided to get a reduced rate by sleeping on the
tables. Fortunately, the Madison Hut policy was more open-
ended than that of Mizpah. We were given a campsite by a
stream that flowed down the mountain. As a precautionary
measure, our names and addresses were kept on file at the hut.
It was ten steep minutes to the site. Someone had chopped
down a couple of pine trees and built a log bench. Some of
the brush was hacked down, but we did not consider this an
act of vandalism. If the site had been any smaller, there would
have been no room for a tent.

What we did consider an abuse was a pile of human offal
deposited in the center of the Trail and decorated wantonly
with toilet paper. We reported the scene to the Madison hutmaster and were asked to do our best in cleaning up the mess
on the way back. In such instances, we could hardly blame

the AMC hutboys for their opinion of tenters. Even animals, except for the maladroit coon at the Dartmouth Outing Club Cabin back at Mt. Moosilauke, were neater in their excretory processes.

We walked up to the hut for dinner. Chicken. Although it tasted good, we wished the huts would co-ordinate their meals so that hikers would not be eating the same courses two and three nights in a row. The Madison Hut had an entirely different atmosphere from that at Lakes-of-the-Clouds. The hutboys were slightly crazy. Who wouldn't be, feeding fifty people every night? For each course the hutmaster blew his whistle. The ten at the table behind us scarffed up food as if there were no tomorrow. Not even we could keep up with them. They consumed ten large serving dishes of beets. We overheard the hutboy say, "I mean, it's true, all you can eat, but remember, every plate has to be empty before you leave."

At the end of the meal another blow from the whistle and a shout resounded from the kitchen: "Alka–Seltzer!"

Doug, the hutmaster, MC'd the after-dinner routine among his energetic kitchen crew:

"Hey, Doug, is it all right for the guests to use the blankets?"

"Yes, they can open the blankets on the bunks because we'll show them how to fold them in the morning. [Laughs]"

"Hey, Doug, what time is sunset?"

"Just before it gets dark. [Laughs]"

"Hey, Doug, are there any more beets?"

"Beats me. [Laughs]"

"Hey, Doug, what'll we serve at nine o'clock tonight?"

"Coffee, tea, cocoa, and leftover beets. [Boos]"

A couple we met on the trail that afternoon showed us a few rock specimens they picked up. From Mt. Clay we saw them scrambling off the Trail toward a pure white rock outcrop. Several of these were set off from the otherwise gray formations. They thought this specimen was granite, but one of the hutboys, a student of geology, dispelled their illusions when he identified it as white quartzite.

We also presented the budding geologist with what we believed an invaluable fossil no larger than a fingernail. We spotted this specimen while walking in a reverie from the remotest periods of glaciation to modern man. Our disappointment was intense as we learned that what could have been a trilobite was melted buckshot. To cheer us up, the hutboy added that it was *very old* buckshot.

Mt. Madison is a jet-nosed peak, composed of beachball rocks, millions of them piled like display oranges. When we reached the top, we dropped a pebble down the side to test whether the peak was as perilous as it looked. It wasn't.

For the last two days we walked in sight of Tuckerman Ravine. This dramatic glacier cirque, like a mountain chute, is a thousand feet deep, half a mile wide, and a mile in length. Daring skiers weave over its snows until late May, though avalanches are common. When the snows melt, the resulting river often forms what is called a "snow arch" spanning the ravine. One such arch was measured at 266 feet long, 84 feet wide and 40 feet high. Crossing the arch is an adventure of courage. The extreme danger involved has already taken one life.

Our last day in the Presidentials was sunny, the sky van Gogh blue. We came down out of the White Mountains and into Pinkham Notch, local headquarters of the Appalachian Mountain Club. Thru-hikers regard Pinkham Notch as an official sign-in station. A special register was provided for Appalachian Trail hikers. We were not properly dressed or mentally prepared for hashing out our ideas on recreation management just then. Later, however, we were to air our opinions with Joel White, the hut system manager, and Ken Olsen, recreation management director of communications. Ken explained that the number of hikers in the White Mountains was phenomenal. The AMC recently added a think-tank researcher to focus solely on recreation management problems.

More than 35,000 people stay overnight at the huts each year. At $16.75 per person, which includes a trail lunch, the collection of funds from huts could total $586,250. Hutboys are paid salaries of about $120 a month. In addition, the dues from the 18,000 AMC membership are spent on maintaining trails, payment of the trail crew, and helicopters for removing sewage from the huts. With porridge and pancakes for breakfast, and other shortcuts, the AMC's expenses seem unlikely to total nearly $600,000.

The need for the hut system would be obvious to anyone who has hiked with the crowds along the Presidential Range. A majority of the people in the mountains these days prefer a hot dinner prepared by someone else, a solid roof overhead at night, and a hot breakfast the next morning. Certainly, such luxuries eliminate backaches from overloaded packs and reduce the wear and tear on mountain tundra that requires decades to restore once it has been scarred by the mindless and inexperienced.

An AMC official in Boston later explained that increasing numbers are using the outdoors. The AMC is involved in satisfying the interests of the majority. Nevertheless, the club might do well to follow the premise of its own raison d'être, indeed, a tenet of our whole society, namely, to assure this same priority to minority members, those who wish minimal organization in the outdoors.

As far as tenting is concerned, the AMC states, "There are no new sites planned for tenting in the Presidential Range. There does exist a shortage for facilities for backpackers. However, we do not know of any suitable sites for new facilities."

Time after time we heard from officials those tired phrases —nobody knows the solution, the situation is all confused. For how long? The most graphic anomaly was told us at Mizpah

Hut. "We're trying to stop erosion of the environment," the caretaker said. Two days later we saw the entire side of Wildcat Mountain blatantly—but profitably—scarred with the gargantuan swaths of ski trails. That's stopping the erosion of the White Mountains?

In across-the-table talks with representatives of the AMC we proposed the incorporation of an arrangement similar to the system of caretakers and primitive campsites operated by the Green Mountain Club of Vermont. Dissemination of information on lesser-known trails; also, promoting use of the area in early spring and late fall might relieve the problem.

For example, after we came down from the White Mountains and crossed the Androscoggin River, the number of hikers dwindled to an occasional loner. This section of New Hampshire was equally appealing, and just as rugged and wild, as the Presidentials.

As for us, we had paid full admission. The crowds were gone. Now we had the house to ourselves.

Rangeley

Big Ho.
Mt.

New Hampshire

Maine

Sabbath
Day Pond

Black Brook

Umbagog
Valley

Squirrel Rock Lean-to

Upton

Mountain Brook

Bald Pate
Mtn.

Grafton Notch

Old Speck Pond
and Mountain

Mahoosuc
Notch

Sunday River

Bethel

Maine

278 MILES

To long-distance hikers all Maine is divided into three parts —Mahoosuc Notch, the swamps, Mt. Katahdin. Mahoosuc Notch, the cutting edge of tripartite Maine, is a boulder-filled gorge a little less than a mile long that takes most hikers three to four hours to negotiate. No hiker coming south described this gorge except in vague terms like "It's something, all right," followed by facial contortions and ambiguous exhalations.

No wonder we entered Maine with creeping trepidation. The guidebook touted the first two days of hiking from the New Hampshire–Maine border to Grafton Notch as the most strenuous since Stekoah in North Carolina. The spectre of Mahoosuc clouded our expectations of wilderness Maine, but once deeper into the state we saw firsthand the splendors of the high ridges. We walked miles of balds and open summits from where we saw the Presidential Range and the White Mountains to the south. As we climbed the south peak of Goose Eye Mountain (3,795 feet), we rested on a wild blueberry and cranberry patch in the sun. Once again we were losing ourselves to the woods. The city noises were gone and, in fact, the cities themselves. We climbed several extremely steep rock sides that demanded fingertip control and careful footing, but this was preparation for Mahoosuc Notch.

The one steep mile descent into the Notch, a pinched and jumbled ravine, brought us to two girls who hiked through from the other direction. They sat under a canopy of conifers and were eating peanut butter and jelly sandwiches. "Where does it begin?" we asked.

"Right down there," one of them said, pointing. "We started at noon and just finished."

It was three o'clock. "Pretty rough?"

"Yeah," they said, "but you should have it easy. Your packs look lighter. We're carrying about thirty-five pounds apiece. We had to take ours off all the time to climb over the boulders. You have to climb through tunnels. It's crazy."

"How do you know when you've finished?"

"Oh, believe us, you'll know."

From all the buildup the Notch sounded as if it were second cousin to the Grand Canyon. In reality, it was a muddle of jagged mountain-face rocks that had fallen from the sheer cliffs above.

We entered the Notch with our spirits high for the challenge and immediately faced a butt of boulders. Gingerly, we climbed over them and faced another set. Over these we climbed and faced another. Up and over, to the side, around the edges, across the ledges we climbed, creeping slowly, holding each other for safety, pushing and pulling each other for help. The Trail was blazed through rock tunnels scarcely large enough for our bodies, let alone our packs. Going was slow.

The sun was hot and bright, but the Notch was fifteen degrees cooler than the ridges. Huge chunks of ice trapped from last winter were lodged beneath the boulders. Farther on we heard the echoes of a subterranean river.

At times we walked on crumbling earthfill between rocks. Gloves protected our hands when our grips slipped. The only time we were forced to remove our packs came when the trail led us through a block of boulders that stretched across the entire Notch. The passageway was too steep and narrow for packs and bodies together, so we took off our packs and pushed ourselves and gear up and over, all the while hearing the gurgling of the underground torrent.

No number of geologic eras during which the boulders of Mahoosuc Notch had not budged an inch could stave off the wild thoughts of having the caves we crawled through suddenly collapse, squashing us before we finished the Trail, or worse, half-squashing us. We hurried through those dark dripping caverns with the river rumbling beneath us and the prospect of an earthquake a dreadful moment ahead.

Figuring our linear progress was impossible since we climbed vertically as much or more than we progressed horizontally. However, the girls were right. The end of the Notch came when the river broke into the open. "You're almost finished when you can see the river," the girls had said. The Notch took us exactly two hours to maneuver. Had we a bottle of champagne we would have christened the gorge in style. As it was, we simply renamed it Mahoosuc Crotch.

When we read in the guidebook that Mahoosuc Notch was one of a pair, we found an open beech forest and camped for the night. The morning dawned, and down the hill we went through brown leaves and gray trunks to a branch of the Sunday River, where we washed in the cold water like an Adam and Eve.

Luckily, Mahoosuc Notch Two was merely the emerging Trail from Notch One. The climb was steady, but easier, to a set of summits in the Mahoosuc Range before the descent to Old Speck Pond. At the lean-to there the caretaker, a hefty mountain girl, was the only official woman on her own we ever saw on the Trail. Unfortunately, the New Hampshire and Maine caretakers had reliable information only about their own shelters. Not one was able to tell us of nearby food sources. For all we knew, we could have been in the Yukon Territory.

From the summit of Old Speck Mountain (4,250 feet) to Grafton Notch is a descent of more than 2,600 feet in 1.65 miles. Later we learned that a newly constructed Trail followed a more gradual descent than the one we took. By the time we reached Maine Highway 26, our knees trembled uncontrollably, like unmolded jello. What Mahoosuc Notch did to our arms, Old Speck did to our knees.

No longer were we within a stone's throw of small towns. Bethel, which by the map seemed to be the only town large enough to have a store, was twenty miles away. On the highway we found cars were as rare as towns, but finally we were on the front lawn of a Bethel church and about to spoon into a half gallon of fudge ripple when a man shouted, "You can't sit here. This is private property. It belongs to my tourist home, and I just mowed the lawn."

The man did not know about Old Speck. We jangled our weary knees across the street to the hot asphalt of the IGA market. We tried not to notice another man approaching, although his dapper figure and mustache looked like less trouble.

"You kids on the Trail?"

We nodded with mouthfuls of fudge ripple.

"Wonderful," he said. "You must have legs of iron. Tell you what, I'll take you back to the Trail."

Walter Cherry and his wife, Emily, drove us twenty miles out of their way to the Trail at Mt. Baldpate (3,812 feet) simply because we were hikers and tonight was a sunset they didn't want to miss. "I've hiked all these mountains around here," Walter said. "I know them and love them. This valley is twenty thousand years old, and sometimes in my more mystical moments I like to think that when I die my soul will be around here."

As we drove, the two of them pointed out the direction of lush waterfalls and little-known campsites screened from the highway. If only we had a couple of extra days . . . .

"I used to climb up the north side of Old Speck when I was younger," Walter said. "My father and I would follow the flume in the spring and watch the surge of new water crash down that mountain."

Before we stepped back onto the Trail, he added, "We envy you your trip. You've seen a lot of wonders."

Those few words remained with us. He was right and he said it right. We indeed saw a lot of wonders in all fourteen states, in fact, every day. The wonders were as magnificent as the 150-year-old white pine tree we slept by two nights later, but also included the four-inch Indian pipes we saw in Virginia. The wonders were as mighty as the Presidential Range, as delicate as British soldier lichens that grew under the umbrellas of scarlet saucer mushrooms. The wonders were everywhere, from the thunderous weather in Georgia to the wispy fog of the Great Smokies and the brilliance of Mt. Greylock in Massachusetts. All we had to do was to see what myriad life forms and shapes and colors we walked through. It was easy, once we unlocked our eyes and resurrected the spirits of our growing-up days. We did this early on the Trail, but Walter Cherry in Maine helped to define the perspective.

No less a wonder was Mountain Brook, sumptuous in its gold water purling over the rocks, melting like clear wax into crystalline pools. It flowed over moss-splotched boulders in a mansion of pines, maples, and hemlocks. In the morning the brook woke us ever so gently. It was difficult to distinguish between its rising vapor and satiny sounds. Maple leaves in one of its pools reflected chartreuse. Greens and browns and reds were uncontrollably brilliant as the sun rose an eastern fan through the woods. The day was perfect, the lesson familiar: a delight of long-distance hiking was that the days picked you instead of the reverse. The nights, too.

MINOAN MOON

My favorite enters,
young and pale at the sacrificial center.
Earth moves slowly, faster, charges.
I watch the bull-leaper tense,
grab the horned mountains and
vault safely to the other side.

My love is captive.
My love is alive.

The wonders continued to unfold, not the least of them the six red bunch berries conspicuous in those Maine woods. We passed another friend, Black Brook, a distinguished wide cavalier of a brook that gave us deep pools of bubbles and polished rock faces. The bubbles tingled our perspiring faces as we opened our eyes underwater to see the pebbles magnified. For a quarter-hour we sat in the middle of this cascade to watch the chocolate browns and moss greens slide off the boulders in never-ending succulent textures.

One rich day after another opened upon us. The morning shade was cold, but the sunlight, warm. Robust stands of paper birch, with sunlight shredding through unrolled bark, fluttered their leaves in the distance. Some maples, speeding toward autumn, were topped with leaves as red as rubies. The woods were so quiet we heard the brushing of an oak leaf against a neighboring pine.

The climb down Old Speck caused a setback in Julia's side. The pain that subsided after Hanover now returned, so we walked the valley floor awhile. It was windy, foggy, and cold, but the change of scenery reassured us. We walked past fields of wild asters and goldenrod. Eventually, the sun shimmered through the fog, spotlighting old apple trees offering their fruit.

At Fred's General Store in Upton, we could tell by Fred's answers that a hard New England winter was expected. "Got any cheese, Fred?"

"Humph."

"Say, how far is it by the Andover B Hill Road to the Appalachian Trail?"

Fred departed into the back room. We picked up our supplies and waited until he finished whatever he was doing. Then, wordless as Fred, we squared our debt with Fred's General Store.

Since neither of us was feeling particularly chipper, we plopped down at a convenient picnic table overlooking Umbago Valley, a treasure of sunlight, lakes, and meadows. We fixed a second breakfast of wild applesauce—which, despite the worms, was tasty with cinnamon—and lightweight brown sugar substitute.

On the Trail at Squirrel Rock Lean-to, we stopped for lunch, but the flies around the trash drove us on. Comments were tacked on the wall of the shelter:

8/9 Good shelter. Nice snake lives in the fireplace.

8/15 Heading for Katahdin. Thoroughly disgusted with all the garbage, cans, and glass around here. This place needs some "Carry-in Carry-out" signs. Then hopefully a few clowns might wise up. We're taking out as much as we can, but it would take a dumptruck to clean this place up.

8/15 This place is gross!

A few hours later we crossed the narrow connecting outlet between Long Pond and Sabbath–Day Pond. An old boat was banked in front of the shelter for hikers. We rowed the waters of Sabbath–Day, which matched the deepness of the sky. The low-lying hills of conifers crevicing to a shallow V across the lake might have been an illustrator's model for a fantasy. The great blue heron that flew by with crooked neck was inevitable for this storybook scene. Four-foot stems shot upward from the bottom of the pond toward sunlight and yielded a lily pad on top to carry the sunlight back down to the roots.

We sunbathed and spied on the fish and long slithery blood suckers under the shore grottos. The few clouds above evaporated, and what remained was an absolutely color-bursting blue day.

Onward we trekked, and came to what the guidebook referred to as the Houghton Fire Road. It was nothing but a lumber road in operation. No one had camouflaged the trucks, bulldozers, Caterpillars, and cranes. After the harmonies of Sabbath–Day Pond a mile away, this sight was appalling. The woods were gutted with tractor-slashes. Every birch, especially the yellow birch, had been removed. The area was an ugly rip through the land. Trees angled helter-skelter in death poses in the erosion the rains produced. We saw no new growth or re-planting. What was more, the mobile housing units for logging operations bore no identification. The company was nameless, like a rapist. The offense we saw here was as unconscionable as the offense we had smelled in Gorham, New Hampshire, through which the chemical-saturated Androscoggin River flows.

Several years ago a Presidential panel in a lengthy report urged that more timber be cut. In conjunction with this proposal, the U.S. Forest Service planned to allow 11.8 billion board feet of lumber to be taken from national forests. Forty per cent of this harvest would be by "scatter cutting" and sixty per cent by "clear cut." The report said that, "if properly applied, clear cutting does not lead to soil erosion, nutrient depletion, wildlife habitat damage, or stream deterioration." From our observations thus far in the Maine woods, the method was not "properly applied." The soil was eroding.

One cannot walk through Maine without being affected by some facet of the paper companies. Ninety-eight per cent of Maine's forest land is privately owned. Twelve corporations together own 52 per cent of the land in Maine, and Maine contains more than 33,000 square miles. One of the Presidential panelists who urged more timber cutting of the nation's forests was a member of the National Forest Products Association, which charges that wilderness classification is the work of a minority of outdoor elitists who want to reserve land for their exclusive enjoyment. In 1969 and 1971 Maine passed the Maine Wildlands Laws, which created a system of zoning and periodic review of its 5,000 streams, 2,500 lakes, 1,300 wooded islands, and all lands above 2,500 feet elevation. As a restraint on the paper companies, however, the law may not be as strong as it seems. What logging company has extensive holdings in Maine above 2,500 feet?

On the Houghton Fire Road the pain in Julia's side showed further signs of recurrence. Fortunately, Rangeley (no exception to the rule that towns were in the valleys and the Trail followed the mountain crests) was close by. We had planned to stay overnight, as we had in Hanover, but a trip to the doctor again delayed our plans. A potent dose of penicillin was administered to knock out any incipient infection.

"After Rangeley," the doctor warned, "there's not a town until Monson. Lay low a couple of days. If this doesn't knock the infection out, we're faced with something serious. You won't feel like climbing anyway."

The Rangeley Inn was old fashioned and comfortable with a deep bathtub. We retired our legs for a long weekend. The miracle drug worked, and we eased into the Bigelow Mountain Range.

With the Big Horn Mountains in the fog, Little Bigelow Mountain provided no views. Only at Flagstaff Lake were we able to see any distance. The lake was enormous and loud, with high waves pounding driftwood against the shore.

The Bigelow Mountain Range has long been a target for the Flagstaff Corporation, which would like to open there the largest four-season resort area in the East. In 1935, the State of Maine was given the opportunity to purchase this area for a state park, but it never did. Developers have been after these mountains ever since, and they are making progress. Professor Hubert Vogelemann of the University of Vermont, after watching his home state's mountains being gouged by developers, warned the Maine Land Use Resources Commission against the Bigelow development. "Unless your fingers get burned a little," he said, "you don't learn to stay away from the stove. They should have learned what happened to us."

Although no commitment to the value a wilderness area provides has been evidenced by the would-be developers of the region, the energy crisis and general inflation may still preserve the Bigelow mountain range. As it stands, however, the chain sawyers are gassing up.

At Jerome Brook Lean-to we met a hiker from Nova Scotia and his cousin plunging on to Mt. Katahdin before school started. They were carrying a two-pound cucumber.

In a back-fence barter, we exchanged a few yards of our toilet paper for a few ounces of their rolled oats before leaving them to exclaim again over their giant cuke.

We were eating unusual fare these days. Our lunches consisted of olive butter and English cream crackers. One dinner was unique, a combination of dehydrated vegetable soup with sour cream mix plus instant potato dumplings. The result was a ponderous, vaguely Hungarian goulash that latched onto our stomachs well into the next day.

At West Carry Pond Camp we planned to make arrangements to be ferried across the Kennebec River, since no telephone was available until Caratunk on the far side of the stream. We decided that, although wading the Kennebec would be more adventuresome, we really could not afford the risk of losing the flute or any other equipment at this point in our hike. We couldn't find the Camp, and so stopped at a cabin to ask. The guidebook was wrong. The West Carry Pond Camp no longer existed, but Mel and Wilma Cobb, who owned the cabin, let us use their telephone. Three operators couldn't find the number of ferryman Harold Smith. Finally, by talking at random to a stranger in Caratunk, we got hold of Harold Smith's number. His wife answered, and told us Harold was out ferrying a hiker across river. Through her we made plans to meet him two mornings later at nine o'clock where the Trail crossed the Kennebec. The Cobbs offered us homemade blackberry cordial, which electrified our empty stomachs after a day of walking, and invited us to tent next to their cabin.

In tribute to the Down Easters, the water in West Carry Pond was still pure. The Cobbs said the pond had been tested several times. They drank it, we drank it, everybody drank it. Was it outrageous to wish that all our country could have ponds like those in Maine?

The Cobbs' outhouse was a conversation piece, too. It was decorated by handsome photographs around an eye-level window looking out over the lake. On the door bright lettering spelled out: *Impeach Nixon.*

Pierce Pond, after Sabbath–Day Pond, was our second Maine favorite. We came to its banks just before sunset, and although we planned to camp along the Kennebec River to be sure we were not late for our appointment with Harold Smith, the ferryman, the setting changed our minds. Points jutted into the warm water, forming ladders into the recesses. We skinny-dipped in the twilight and pitched the tent on the downy grass, nicknaming our site Dragon Flight Runway, for from here the dragonflies took off into their skidding turns over the water.

On our quiet sunrise walk 3½ miles to the Kennebec, we spotted deep moose tracks in the mud for the first time, but we heard no sounds and saw no moose. The river was used for logging, and after nine o'clock the dam upriver was opened to float logs downstream. Crossing at that time was extremely dangerous. The depth reached only six feet, but the current was fast. The crossing was a distance of $\frac{2}{10}$ mile.

When we arrived at the river crossing, one hiker had just waded across and was resting on the pebble shore. Another lone hiker waded across, walking slowly with a staff. We were disappointed to discover that the Kennebec looked easily conquerable by foot. "How you going across?" the hiker asked, wringing out his socks.

"The ferryman."

"That's eight dollars for both of you, isn't it?"

"Yes, but we heard that after nine o'clock crossing could be dangerous."

He eyed us as if we were hiking on a Guggenheim.

On the other side we saw a pickup truck. Someone called across in a husky voice. "Sherman? Sherman, is that you?" The man gestured cryptically. The wind caught a few words for us. "Downriver at log jam. Meet at point."

We yelled back, trying to verify these directions, but the

wind blew against us. We headed along the river until we came to the log jam and waited. Harold Smith stood in his flatbottom dinghy and poled his way across. He made a Plutonian silhouette, standing up, pushing against the current with a long, oak pole that he stabbed into the water: a Charon on the river Styx. Already the day was hot, but Harold wore a red wool long-sleeved shirt, suspenders, red-striped hunting socks, and L. L. Bean boots. These "Maine boots" were made of rubber soles and lightweight leather tops. Completely waterproof, they were good for bogs, and we often wished for a pair while hiking through this state.

Harold Smith was as colorful as his clothing. As he poled us through the water, which had not risen one iota since the other hikers waded across, he told us all he could during the dollar-a-minute ride. Rather, he shouted, for either his wife was hard of hearing or else he had grown accustomed to talking over the river current.

"You have to be a licensed Maine guide to ferry hikers," he said, his voice rolling downriver. "You can't be anybody. I told the AT Conference that we needed a telephone line from the south shore to Caratunk so that you hikers don't have to find a phone someplace three or four days ahead of time. Hikers get stranded in a storm and then what am I supposed to do? One time somebody from Boston called me up and made reservations to cross, so I went and waited for him but he never did show. I went back at the same time for three days, but he never came. They don't bother to tell you when they want to cancel."

Harold poled through the water with the nonchalance of a Venetian gondolier. "Oh, yes, and someone should inform them at the Appalachian Club that I'm the ferryman now. Why, my predecessor went down to the mill last year and people are still asking for *his* predecessor, who died years ago. Don't they have a magazine or something?"

Harold was also worried about the new generation in

Maine. "And not just hippies either," he said. "They throw rocks at my boat. Even shoot it. Used to be you didn't have to lock up everything around here. Used to be you could leave things without chaining them, but not now." The boat scraped shore. It was a smooth trip. Harold paddled back to a small island to hoist pole, paddle, and anchor to dry land. "Why, one time some people from out of state, New York or someplace," he hollered, "came up here and stole snapbeans right out of my garden. Shows what they know. Wasn't even ripe."

We stood near his pickup truck. "How old are you, Harold?" we asked our ferryman, hardy in body and spirit, standing proud.

"Seventy," he said. "Say, I'll drive you to Caratunk. It's just down street."

On the way we told him we were going to write a book about the Trail. "Oops. Well, if you put me in it, don't tell everybody I'm pessimistic. Say he was genial and always laughing."

At the far end of Moxie Pond, six hikers congregated at Joe's Hole Brook Lean-to. Our two friends, with whom we bartered toilet paper for rolled oats, were drying their equipment in the clammy air. The river was beaver dammed and looked unappetizing, but the two hikers weren't particular.

The other party of four was moving on. They were out for a weekend and didn't like the water either. One man carried a two-pound axe, the other a small latrine shovel. All wore sunglasses, though it was dark and on the verge of drizzling. Their dog, Star, a lab mongrel, probably used to city apartments, trotted ahead, backtracked, panted at our heels, galloped ahead again. Afraid they would reach the water source and tent site at Bald Mountain Brook behind us, one hand-holding couple blocked the Trail, but we were conditioned to a faster pace and politely begged their pardon.

Bald Mountain Brook was clear and, as we expected, tenting space plentiful. Star bounded over to see what was cooking as his owners set up their tents and changed into carrot-orange rainsuits. As we prepared Danish ham and brown rice, Star kept guard with ears alert, eyes begging, nose twitching, tail wagging. One of the disconsolate girls walked past our tent to the river. Her companions were having fun digging latrines.

The next morning the playful mongrel was nowhere in sight. In peace we hiked the 2.4 miles up Moxie Bald (2,630 feet). At the summit we rounded a stand of fir and Star charged down the trail to welcome us to his mountain. "Star, go home!" we entreated. Useless. The dog was in his element. Accompanied by this wayward dog, who chased dragonflies and chipmunks, we hiked on to the fire warden's cabin. Unlike the loner canines we met in the South, Star was innocent and city-bred. We arranged with the fire warden to keep him tied up until his owners arrived.

The walk over Moxie Bald was a refreshing divertissement. From here we could see the knife-edge of Katahdin, our ultimate goal, sixty miles distant as the crow flies, more than twice that by the Trail. The closeness of Katahdin strengthened our push forward. The end was indeed in sight, a reality that didn't exist a thousand miles ago, even a hundred miles. We marched on. Later we revealed to each other that individually we harbored dreams of never leaving the Trail. What began as a hike turned into a way of life. What would we do after climbing Katahdin? We even discussed the possibility of living on the Trail, like an American Indian whom we heard about. Apparently, for ten years he had been living on the Trail and supporting himself with odd jobs on nearby farms and in small towns.

For the moment, we considered the balds, a stretch of terraces sculptured with blueberry and cranberry bushes. The wind stopped blowing as we descended to the woodlands.

Hot August sun mixed with the muggy air to burn and boil us at the same time. The Trail led us through overgrown swamps where we tramped and bushwhacked through thickets tangling high overhead. Old lumbering haul roads, totally devoid of tree protection, added to the sweltering heat. It was not fun.

As if the heat and thickets were not enough, south of Monson the Trail took us past ugly scars of lumbering debris and destruction. Companies, such as Scott Paper and the Great Northern Paper Company, were helping to make the Maine we saw look like a game of pick-up sticks. Mighty tree poles lay askew in contempt of the living processes, a self-indictment of man's myopic place on the planet.

To top it off, the rains hit. More importantly, the rains hit the hills and mountains surrounding us. The waters collected, rushed downhill, filled and flooded the streams and swamps of the flatlands where the Appalachian Trail now led us. We discovered what the lowlands of Maine were really like.

At Monson on August 31, we realized that in a week or so our hike would be over. We also realized that we would have to carry more food than we ever previously packed. No stores existed between Monson and Baxter State Park. This small town, a kind of Hot Springs, North Carolina, of the Pine Tree State, was situated on the shores of Lake Hebron. We met a dozen hikers at the post office and café before setting up our tent at the Boy Scout camp by the lake. The town had no motel. Three more hikers arrived, and so did the rain. We washed in the lake and made ourselves as comfortable as possible.

We calculated our menus and snacks with the greatest of care, figuring how much dry milk we'd need, and trying to find the lightest, most nutritious food in town. We discarded all excess baggage and containers, honing our packs down to the skinniest minimum for these last seven days. We needed to average fifteen miles a day to have enough food until the Abol Bridge camp store adjacent Baxter Park.

After three straight days of rain, we could postpone the disembarkation no longer. Into the woods we went and into the muck, too. The sky was clear but the Trail was submerged. For long stretches we were forced to walk on high ground far to the side of the Trail. Then the drizzle came, and eventually turned to steady rain. Again we bushwhacked through swamps and flooded flatlands, slopping to our boot tops too many times to keep them dry. Mud and weeds stuck to the leather.

At Little Wilson Stream, we stood on a foggy embankment and stared into a roaring, flooded waterway that provided no visible crossing. The rocky bank was covered with a slippery film from the rains. This time no rocks provided an assured bridge. Farther upstream, the guidebook told us, were the slate abutments of a dam where the old stage road from Monson crossed the stream. This was the site of the Savage Mills in 1824. Such information was hardly useful now.

Like Paul Bunyans, we hefted dead pine trees down the bank. Four of these thrown across formed an unstable but feasible bridge spanning three-quarters of the river. The Kennebec looked harmless in comparison to this raging, swollen stream. We crossed separately. The water washed over our boots as we stepped onto the makeshift walkway. One of the trunks broke loose and bobbed in the rapids. Our makeshift staffs on the up-current side wobbled on the slippery river bottom. Overhead, we held onto a branch that arched halfway across the stream. We had jumped wider spans than the remaining three feet of this catwalk, but always before we had the momentum of a running leap. The pine trunks were slippery and kept shifting under the weight of the eddies. Both of us jumped, slid in the mud, regained balance, and then were home free on terra firma. If this country was so flooded in autumn, what was it like in spring?

Sopping wet after crossing four tributaries to the same stream in a half mile, we came to Maine Forest Service's Little Wilson Campsite. We hiked eleven miles that day and saw no one. To our surprise after emerging from the woods, the campground was full of trailers, kids, hot dogs, motor bikes, the works. It was Labor Day weekend.

Part of the inundation of the Appalachian Trail that we had observed resulted from beaver dams. These fifty-pound rodents build mud-and-branch lodges with underwater entrances for security. If the spot they choose for the lodge is too shallow, they build dams to deepen the water. The dams are a nuisance sometimes, but in the overall scheme of nature they provide incalculable benefits in flood control, as well as providing good firebreaks and maintaining water level in dry seasons. Beaver dams also flood meadows, creating what naturalists term "edge effects"—habitats for grouse, woodcock, deer, and other wildlife thriving in semi-open areas. Tudor Richards, executive director of the Audubon Society in New Hampshire, said, "The return of the beaver probably has done more to improve wildlife habitat in New England than anything else that has happened in the last three hundred years—with the possible exception of some major land use changes."

Whatever the long-range benefits of beaver dams, we felt their immediate effects on our boots. Water was all around us—on the ground, in the sky, on the brush we walked through. What happened the next few days neither of us would ever forget. This section of the Trail traversed the Barren–Chairback Mountain Range, which included Barren Mountain (2,266 feet) and four lesser peaks around Long Pond. When we saw that these mountains were in the rain clouds, we plotted a shortcut by taking the new St. Regis Tote Road. Between 1950–55 the old Trail followed this tote road, which had been used for lumbering operations. According to the guidebook, old blaze marks were still visible.

We skirted Barren Mountain with the hope of following the old Trail to hook up with the regular Trail at Long Pond, a mistake. After two false starts down other overgrown tote roads, we spotted some faded blazes. Two hours later, two hours of bushwhacking and muckalucking through four miles of overgrown bogs, we came to a dead end. The tote road split and dwindled into three rutted directions, each camouflaged with goldenrod and asters. We split up to search for more blazes. During the fifteen-minute search, Steve found a monstrous bull moose, but no blazes.

By lunch time we came half circle to Wilder Brook, which, we presumed through careful calculation, led to our destination of Long Pond. So impelled were we to outmaneuver the rain that we seriously considered wading upstream through the dense wilderness to Long Pond and rejoining the Trail there. Neither of us liked to admit defeat. We knew that by the time we reached Barren Mountain again it would be late afternoon. Our supplies allowed seven days, no more, and at the rate we were going we would be in danger if we did not make progress. With heads down we backtracked the four miles we had supposedly shortcut.

On our return, Long Pond Stream was too flooded to cross. Then at four in the afternoon we reached the blue-blaze trail that led to a bridge across Long Pond Stream at the head of a gorge and Slugundy Falls. The bridge was a narrow foot of split logs with a crude handrail, all suspended by cable. The drop from the bridge into the gorge was approximately thirty feet. Handholds and bootsteps were slippery. We inched across, carefully placing one foot in front of the other.

At nightfall we reached Cloud Pond Lean-to. By this time we had hiked eighteen miles, eight of them for naught. Cloud Pond Lean-to was isolated and deserted. The tent sites were slanting. By the time our dinner was cooked, it was closet dark. Once more we mistakenly parked downwind of the latrines and the insolences of bygone hikers. Our bodies were sore. The rains poured forth before we went to sleep.

In the morning the rain still beat down through the pine trees and onto the pond like an electric shock. A sudden cloudburst hit us just as we took down the tent. We dashed into the shelter. The pond, only feet away, was scarcely visible through the downpour. Our clothes were soaked. The tent was a soggy mass of clinging nylon. We jammed it into its bag, water and all. Luckily our sleeping bags were only damp.

The shelter was a hybrid of a horse's stall and a sawmill: the floor was spread with sawdust and shavings, and the roof was too low for us to stand up straight. Since no bunks were built to put gear on, sawdust stuck to pots, pans, jeans, boots, and us. We looked like giant eggplants rolled in bread crumbs. The roof leaked and the rain did not subside. The weather had turned cold. The cold magnified our appetites. Our seven-day food supply had already dwindled to five, and we were behind our daily mileage projection.

To pass the time we read scraps of paper as we waited for the rain to stop. Two days before we arrived two hikers wrote that they passed someone on the Trail who seemed to be lagging. They offered him a candy bar and he lackadaisically took it. They reached the lean-to and were preparing their dinner when they realized the hiker they passed should have arrived, too. They went looking for him, found him unconscious, and carried him back to the lean-to. He regained consciousness long enough to tell them he was a diabetic and hadn't packed along any insulin. One hiker stayed with him while the other jogged back to a highway and hitched a ride to Monson. A helicopter was sent in for the diabetic hiker the next morning.

This news added little cheer. The rain continued to pelt the mountain, but we sidled out onto the Trail anyway, determined to push on, now or never. This was our last leg, and we had been through too much to give up easily. We hiked half a mile and clocked ourselves. The Trail was a series of rivulets, flooded and muddy even in these mountain peaks. We progressed at a mile an hour.

It was then, sitting in the rain, arguing, weighing, balancing, meditating, that we decided to turn back to Monson. The decision was difficult. However, everything indicated it was right. Being helicoptered out of Maine was avoidable, as was risking our lives to impatience and haste like the young boy who had drowned in Vermont.

Backtracking was a downhearted process. We unwalked all the hard miles we had covered. Five straight days of rain flooded the Trail. The gorge with the cable bridge over Long Pond Stream was more violent and intimidating than the day before. The roar of the stream, a seething miniature Niagara Falls, could be heard against the rock walls halfway down Barren Mountain. Crossing the narrow bridge over those roiling waters frightened us. We checked and double-checked our packs and hitched them tight against our bodies so they would not throw us off balance.

In a way, we were relieved to see the friendly café, laundromat, and comfortable setting of Monson. On the other hand, we didn't exactly know what to do next. Out of the mountains it was not raining, and we doubted our decision, that is, until we met hikers Bill and Julie, and their dog. Over a hamburger we meshed our situations: we drove their Volkswagen bus to Baxter State Park while they tried their luck through the sludge.

The 200,000-acre Baxter Park was a gift from former Maine Governor Percival P. Baxter. In 1930 he made his first land purchase, which included Mt. Katahdin (5,268 feet). During the next thirty years, he added land to this first core purchase. Today, the park is extremely popular and reservations must be made, especially before Labor Day. Nevertheless, we took our chances. A few tent sites were set aside for thru-hikers at Katahdin Stream Campground.

The top of Katahdin was an eight- to ten-hour hike. We arrived in the Park too late to start out. Instead, we met the Lothar family, a couple with their ten-year-old daughter, who we heard were hiking the entire Trail, though we had never crossed camps with them. Inventive Mrs. Lothar made their three-man tent as well as their jeans, zippered at the thighs for easy transformation into cutoffs if the weather got too hot. The family also hiked with handmade staffs tipped with rubber chair-leg plugs for a better grip on mountains.

The next morning was foggy, the usual weather condition. We continued as planned, both carrying our Peterborough, New Hampshire, library bags as day packs with lunch, snacks, a few Band-Aids, flute, and the marigold seeds which we had carried all the way from Springer Mountain, back in Georgia. The Lothars tromped by single file in the rain toward the mountain. When we reached the ranger's cabin, we saw their packs lined up against the wall. We signed in, for Katahdin was a dangerous mountain, and the rangers kept tabs on all hikers. As we were leaving, the ranger asked where we were going.

"We're thru-hikers," we said, anticipating authority's voice and hoping this fact would spare us.

"Well, all the trails are closed until the summit clears."

One mishap after another was focusing in on us. The day before, a one-hundred-pound butane tank accidentally leaked under high pressure ten feet from our borrowed van, but luckily did not explode. The previous night the limb we hung our food on broke and nearly cracked our skulls. Now we weren't allowed to hike Katahdin. We argued, "But the Lothars went up."

"They'll be back down. I didn't see them or I wouldn't have let them go. It's raining up there."

Perhaps this dictum was a blessing in disguise. Now we could do our backtracking, climb Whitecap (3,707 feet), Boardman (2,204 feet), and Joe Mary (2,904 feet) mountains. After a morning of driving back-country roads in the rain, we arrived at West Branch Pond Camps at the base of Whitecap.

Not a soul was in sight at Kealiher's camp. A horse stood

under a tree to lighten the burden of beating rain. Finally, Mr. Kealiher appeared, and tried to dissuade us from hiking Whitecap in such adverse conditions. "I've never seen the Trail this muddy," he said. "You come back by here for coffee afterward. You'll need it." He wanted to know if we got back down the mountain all right.

We climbed Whitecap through the beaver dams at the base of its mushy bottom, up the watery side, and to the top of its stormy summit. The wind blew the rain horizontally at about 35–40 miles per hour. The trunks of pine trees were bending in a wind of at least seven on the Beaufort scale, near gale force.

Shivering too much even to eat snacks, we turned around at once and headed back. We descended as if by some compulsion we had fulfilled our duty of hiking this peak. In Mr. Kealiher's log cabin dining room, hot coffee and warm fresh rhubarb cobbler with udder-fresh cream thawed us out. Afterward, we stood talking in the kitchen. Mrs. Kealiher was convalescing and help was needed. The temptation to live in such a setting was strong, but we had a few miles to go before Katahdin.

On September 7, when we finally were allowed access to the heights of Katahdin, the fog partially lifted. Up the steep boulder edge of the mountain we climbed, grabbing onto the metal handholds, balancing on the flank of this mammoth oblong block. Such a fitting mountain to end the Trail.

The Spur was a nearly vertical ascent before it leveled off onto a surrealistic plateau of rocks and tundra grass. Like our conditioning mountain in New Hampshire, Katahdin was a monadnock, that is, a solitary mountain surrounded by a peneplain.

On the top, this 1½-mile-long mesa was a kind of launching pad to another and better world. Below us were the myraid ponds and lakes we skirted. The sun hit first one, then another, signaling the clouds to move in oversize formations. How happy we were, for this was our goal, and yet how sad and questioning, too. Could we possibly sleep among four walls day after day? Could city life be anything but dull after this?

We passed another couple who saw the smiles on our faces and guessed we were thru-hikers. "Congratulations," they said. We were ecstatic, but what did this all mean? We knew that we learned more about nature than we ever learned in books. In Georgia we started off thinking only of one step after the other. By Harpers Ferry the ideas, causes, beliefs, of all those we met and all that we saw became integrated into new commitments. The four and a half months on the Trail trained us to honor the land and seek its majesty, yet something more happened to us that we did not anticipate. Through direct experience we felt the impact of crucial issues that never before really touched us—the attitude of hikers and industrialists alike toward pollution, the urgency of recreation management, the need of personal privacy, the importance of aesthetics, the responsibility of organizations for their goals, the responsibility of individuals to see that the goals are achieved.

Past Thoreau Spring we hiked, and up the last of our two thousand miles. A short sleet storm blew over, and so in the clouds we took out the packet of marigold seeds we had carried from Springer Mountain in Georgia. With abandon we cast them to the four winds. They all blew north.

Appendix I

THREE HIKERS

We asked three other hikers who walked the Appalachian Trail from Georgia to Maine the same year we did to send us impressions of their hikes. Each of them hiked the Trail for different reasons. Each of them came out on top of Mt. Katahdin.

WARREN DOYLE

Many people have questioned my motives behind walking the AT in such a short time (66½ days). Nature, in my opinion, was created to assist man in fulfilling his wants or satisfying his needs, whether they involve a quest for natural beauty, solitude, simplicity, physical exercise or achievement. I set upon this particular trek with the last type of quest foremost on my mind. The addition of the temporal dimension only increased the difficulty inherent in walking the whole AT.

I knew and accepted the fact that this approach would tax my mental and physical capacities to their limits. Nature was to serve as a vehicle for self-education; the AT would be "required reading" under the topic heading of "Personal Growth." I was going to learn just who I thought I was, how much I felt I could take, and, more importantly, how much I reasoned I could give. It turned out to be a successful character-confirmation experiment.

Another popular question concerns what I felt were the keys to this unique accomplishment. Basically, the answer boils down to four things: planning, psychological preparation, gutsy perseverance, and "a little help from my friends." Planning was meticulous and almost as exciting as the hike itself. It represented a culmination of personal organizational skills developed over the years. I forsook any type of formal physical training and applied my energy to "psyching" myself. I approached the hike expecting the worst. I got it—and even more. Not only was I stripped of physical fat (32 pounds) but emotional fat as well.

I cried out of loneliness and from the pressures of the "time-table." Many nights were spent in restless anxiety brought about by the realization that I was behind schedule. The albatross around my neck was obese, and beauty was everywhere but not the time to drink. Perseverance got me through the actual hike. I became obsessed with the goal. There was no other way I could have accomplished it. Steadfast determination pushed me through rain, mud, heat waves, inflamed tonsils, fever, and the tediousness of walking fifteen hours and more day after day. I couldn't afford the time or effort to be concerned with my personal comfort.

My help from friends came from four main sources. My father followed me with the family car for a month. His companionship, common sense philosophy, and warm meals made the arduous task somewhat easier. I only hope that I can do the same for my future offspring. My mom did her share of worrying, but gave encouragement anyway. Love motivates us all. My fiancée with her homemade bread, encouraging words over the telephone and inspiring-to-tears letters, gave me the unique feeling of actually being alone but still loved from afar. Cards and letters from friends and unknown people from my hometown area contributed something fresh to an otherwise boring routine.

I'm proud of what I've done. I did it honestly. I can walk tall now. I did not conquer the Trail; man can never conquer Nature. I utilized the AT to conquer myself. In technical terms, it took 66½ days, and I averaged 30.6 miles per day while spending an average time of 15 hours 20 minutes walking each day.

More important, though, was the outcome in personal terms. I know more about what is and isn't important now. I see more trivialities around me, and I question more frequently. I've become more dissatisfied with how far man has separated himself from the natural way of living. Our society is going down under waves of artificialities and strong currents of conformity, which carry the pollution of mediocrity.

I feel an obligation to the AT for giving me this enlightening experience. When my degree requirements are completed, I plan to devote some of my time and energy to maintaining a section of the Trail. I want to become involved in the ATC. I plan to hike the AT two more times in my life, once with my children and once after I retire. This will give me two additional perspectives of how to approach the AT.

DAN WELCH

As a retired thru-hiker, I do have some strong feelings about the Appalachian Trail. First, since the Appalachian Trail is now officially designated a National Scenic Trail, it belongs in spirit, if not in fact, to all the people of the United States, not just to a small group of Trail club members. Second, despite its deficiencies, wherever the AT leads along the length of the Appalachians, it proves to be the most popular trail—I suspect because many people come to sample the magic only the famous 2,000-mile foot trail can offer.

We all come to explore the Appalachians, their peaks and ridges, their intervals and hollows, possibly to spot a golden eagle or a spruce grouse, or to spot a moose or black bear.

I found the Trail to be like a quaint little red schoolhouse without walls—one whose wonders never cease. It's the quiet wonders that suck you back, the taste of ripe huckleberries, the first lonely flower of spring, the fragrant smell of balsam, and the long rows of old stone fences.

These wonders occur in the most unexpected and unremarkable localities; yet far too many volunteer Trail routers, due to their immaturity and insensitivity, have failed to improve the Trail route with the passing years, allowing much of the Trail within their control to continue along mountain ridge crests, tediously ascending straight up nearly every local peak and molehill. Much of this sad routing, sometimes over the roughest available footway with a smooth alternative only a hundred feet to the side, I suspect is done in the name of a view, or was planned by some local hiking jock seeking pleasure in the tough physical effort required to make it to the top. The peaceful valleys, the tumbling brooks, the quiet glens are all cast aside for the more "spectacular."

I have nothing against peaks, but enough is enough. It can be fun looking up, too! Each national forest, national park, state park, or other distinctive region (or "enclave," I call it, for lack of a better word), has a characteristic look or flavor about itself. In the southern Appalachians, and to a limited extent in the Green Mountains, Vermont, and in New Hampshire intermountain enclaves, skilled workers have pieced together remarkable lengths of a pleasant foot trail that passes through nearly every type of area suitable for hiking. These enclaves were a joy to walk, giving me great pleasure and an inner confidence that I had seen all the significant features characteristic of that enclave.

I wish I had this confidence about other enclaves I traversed, many times with undue physical strain. Our Appalachian Trail deserves the best, most varied, and interesting routing possible. All the skills needed for better Trail routing are available. All it requires is that we demand it.

CARL WINDLE

This was my first time at backpacking. Sergeant Butler, co-chairman for the Swansea (Massachusetts) Heart Fund, along with his wife Ethel and members of the police force and community, got pledges for each mile I walked. Approximately $2,700 was raised. The Butlers also mailed all my packages of food and clothing to my thirteen pickup points. They were coordinating the whole trip.

Rain, mud, wet feet, blisters, wind-swept ridges, swollen tendons, pack straps digging into my shoulders; out of food, money, water; diarrhea, getting lost, taking wrong trail; discouraging people, dogs, fever, mental fatigue; always hungry, always thirsty, Trail always going over the toughest parts, rattlesnakes, copperheads, rocks of Pennsylvania, bad water of New York, New Jersey, bad Trail markings of southwestern Virginia, floods of Vermont, White Mountain day hikers and their remarks; gnats on top of mountains, blackflies halfway down and mosquitoes at the bottom, shelters taken down because of vandals, raccoons and porcupines trying to get into the pack, mice of Georgia, North Carolina shelters (always after Alpen cereal), hot sun of Pennsylvania, heat exhaustion.

The Trail was certainly not a picnic or a chance to take a lovely stroll, as others would have you believe, but a rugged undertaking. There are many beautiful views, but to get to them you have to work hard.

Sometimes the solitude was too much and I felt alone. The call of the towhee, *Drink your tea*, followed me from Georgia to Velvet Rocks, just north of Hanover, N.H., and then no more.

People were interesting. Harry Thomas (Majawsha), a Winnebago Indian, has been on the Trail for ten years, going into towns for work in the winter, and has finished the Trail once.

The push to make the whole Trail and the constant thought, Will my body hold up, and if so, will my mind? The Good Lord watched over me and helped me through all the obstacles and difficulties. Without Him and the Butler family, my Dad, Mom, and sister, as well as the efforts and support of my community, I would have never made it.

I started April 13, 1973, and finished July 24, 1973, averaging a little better than 20 miles a day.

When at the end, I was shocked and it was hard to believe it finally ended. The last blaze. And so I made it and I know that in my heart some day I will walk that Trail again.

Appendix II

GEAR

The items that we wore and carried in our packs at the end of our hike:

FOOD:

Rye Crisp crackers
Instant coffee
Dehydrated vegetable soup
Substitute sugar
Salt and pepper
Eleven tea bags
Spaghetti sauce mix
White rice
Instant pudding
Rolled oats

Instant hot cereal
Golden raisins
Nuts
Substitute brown sugar
Quick-cooking barley
Powdered milk
Spices (bouillon cubes, garlic, nutmeg, oregano, dill, basil, cinnamon, bay leaves)

CLOTHING:

Sweat shirt
Three pair wool socks
Turtleneck sweater
Slippers
Jeans
Bandanas
Ponchos
Navy sweater
Windbreakers

Sleeveless top
One pair cotton socks
Moccasins
Boots
Underwear
T-shirt
Bikini
White long-sleeve shirt
Chippewa boots

PERSONAL EFFECTS:

Pocket Kleenex
Sunglasses
Toothpaste
Tampax
Dental floss
Soap

Toilet paper
Toothbrushes
Hairbrushes
Handcream
Perfume
Drawing ink and pens

Drawing pads
Stamps
Coin purse
Maps of Baxter Park
Recorder
Checkbook
Ballpoint pen

Journals
Identification
Address book
Sheet music
Flute
Travelers checks
Shampoo

MEDICINE KIT:

Elastic roll bandage
Large adhesive patch
Ben-Gay
Thermometer
Halozone tablets
Antibiotic ointment
Salt tablets
Vitamin C and iron pills
First-aid cream

Darvon
Excedrin
Sewing scissors
Blistex
Corn pads
Allergy pills
Band-Aids
Cutters Insect Foam

COOKING EQUIPMENT:

Primus Stove
1 pint fuel
Brillo pads
1 large pot
1 frying pan
2 forks
1 pot handle
Sponge

Matches
Grudge cloth
1 small pot
2 lids
2 spoons
1 dish
2 thermal cups

CAMPSITE EQUIPMENT:

1 Gerry Lodgepole tent
2 1-quart canteens
2 inflatable pillows
Flannel pillow cases
Collapsible water jug
3 plastic tote bags
50-foot nylon rope
2 down sleeping bags
Ensolite sleeping pads
Plastic tablecloth

2 pocket flashlights
2 stretch ropes
Whisk broom
2 whistles
Swiss Army knife
Camp kit (thread, needles, safety pins, rubber bands, elastic for tent poles, knife sharpener, fishing line and hooks)

Appendix III

ANSWERS

Preparation and conditioning time: *two months.*

Expenses for two: *per diem* $ *7.71*
                  total (142 days   *$1,095.00*
                  on the trail)

Body weight:

	BEFORE	AFTER
Julia	*106*	*112*
Steve	*160*	*154*

Pack weight: *Julia 23–28 lbs.*
                 Steve 32–38 lbs.

Boots to walk 2,000 miles: *one pair each.*

Average mileage: *15 miles per day.*
                     Fastest—22 miles a day in Shenandoah National Park

                     Slowest—8 miles per day in Stekoah, N.C.; White Mts., N.H.; Mahoosuc, Me. (or about 1 mile per hour).

Began: *April 11*

Finished: *September 7 (150 days)*

Extreme verified temperatures: *18 degrees, Big Stamp Gap, Georgia.*
                                   101 degrees, Woodstock, N.H.

State easiest to walk: *Connecticut*
Most tedious: *Pennsylvania*
Most deer sighted: *Virginia and New York*
No deer sighted: *Maine and New Hampshire*
Most people: *White Mountains, N.H.*
Least people: *Georgia*
What we should have taken but didn't: *blackfly hoods.*
What we did take but shouldn't have: *pocket signal mirror*
complicated compass
waterproof match holder
State with most Trail mileage: *Virginia (452 miles)*
State with least mileage: *West Virginia (10 miles)*
Serious injuries: *none.*
Amount of money found on Trail: *$1.84.*
Would we hike it again?: *Yes.*

Appendix IV

PARKS AND FORESTS
ON AND NEAR THE TRAIL

† National Parks
* National Forests

GEORGIA:

Amicalola Falls State Park
Winfield Scott State Park
Vogel State Park
Chattahoochee National Forest *

NORTH CAROLINA:

Nantahala National Forest *
Great Smoky Mountains National Park †

TENNESSEE:

Pisgah National Forest *
Cherokee National Forest *

VIRGINIA:

Mount Rogers State Park
Jefferson National Forest *
George Washington National Forest *
Blue Ridge Parkway
Shenandoah National Park †
Skyline Drive

WEST VIRGINIA:

Harpers Ferry National Historical Park

MARYLAND:

Gathland State Park
Washington Monument State Park

PENNSYLVANIA:
: Michaux State Park
Caledonia State Park
Pine Grove Furnace State Park
St. Anthony's Game Preserve

NEW JERSEY:
: Delaware Water Gap National Recreation Area
Worthington State Forest
Stokes State Forest
High Point State Park
Wawayanda State Forest

NEW YORK:
: Harriman State Park
Palisades Interstate Parkway
Fahnestock State Park

CONNECTICUT:
: Macedonia Brook State Park
Mohawk Mountain State Forest

MASSACHUSETTS:
: October Mountain State Forest
Greylock State Reserve

VERMONT:
: Green Mountain National Forest *

NEW HAMPSHIRE:
: White Mountain National Forest *
Franconia Notch State Park
Crawford Notch State Park

MAINE:
: Grafton Notch State Park
Baxter State Park

Appendix V

GOOD READING

Allen, Arthur (text) and Kellogg, Peter Paul (record), *Birdsongs in Your Garden*. A Cornell Lab of Ornithology Book Album, Boston, Houghton Mifflin Company, 1963.

Appalachian Mountain Club, *Mountain Flowers of New England*. Boston, Appalachian Mountain Club, 1964.

Appalachian Trail Conference, Inc., *The Appalachian Trail*. Publication No. 5, 8th edition, Washington, D.C., 1970.

————, *Appalachian Trail: A History and Anthology*. Harpers Ferry, W. Va., 1976.

Bartram, William, *Travels of William Bartram*, edited by Mark Van Doren. New York, Dover, 1928.

Bleything, Dennis, *Edible Plants in the Wilderness*, Vol. I. Beaverton, Oregon, Life Support Technology, Inc., 1972.

Brooks, Maurice, *The Appalachians*. Boston, Houghton Mifflin Company, 1965.

Brooks, Paul, *Roadless Area*. New York, Alfred A. Knopf, 1964.

Brown, Cora, *et al.*, *Outdoor Cooking*. Greystone Press, New York, 1940.

Coker, Robert, *Streams, Lakes, Ponds*. New York, Harper & Row, 1968.

Douglas, William O., *My Wilderness, East to Katahdin*. New York, Doubleday, 1961.

Fisher, Ronald M., *The Appalachian Trail*. Washington, D.C., National Geographic Society, 1972.

Fletcher, Colin, *The Man Who Walked Through Time*. New York, Alfred A. Knopf, 1967.

240

Garvey, Edward B., *Appalachian Hiker; Adventure of a Lifetime*. Oakton, Virginia, Appalachian Books, 1971.

Hare, James, editor, *Hiking the Appalachian Trail* (two volumes). Emmaus, Pennsylvania, Rodale Press, 1975.

Headstrom, Richard, *Whose Track Is It?* New York, Ives Washburn, Inc., 1971.

Montgomery, F. H., *Trees of the Northern United States and Canada*. New York, Frederick Warne & Co., 1970.

Morris, Taylor, *The Walk of the Conscious Ants*. New York, Alfred A. Knopf, 1972.

Peterson, Roger Tory, *A Field Guide to Bird Songs*, text by Arthur Allen and record by Peter Paul Kellogg. Boston, Houghton Mifflin Company, 1968.

————. *How to Know the Birds; An Introduction to Bird Recognition*. New York, New American Library, 1957.

Porter, Eliot and Abbey, Edward, *Appalachian Wilderness: The Great Smoky Mountains*. New York, Ballantine Books, 1973.

Sutton, Ann and Myron, *The Appalachian Trail; Wilderness on the Doorstep*. Philadelphia and New York, Lippincott, 1967.

Teale, Edwin Way, *North with the Spring*. New York, Dodd Mead & Co., 1966.

Thoreau, Henry David, *The Maine Woods*. New York, Bramhall House, 1950.

Wallis, G. B., et al., *The Oxford Book of Food Plants*. New York, Oxford University Press, 1969.

Watts, May Theilgaard, *Flower Finder*. Berkeley, California, Nature Study Guild, 1955.

————, *Master Tree Finder*. Berkeley, California, Nature Study Guild, 1963.

Whitman, Walt, *Complete Poetry and Selected Prose*, James E. Miller, Jr., editor. Boston, Houghton Mifflin, 1959.

Zim, Herbert S. and Martin, Alexander C., *Trees, A Guide to Familiar American Trees*. A Golden Nature Guide. Racine, Wisconsin, Golden Press, Western Publishing Company, Inc., 1956.

Index

243